A-LEVEL AND AS-LEVEL ENGLIS

LONGMAN A AND AS-LEVEL REFERENCE GUIDES

Series editors: Geoff Black and Stuart Wall

TITLES AVAILABLE
Biology
Chemistry
English
Geography
Mathematics
Physics

A-LEVEL
AND AS-LEVEL

LONGMAN
REFERENCE
GUIDES

ENGLISH

Barbara and George Keith
with additional material by Stuart Sillars

Longman

Longman Group UK Limited,
Longman House, Burnt Mill, Harlow,
Essex CM20 2JE, England
and Associated Companies throughout the world.

First published 1991

British Library Cataloguing in Publication Data

Keith, George
English. – (Longman A–Level reference guides)
1. England. Secondary schools. Curriculum subjects: English
I. Title II. Sillars, Stuart, *1951–*
802.76

ISBN 0–582–06396–5

Designed and produced by
The Pen and Ink Book Company,
Huntingdon, Cambridgeshire.
Set in 10/12pt Century Old Style.

Printed in Singapore

ACKNOWLEDGEMENTS

The authors would like to express their thanks to Geoff Black and Stuart Wall for their support and advice, and to Annette Smith who typed the manuscript.

The poem by e.e. cummings is reproduced by kind permission of Grafton Books Limited.

HOW TO USE THIS BOOK

Throughout yourA-level and AS-level course you will be coming across terms, ideas and definitions that are unfamiliar to you. The Longman Reference Guides provide a quick, easy-to-use source of information, fact and opinion. Each main term is listed alphabetically and, where appropriate, cross-referenced to related terms.

- Where a term or phrase appears in **different type** you can look up a separate entry under that heading elsewhere in the book.
- Where a term or phrase appears in **different type** and is set between two arrowhead symbols ◀ ▶, it is particularly recommended that you turn to the entry for that heading.

A

ABSTRACT

1 An abstract is the name given to a brief statement (usually the equivalent of one side of A4) at the beginning of a project, dissertation or thesis. It summarises the contents so that the reader can gain an immediate overview of the argument and scope of the whole work. Here is an example from a JMB A-level English Language project:

> This project investigates the content and style of teachers' comments on end of term school reports. The study was undertaken with the co-operation of 7 main subject teachers and examined their comments on 30 fifth year reports. A grammatical analysis of teachers' statements is follwed by an analysis of particular words used. There is also a discussion of ways in which meanings are implied as well as explicitly stated. Finally the report discusses the existence of a particular code in which school reports are written and attempts to identify some of the functions of language in school reports.

2 Abstract is also a word frequently used to describe things that are not concrete or tangible. Ideas, concepts and theories are all abstract (adjective) or abstractions (plural noun). Abstract art may be defined as art which does not represent everyday objects but which depicts shapes or geometric structures abstracted from everyday objects. Mathematics is abstract; so too is language, which is sometimes referred to as the supreme abstraction. The history of Western philosophy may be described as the history of a series of abstract nouns e.g. justice, freedom, love, truth, knowledge, goodness. Metaphysics is a term that is also used to describe philosophical abstractions. The word is derived from its use by Aristotle who, after completing a book on the known physical world, *Physics*, called his next book, on aspects of the non-physical world, *Metaphysics*. All he meant by his title was, 'the book written after *Physics*'.

Explanations of how abstractions, or abstract nouns, have meaning (**semantics**) is an area where philosophy and linguistics frequently meet. Linguistic philosophers, following **Ludwig Wittgenstein** and **A.J. Ayer** always treat abstractions with great caution. Some have gone so far as to debunk metaphysical entities as nonsense. Wittgenstein argued that grammar was not a sure guide to meaning. Just because you can say something, it is not necessarily true. This kind of healthy scepticism serves linguistics well and gives rise to such sensible maxims as:

> *The meaning of a word is its function* (i.e. you should understand the meaning of words like *freedom* or *beauty* by the ways in which they are being used).
> *The truth of a statement lies in its verifiability of falsifiability* (i.e. 'truth' does not have to be absolute, it is dependent upon how we would test it).

ABSURD

While this normally means ridiculous, in the theatre it refers to a particular kind of play, written in the middle of the twentieth century and concentrating on making moral or philosophical points through plots that are 'absurd' – for example, a giant corpse which keeps growing larger or a choir of weighing machines. Much better to avoid its use apart from in this very special way.

ACCENT

Accent refers to the way a speaker pronounces the sounds of a language. It is largely determined by regional and social influences and can be detected not only in variations of individual phonemes (see **phonology**) but also in characteristic intonation patterns. Studies of accent look for phonological characteristics of a social or regional group.

Accent refers only to sound and should not be thought of as synonymous with *dialect* which is a larger category altogether and includes accent along with lexical, grammatical and semantic features.

The term can also be used to refer to a point of stress in a person's intonation. A word or part of a word may be stressed or accented to convey emphasis. A whole sentence may be accentuated in order to draw special attention to it. Generally speaking, however, it is the regional and social aspects of accent that have aroused most interest and debate. Lamentably, it is also true that issues of social class have overwhelmed our appreciation of regional variety, creating such stereotypes as the idea that northern accents are working class while southern accents are middle class. If you wish to study accent in anything like an objective way it is important to beware of the stereotypes we all have in our minds, and to begin to really listen to what people say and how they say it.

Music hall, films, comedy programmes on the radio, comic songs and monologues have all, over the years, reinforced regional stereotypes:

– the gormless Lancashire lad
– the aggressive Yorkshireman
– the cocky Glaswegian
– the cheeky Cockney
– the Somerset yokel
– the mad Irish joker

Radio comedy and TV soaps depend a great deal upon regional accent for creating community and togetherness, but regional difference is also something that they can exploit for dramatic contrast. You could carry out a survey of current soaps (including *Neighbours*) and radio comedy in terms of accent variety. Who speaks differently from the rest of the main characters?

Accents are important for bonding communities together so that individual members have a stronger sense of identity. Accent differences can be a source of curiosity and pleasure but there are two factors which interfere with our enjoyment of variety. One is insecurity. The very fact that accents bind us together can create a sense of suspicion or caution when we encounter a different accent. Other people's accents are so immediately obvious and introduce an all pervasive new element into everyday contacts. If a degree of enmity develops the different accent becomes threatening, intrusive, irritating. Under such circumstances the usual reaction is to poke fun at the obvious target. In our history, collective insecurity has often been engendered by foreign influences and it is not surprising that we have comic stereotyped accents for Germans, French, Americans, Russians. None of us will have any difficulty mimicking in our minds the way English is spoken by the stereotypes but they are only stereotypes and not real speakers. The TV programme *'Allo, 'Allo* creates enormous fun with its stereotyped accents. It even has a British agent posing as a French gendarme, speaking English as though it were French pronounced very badly!

Accent is such an important bonding agent that it is not at all unusual for people to assimilate the prevailing accent into their own way of speaking. Students from Nottingham, studying at Aberystwyth, can develop Welsh accents; teachers from Southern English counties, working in Newcastle, begin to speak so-called Geordie.

The tension between insecurity and curiousity is likely to remain but it should not prevent us from trying to get behind the stereotypes. It is in fact a very profitable area for a language study project investigating people's reactions and attitudes. A useful starting point is provided by two BBC recordings (LP and cassette) called 'English With an Accent' and 'English Dialects'. The one gives examples of English spoken by a wide variety of speakers for whom English is a second language, the other gives examples of English spoken by people from different regions of Britain. Both recordings contain everyday talk and can provide the basis of a very enjoyable and instructive guessing game.

The second factor that complicates and skews our assessment and appreciation of English accents is socio-economic. Some years ago the distinguished historian of culture and society in Britain, Raymond Williams, protested at the term 'Home Counties' meaning those counties bordering on London. The same concept lay behind the BBC's old name for Radio Four, 'the Home Service'. Whose home? asked Williams. It certainly was not his home since he came from the Welsh border. Nor was it the home of Northerners, or Cornishfolk, or East Anglians. He went on to argue that the sheer force of economic activity and social prestige in and around London has generated great political power which in turn has regionalised Scotland, Wales, the North West, the North East, East Anglia, the South West in what amounts to an outer circle around the so called Home Counties. They did not choose to call themselves regions they have been designated as such. This is a fascinating socio-economic argument and it gives a perspective to one of our national language pre-occupations, namely *Received Pronunciation* (RP). The other national language pre-occupation is the notion of *Standard English* which should not be confused with RP for the same reason that accent should not be confused with dialect. Standard English is discussed under **dialect**.

Received Pronunciation is an idea, some would say an ideal. It is quite different from the well known 'upper class' or 'well off' stereotypes:

- the Oxford English of the nineteen twenties
- the 'cut glass' accent of a Mayfair hostess
- the caricatured retired army colonel
- the special telephone voice aunties put on
- the strained, careful voice of a suburban snob (who has had elocution lessons)
- the yuppie stereotypes beginning to appear in TV comedy
- the county set (and 'Sloane Rangers')
- some clergymen of the old school
- the voice that young English film actresses seemed to acquire in the 30's and 40's.

RP is also known as 'Queen's English' or 'BBC English'. It is the kind of speech that is described in such everyday remarks as:

He speaks like an educated man.
She talks properly.
I like to hear good, plain English.

RP is the English accent of educated, professional groups. It is not something imposed but something that has developed through generations of educated people talking together. There is no doubt that it is reinformed by social institutions such as universities, the BBC, the Civil Service, the legal profession, the world of business. It is regionally neutral, it is more easily understood by people learning to speak English and it facilitates communication across different cultures. It should not be regarded as the 'Best English' which would be to make the same mistake that underlies the concept of 'Home Counties'. It is nevertheless true that RP has come to be associated with the counties around London, but that is governed by political and economic factors not linguistic ones. Many highly educated speakers today resist RP because of the way in which it can be used to devalue regional accents, and continue to speak Standard English (see **dialect**) with their own regional accent.

Many linguists would argue that accent is an inescapable fact of language and that everybody will have one. The fact that however hard some may try to eliminate an accent they can never be sure it will not betray them at some point, is taken as evidence. Practised phoneticians have no difficulty in identifying the regional origins of BBC national news readers.

The whole issue of RP is fuelled by social prejudice and insecurity. What has happened historically is that more and more people are communicating very effectively in modified regional accents and that is typically how languages change, through common practice and adaptation rather than prescription and legislation. The question of RP is a national language pre-occupation in the sense that social distinctions and educational prejudice have bred in several generations a sense of deficiency about the way they speak. It is also part of a recognition that language gives power, and that power has traditionally spoken with an RP voice.

ACOUSTIC PHONETICS

◀ Phonetics ▶

ACTION

ACTION IN DRAMA

This refers to whatever is happening on stage, not only something which is 'active'. It's quite valid, therefore, to talk of the 'action' of a play even in those of, say, Samuel Beckett, where very little actually 'happens'.

While you are reading a play or passage, you will of course aim to gain an idea of what is actually *happening* in the scene. Sometimes the stage directions will help here – but more often you will need to work out what is going on from the words of the characters.

Look especially for signs of *movement* and *development* during the scene – how far things have changed from the situation at the beginning to that at the end. Sometimes action will be rapid, as in the short battle scenes of Shakespeare's history plays, or the comic scenes in Marlowe's *Doctor Faustus*. In other plays, for instance Shaw's *Heartbreak House*, there's less action than a series of views of a current phase of civilisation.

ADAPTATIONS

Many novels have been adapted into different forms. Stage plays, films and radio performances have frequently been made of well known (and some less well known) novels, and properly used these can be of value to you when revising.

Be careful, however, when watching films or stage adaptations. *Stage plays* will inevitably have to leave out certain parts of the action, especially in novels which are very long or which contain action that takes place in complex or frequently-changing settings. Very often, too, they will omit sub-plots or other aspects of the action, simply for reasons of time. Overall, they may present a version of the novel that is shorter in length and thinner in texture.

Much the same is true of *films*. They may deliberately extend the range of a novel, using locations or exteriors where the novel is concerned with the inner life of the characters. Some may concentrate on setting and visual effect to the detriment of deeper themes and ideas: some recent British films of E. M.

Forster's novels, for example, have tended to do this. Beware of something visually stunning and intellectually thin.

Radio adaptations are often the most successful treatments of novels. They frequently combine the use of a narrator with dramatised action, thus keeping the narrative voice and nature of the original and adding to it further dimensions of the characters. They are often far closer to the spirit of the original, too. Make a point, then, of checking to see if an adaptation of a novel you're studying is due to be broadcast. Radio 4 is the best place to look for the more popular serious novels, but Radio 3 sometimes has adaptations as well, so a close scrutiny of *Radio Times* or its equivalent may be a fruitful exercise.

ADDRESS

In linguistics address, or mode of address, refers to the ways in which people address or refer to each other in conversation or writing. e.g. Eh you; excuse me; sir; mate; luv; ducky; pet; Dear Sir or Madam; My learned friend; Your Lordship; Madam Chair; the Honourable Member for Warrington.

ADJECTIVES

Adjectives are a class of words that describe nouns. They can occur before the noun (e.g. the green hat), which is called the *attributive* position, or after the noun (e.g. the hat is green), which is called the *predicative* position because it is connected to the noun by a finite verb.

Adjectives are also distinguished by degrees:

good	fast	open	(positive degree)
better	faster	more open	(comparative degree)
best	fastest	most open	(superlative degree).

The term *adjectival(s)* is also used to denote words acting as adjectives but which are more likely to occur in another word class:

the *summer* house
the *walk*way
the *bus* seat
the *school* playground
the *college* curriculum.

ADJUNCT

A useful grammatical term to describe information in a sentence that can be moved or removed without affecting the structure of the sentence. Consider the following sentence:

The students organised a demonstration last term.

The students	= the subject of the sentence	(S)
organised	= the main verb	(V)
a demonstration	= the object of the main verb	(O)
last term	= the adjunct	(A).

Thus the pattern of this sentence may be written SVOA. Note that it could be ASVO or SAVO or SVAO. The word adjunct literally means 'joined to', and in most cases adjuncts are **adverbs**.

ADVERBS

Adverbs are a class of words which describe the action of the verb. Commonly they are signalled by the suffix −ly as in 'sadly', 'madly', 'badly' but many adverbs do not take this form (e.g. afterwards, then, fast, soon).

It is usual to classify the variety of adverbs in the following way:

He went *quickly* (manner).
Why did you go *there*? (place).
Tomorrow we go to Italy (time).
She is *very* tired (degree).

Given that the verb has a key role in sentences anything that modifies it plays a significant role in the overall meaning. Adverbs also modify whole sentences and are sometimes referred to as *adverbials*. The best way to distinguish between the two words is to treat adverbs as a word class and adverbials as *sentence connectors* or as *interpersonal features*. In both cases they allow the speaker or writer to insert a comment, express an attitude or indicate a point of view. Words like 'however', 'moreover', 'actually', 'in short', 'consequently' or 'as a consequence of this' make connections between sentences. Words like 'frankly', 'supposedly', 'possibly' establish an interpersonal connection between writer and reader, speaker and listener. They express a point of view.

AFFIXATION

This is the familiar process in English whereby the meaning of a word may be modified by the addition (affixation) of something to the beginning or the end of the word. Collectively these additions are called affixes and may be divided into *prefixes* (occurring at the beginning) and *suffixes* (occurring at the end). In **morphology** affixes are referred to as bound **morphemes**.

Some affixes used in English (e.g. −ology, psycho−, phono−, −graph, bio−, geo−) are derived from Ancient Greek but you should also observe everyday affixes like −ment, re−, −ly, which are equally important and much more common. Affixes borrowed from Greek and Latin are frequently found in philosophy, science and technology, and in medicine.

AFFRICATE

A sound produced in English by a combination of expelled air and friction.
The initial sound of *ch*op, *ch*ap, *ch*icken, *ch*alk is an affricate.
The initial sound in *j*udge, *j*ust, *J*apan, *j*oke, *j*olly is also an affricate.

ALEXANDRINE

◀ Metre ▶

ALIENATION OR A-EFFECT

A device created by the playwright Bertolt Brecht with the aim of preventing the audience from becoming too involved with the characters and actions of his plays, and so seeing them as 'real' instead of theatrical embodiments of ideas or moral standpoints.

This is really only one term for something that writers have been doing for centuries: the *chorus* in Greek drama can have the same effect, and many eighteenth-century novelists deliberately break the reader's sense of involvement by addressing him or her directly to make points about the characters.

ALLEGORY

An allegory is a story which exists on two levels at once. Generally a story is presented which can be taken at a straightforward literal level, but, when examined more deeply it is an exact parallel to a series of other events. This enables an elaborate commentary to be made upon the events being presented by implication only. George Orwell's *Animal Farm*, for instance, is an exact allegory of the events of the Russian revolution which reaches damning conclusions about the consequences of the seizure of power by the people; on the contrary, John Bunyan's *The Pigrim's Progress* is an allegory of the trials and sufferings that are undergone by the Christian soul in its progress through the earth which shows that, despite them all, it will receive blessing and satisfaction in heaven.

ALLITERATION

The repetition of the same consonant, usually at the beginning of a series of words. Students often feel that there is a kind of mystic power about alliteration when generally there isn't: it's a rather crude device to convey some degree of fluency. At times, however, it can have an important function in underlining meaning or creating effect. In the line 'I'll have him poisoned with a pot of ale' the repeated *p* sounds suggest venom and anger which well creates the mood of the speaker.

ALLOGRAPH

An allograph is simply a variant form of an alphabetical letter produced by differences of handwriting or typeface.

The following are all allographs of the letters b and g.

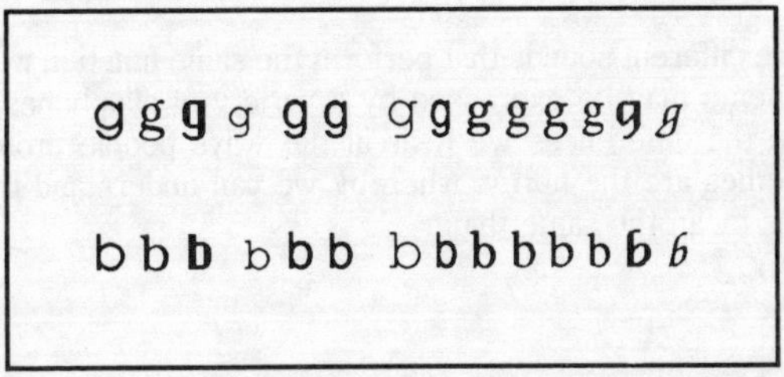

Fig. A.1

ALLOMORPH

This is a term used in **morphology** to identify a change in the form of a linguistic unit without a change in its meaning. The negative prefix in–, for example, means 'not' (as does un–). It occurs in words, like inadmissable, inattentive, inorganic, inexcusable. But in words like 'impossible', 'imbalance', 'impervious', 'impropriety' its pronunciation changes but the meaning remains the same. Thus 'im–' is an allomorph of 'in–'. Similarly 'in–', 'un–' and 'not' are all allomorphs. When English assimilates a word from another language problems are sometimes caused by the mismatch between the morphological rules of that language and the morphological rules of English. Greek and Latin borrowings raise well known problems. In English the plural, for example is usually formed by the addition of a suffix –s (e.g. cat, cats). Latin forms its plurals in different ways, as does Ancient Greek e.g.:

Singular	**Plural**
phenomenon	phenomena (Gk)
criterion	criteria (Gk)
curriculum	curricula (Latin)
datum	data (Latin)
syllabus	syllabi (Latin).

All these words are not uncommon in English use and their plural suffixes may be regarded as allomorphs of the English plural –s. Frequently though they give rise to irregularity in use, with varying degrees of public approval and disapproval. 'Criteria' is sometimes used when 'criterion' is meant. A pause is sometimes noticeable while English speakers try to remember which is which. Many English speakers however are uncomfortable with a word like 'syllabi' and prefer to speak or to write 'syllabuses' (note here that '–es' is a native allomorph of –s). 'Datum' is rarely used in English though it is the correct singular form in Latin. The plural form 'data' seems to have been grouped with words like 'fish' and 'sheep' as an acceptable singular as well as plural form when used in English.

ALLOPHONE

Allophones are different sounds that perform the same function within a word. A single phoneme may be expressed by a variety of allophones. Allophonic variations are the differences we hear in the ways people pronounce their words. Phonemes are the norms whereby we can understand that different pronunciations mean the same thing.

◀ Phonology ▶

ALLUSION

An allusion in a literary text is a reference to someone or something which brings in a series of associations which extend the meaning of the poem and enrich its significance.

> Apollo hunted Daphne so,
> Only that she might laurel grow;
> And Pan did after Syrinx speed,
> Not as a nymph, but for a reed.

These lines, from 'The Garden' by Andrew Marvell, refer to two pursuits from classical mythology. Apollo 'hunted Daphne' who, to avoid being raped, turned into a laurel; Syrinx, when pursued by Pan, was changed to a reed. These are allusions which someone with a classical education – like that which Marvell's original readers would have had – would recognise.

What is more important, though, is what the allusions *achieve*: why does Marvell use them? Here, the answer is to make a witty comment on the attractiveness of the garden. The Greek gods pursued the nymphs not for sexual gratification, Marvell suggests, but simply so that they would turn into plants. The pleasure of a garden, then, is wittily said to be greater than that of love, and Marvell has used allusion to a strikingly comic end.

In an exam, it's unlikely that you'd be given a poem to write about which has allusions as complex as these. If you are given such a poem, the allusions will probably be identified in a note. What matters, though, is not simply *identifying* the allusions – rather, as with changes of grammar and syntax, you must *say what they are used for*, and what they *contribute* to the poem as a whole.

The best way to prepare for allusions and references is to read as widely as you can, trying to extend your knowledge into all kinds of areas. Don't worry if you come across something that you don't recognise in the exam: think hard, and try to find an explanation which fits with the context and tone of the rest of the poem.

AMBIGUITY

The ability of words and sentences to express more than one meaning is both an advantage and a disadvantage. In everyday writing it is usual to take care not to introduce ambiguities and to hope that none have crept in unnoticed. The chief reasons for this are to keep information accurate and to make sure that specified actions or outcomes will be clearly understood. Instructions, declared intentions and practical purposes depend upon avoidance of ambiguity.

Poets, novelists and playwrights, on the other hand, deliberately exploit possibilities for ambiguity to produce a range of ironic or multi-dimensional effects which readers find stimulating and enjoyable. Humourists often rely on ambiguity (e.g. puns and *double entendres*) and much sexual comedy and impropriety is created by our ability to interpret things 'the wrong way'.

Rather than regard ambiguity in everyday speech as a crime or a sin, we should acknowledge that, in fact, it occurs all the time without causing any problems. What happens is that language users can have an instant capacity for *disambiguating* utterances according to context and according to what has been said previously. We usually identify what is intended and may not even notice an ambiguity until someone smiles or makes a passing reference: e.g.

> All that fuss over such a little thing!
> (The topic of conversation is a cut finger. 'Carry On' films depend upon old chestnuts like this for much of their humour).

Words like 'it' and 'thing' are notorious for giving rise to ambiguity.

The American linguist Noam Chomsky made a special study of ambiguity in language because it was such a frequent phenomenon, and used examples to demonstrate his notion of *surface grammar* and *deep structure grammar*. He considered the sentence:

> Flying aeroplanes can be dangerous

and pointed out that beneath the surface structure of this sentence are two different deep structures. One means, 'being a pilot can be dangerous'; the other means 'aeroplanes in flight can be dangerous'. On paper it might be difficult to decide which meaning is intended, especially out of context, but if such a statement occured in conversation it is highly likely that the participants would automatically know exactly what was intended.

Ambiguity of this kind is sometimes called *syntactic ambiguity*. Another common example occurs when it is not clear to whom, or to what, a pronoun refers e.g.

a) She saw her on *her* way to the cinema.
b) He told him that *his* job was under review.
c) They told them *their* team was the better of the two.

In a) we do not know from the syntax who the second 'her' is referring to.
In b) we are not sure whose job is under review.
In c) we do not know whether 'their' refers to 'they' or 'them'.

Lexical ambiguity

This occurs when the same word has two meanings:

i) Go and ask the butcher if he's got any brains.
ii) He went for a crash course as a driving instructor.

Phonological ambiguity

which occurs in speech:

i) The country hasn't an ocean.
   or
   The country hasn't a notion.
ii) Pity my simplicity.
   or
   Pity mice in Plicity.
iii) It's not the coughin' that carries you off, it's the coffin they carries you off in.

For a discussion of the multiple levels of meaning in literature, see Ambivalence.

◄ Ambivalence ►

AMBIVALENCE

Expression which by deliberate intent has more than one meaning. When Disraeli wrote to an adviser who had sent him the manuscript of a novel 'Thank you for your writing; I shall lose no time in reading it', he could have meant either that he would read it directly or that he would not waste his time on it.

Ambivalence is often a very valuable way of enriching the significance of a text. Andrew Marvell's 'Horation Ode', for example, may be read either as praise or condemnation of Oliver Cromwell, its subject. In texts such as these, there is no single, true 'meaning'; the significance lies in the simultaneous existence of several different attitudes.

Some writers prefer to use the term 'ambiguity' for this quality. As it is used in general speech to mean something which is unclear by accident or through faulty expression, however, it is best replaced by the term 'ambivalent'. In the study of language, too, ambiguous has a specific meaning.

'Multivalent' is a term used where there are more than two possible levels of meaning in a text.

◀ Ambiguity ▶

AMPHIBRACH

◀ Metre ▶

ANAPAEST

◀ Metre ▶

ANAPHORA (AND ANAPHORIC REFERENCE)

This is a grammatical term illustrating the economical nature of the English language. Consider the following:

> The car was a magnificent Bentley from another age. It was John's pride and joy. He had driven it to Monte Carlo many times and actually bought it there in 1936. That was the year of his greatest triumphs.

The underlined words are anaphoric because they refer back to something that the reader has already been told about.

> 'It' refers back to 'The car'.
> 'He' refers back to 'John' (as does 'his').
> 'It' again refers to 'The car' (twice).
> 'There' refers back to Monte Carlo.
> 'That' refers back to 1936.

The ability of a language to be anaphoric means that users do not have to repeat themselves constantly. Sometimes the word *cataphoric* is used for references forward and *exophoric* for references outside the text but there seems to be a general tendency to use anaphoric to cover all references of this kind – whatever the direction of the reference.

ANTONYM

Antonyms are words that express opposites e.g. kind/cruel; generous/mean; in/out.

◀ Meaning ▶

APPLIED LINGUISTICS (AND APPLIED PHONETICS)

Traditionally, academic linguistics has been applied to the practical fields of second language learning, speech therapy, voice training, and the compilation of dictionaries. In more recent years linguistics has increasingly been applied to social studies (hence sociolinguistics) and to areas of pyschology (hence psycholinguistics). There are also some interesting applications of linguistics to aspects of information technology (e.g. computer languages; voice simulation; effects of word processing on writing).

ARCHAISM

The deliberate use of an old-fashioned word or expression, usually to add to the atmosphere of a poem or prose passage. In *The Faerie Queene*, for example, Edmund Spenser uses archaic terms to make the story sound more like an ancient legend, beginning with the line 'A Gentil Knight was pricking on the plaine'; mock-mediaeval language is used by Keats in 'The Eve of St Agnes' for the same reason.

ARTICULATORY PHONETICS

Articulatory phonetics is concerned with how humans make speech sounds.
◀ Phonetics ▶

ASIDE

◀ Elizabethan Stage ▶

ASSIMILATION

In **phonology** assimilation refers to the way in which individual sounds merge with each other when in a continuous sequence. When we speak the words tend to run into each other unlike written words which are spaced on the page. Pauses in speech are for effect, or for breath, or they are caused by hesitation. They do not normally separate the words unless we are speaking very deliberately.

It is this feature which determines the rhythm and intonation of what we say. You may well have already discovered that whilst *phoneme theory* (see **phonology**) is a useful way of identifying the sound segments of English it is the *supra-segmental* features of an accent that are more often noticeable rather than the individual phonemes. Supra-segmental simply means across two or three, or more, phonemes.

Assimilation also occurs within words. Lady Bracknell in Oscar Wilde's *The Importance of Being Earnest* may well have pronounced every phoneme in the word 'handbag', and achieved a famous comic effect, but the pronunciation of the word most frequently heard in everyday use is an assimilation that sounds more like 'hambag'.

'h–a–n–d–b–a–g'.

The term assimilation can also be used to describe ways in which words from foreign languages or other dialects can be absorbed into another language or dialect.

ASSONANCE

The repetition of the same vowel sound in a series of words – for example, in the line 'the brown frown of a drowned town'. Here it suggests dreariness. Like alliteration, the technique is best commented on only when it reveals a particular aspect of the meaning or effect of the line.

AUXILIARIES

Auxiliaries are verb forms derived from 'to be' and 'to have'. They help other verbs to be more precise. An extreme example is contained in the following:

> *Having had* a serious setback, he *will have to have* fully recovered before he *will be able* to fly again.

AUDITORY PHONETICS

Auditory phonetics is concerned with how we hear speech sounds.

◀ Phonetics ▶

AYER, A J

Ayer, a British philosopher (1910–1988) first came to prominence in 1936 when he published *Language, Truth and Logic* which proved a formative influence on British linguistic philosophy. For language to be meaningful Ayer asserted that its propositions must be verifiable by sense experience common to all, or there must be a social convention that determines how a word is being used. In this way Ayer restricted meaning to scientific, logical prepositions and had nothing to say about the language of art, religion or ethics because it was too full of unverifiable expressions of states of feeling, or of what ought to be. Much of his later work, *The Problem of Knowledge* (1956) and *The Central Questions of Philosophy* (1972) continued to explore how we can think and talk philosophically with only language to do it with. His logical positivist view of language was rejected by those whose view of language and philosophy did not outlaw expression of feelings, subjective states and non-physical awareness.

B

BALLAD

A narrative poem, telling its story (often at some length) in a simple, unadorned way, and with a minimum of characterisation and description. Original ballads were often anonymous folk tales, but the style has been copied copiously by many authors. The *Lyrical Ballads* of Wordsworth and Coleridge attempt to use everyday language of the folk tale in a context of serious poetry.

BASIC ENGLISH

Basic English is a concept frequently invoked by political critics, and some educationists, who feel that young people are inadequately educated in their use of language. It is an ideologically loaded concept which assumes that a language can be reduced to a basic minimum which, if teachers concentrated on it, would enable pupils to use English much better. The problem with this reductionist approach is that it is never basic enough. The teaching of routine exercises on nouns, apostrophes, agreement and sentence joining never reaches the deeper level of language production where the problems really lie.

Sometimes people mean by Basic English, 'Standard English' (see **dialect**) but often it is used in a prejudiced way against a regional accent, or against a younger generation whose use of English reflects changes that have recently taken place in the language but which do not directly affect an older generation, e.g. 'They can't even speak basic English!'

In 1944 the government set up a committee on Basic English and an interesting account of its work is given in a Ministry of Education pamphlet *Language: some suggestions for teachers* (HMSO 1954). In the pamphlet, a speech by the 1944 Prime Minister, Winston Churchill, has been converted into Basic English to show how effective it can be.

BATHOS

A rapid collapse from something which is serious, or perhaps serene, to something which is ridiculous. Alexander Pope very often uses bathos to telling effect in his poems, as in this example:

> Here thou, great ANNA! whom three realms obey,
> Dost sometimes counsel take – and sometimes Tea

BIBLIOGRAPHY

If you're writing an extended essay – or even a detailed one of normal length – it's helpful to list the books you've consulted. This should go at the end of the essay, and include the elements shown below. Arrange the books in alphabetical order of author or editor's surname, and include all the details given in the example. Generally speaking, the bibliography will include all the books you've consulted which have significantly aided your research, and of course all the books from which you've quoted.

There are various standard forms for entries in a bibliography, but the following is reliable and clear. This is the order for a book:
Author (surname and initials): Title (underlined): Publisher: Place of Publication: Date of Publication.
An example would look like this:

Carter, D.N.G, Robert Graves: The lasting Poetic Achievement, Macmillan, London, 1989

For an article in a periodical, the order is as follows:
Author: Title of article (in quotation marks): Title of periodical (underlined): Volume and number of periodical: Date of periodical: Page numbers of article.
For example:

Johnson, W.S., 'Memory, landscape, Love: John Ruskin's Poetry and Poetic Criticism', Victorian Poetry, Vol 19 No 1, Spring 1981, pp. 19–34

BI-DIALECTAL

Bi-dialectalism is a term referring to the ability to use two dialects. It is similar to *Bi-lingual*. The term multi-dialectal may also be used.

BLANK VERSE

This is verse written in lines of iambic pentameter which do not rhyme. The most celebrated examples in English are Milton's *Paradise Lost* and Wordsworth's *The Prelude*. Milton chose to use unrhymed verse because he felt – along with many poets before and since – that rhyme was an inferior form of writing.

Blank verse is usually divided into sections, according to its own progress, which are generally called paragraphs. Do not confuse blank verse with **free verse**.

BLOOMFIELD, LEONARD

Eminent American linguist, Leonard Bloomfield (1887–1949) was very influential in pre-war studies of language. Despite the reaction against his rigorously behaviouristic approach to language use and his insistent concentration on structures rather than on meaning and functions, his book *Language* (1933) remains a very readable introduction and his reassuring remark that 'all grammars leak', ought never to be forgotten by students of language.

BRAINSTORMING

◀ Essays ▶

BURLESQUE, PARODY AND PASTICHE

1 A burlesque is an imitation of the style of a serious or elevated piece of writing in a work which has a ridiculous or comic subject. The result is comic because of the great difference between subject and style: usually this difference is used to satirise the subject treated. Samuel Butler's *Hudibras*, for example, is a comic burlesque of a courtly romance – a noble, heroic story of chivalry and valour – which satirises the limited ideas of Puritanism by narrating commonplace events and deeds in a style which is a comic imitation (see **mock-epic**) of heroic poetry.
2 A parody is similar, but is often used about writing which is of greater literary merit – for example, Pope's *The Rape of the Lock* which, though discussing a trivial subject, contains writing of great subtlety and skill.
3 The term pastiche is often used of burlesques or parodies, but properly it is a word assembled from a series of fragments borrowed or stolen from other sources. The sense of incompleteness this often provides can result in the same kind of incongruity apparent in the other forms – but the origin is quite different.

BUSINESS OR STAGE-BUSINESS

This is a term used to refer to parts of the action which call for the characters to perform certain physical acts. In John Arden's *Serjeant Musgrave's Dance*, for example, there is a lot of 'business' which includes assembling a Gatling gun. It's easy to overlook this kind of action, as it's only described in the stage directions. But remember that a paragraph of description may take several minutes to perform on stage – so don't overlook *stage business* in your study of a text, and make sure that you use the term properly when writing about it.

C

CARICATURE

A character whose personality is described in terms of a very small number of features, often grossly exaggerated. Many of Dickens' characters, for example, are grotesques, used to expose or satirise various human failings.

CATHARSIS

The idea that the feelings and desires of the audience are purified by the violent action which occurs in the closing scenes of a tragedy – originally a Greek term but used by the Elizabethans about their own very gory plays. The debate on whether violence on stage rids the audience of their anger, or simply incites them to further violence, is one that has raged for many years and is still current today.

CHARACTER

This is generally used to mean 'a person in a play or novel'. Try not to use it to mean 'what a person's like'; otherwise you end up talking about 'the character of a character'. Try using 'nature' instead.

CHARACTERS IN PLAYS

Dramatic characters are *not* real people, and can't properly be considered outside the theatrical texts of which they are a part. One of the most common reasons why people do badly in exams – when writing about their set texts as well as in critical appreciation papers – is that they write about characters as if they were actual people – so you must avoid this and instead see each one as part of the larger themes and action of the play.

Despite this, you do need to think carefully about the nature of each of the characters who speaks or takes part in the scene you are given for critical appreciation. Do this by studying the following:

- *What they say*. This is the essential information for understanding a character and his or her contribution to the whole play. Look at the kinds of words; the tone and diction of the speeches; the structure of the sentences; the frequency with which he or she speaks; stage directions which accompany the speeches; and the meaning of what he or she actually says and its significance within the situation of the scene. All of these will tell you a great deal about the character.

- *What others say*. What the characters say to and about each other will reveal much about their relationships. Remember, though, that each character will look at things from his or her own viewpoint – so don't assume that they are giving a full or unbiased commentary on each other.
- *How the characters behave towards each other*. Look to see if one character is persistently ignored, or if his or her remarks are treated with respect and immediately acted on. Look, too, at what actions, if any, take place between the characters, since these too will reveal much about their relationships.

CHARACTERS IN NOVELS

Characters in novels are rather similar to characters in plays: they are an essential element of the structure of the whole, but they must not be seen as people in their own right. When making detailed notes about a novel, think about what the characters contribute to the development of the plot and the discussion of themes and ideas which are the novel's concern. You will not be asked to write a simple study of a character from a novel or play in the exam: you may very well be asked what techniques the novelist uses to make him or her real, or what he or she contributes to the discussion of various themes or ideas, and this should be the main focus of your attention when reading in detail.

◀ Drama, Prose ▶

CHOMSKY, NOAM

Noam Chomsky, born in 1928, is one of the world's most distinguished linguists. Professor of Modern Languages and Linguistics at the Massachussets Institute of Technology (MIT), his influence has been so great that we now talk of an intellectual revolution wrought by his work. His name has become a familiar adjective to describe the new perspective he brought to linguistics (Chomskyan). He published a number of significant studies in the 1960s and one of his best known writings is his review in the New York Review of Books (1959) of a book called *Verbal Behaviour* published by the eminent behaviourist psychologist, Professor Burras Skinner. Skinner argued that children learn language in the same way that rats and pigeons learn their behaviour, that is to say, by imitation. Chomsky on the other hand argues that children learn by creative processes since there simply would not be enough time to learn all that they do learn between 0 and 3 years if they had to imitate everything. Furthermore, children produce linguistic constructions which follow rules but which could never have been learned from an adult (e.g. we buyed some mices).

Chomsky's work has had considerable influence on the development of psycholinguistics especially on studies of how language works in the mind and how it affects our thinking.

Chomsky's approach to grammar takes time to learn for though he uses many of the traditional terms (nouns, verbs, etc.) his system of relating the sources of language production (the deep structures) to what we actually utter (the surface structures) is complex and requires considerable practice. (see tree diagrams).

Ironically, it is Chomsky's grammar that has most relevance to educational issues such as becoming a better writer, than the traditional approach to grammar (illustrated under **parsing**). In popular opinion it is parsing that is thought to be most useful to pupils but in fact parsing gets nowhere near the generative source of language where development really takes place. Chomsky's grammar, despite its difficulties, gets at the parts other grammars cannot reach!

CHORUS

Originally a body of performers in Greek drama who recited or chanted lines commenting on the action of the play before them. Nowadays the term is used of any character who acts as commentator in a play. Shakespeare's *Henry V* uses a chorus to set the scene and add dynamism to the play's action.

CLAUSE

A clause may usefully be regarded in the first instance as a unit of coherent thought. If we imagine words, feelings, ideas, grammatical structures all floating about in our minds, a clause occurs when these different elements cohere into a recognisable, meaningful expression. Frustrated anger, for example, could come out as a one word exclamation e.g. *Damn*! or it could take the form of a statement e.g. 'You infuriate me' or a question, e.g. 'What is the meaning of this?' or a command e.g. 'Get out of my sight'. You should notice that a clause has the characteristics of a *simple sentence*. It contains a subject and a finite verb.

It should be distinguished from a *phrase* (or *group*) which is a combination or pattern of words without a finite verb e.g.

- a large, black car belonging to the Mafia
- a little, old lady
- a fond, foolish boy
- tripe and onions
- in a manner of speaking.

Notice that the present participle verbs, 'belonging' and 'speaking', are not finite verbs.

It is perfectly possible to express oneself at length in speech or in writing in single clauses (or simple sentences) without necessarily sounding immature or simple-minded.

Clauses may be connected very economically and effectively by using such familiar words as 'and', 'but' or 'then'.

We went to the pictures, *then* we went for a Chinese meal.
I'm not very goot at tennis *but* I'd like to join the tennis club.
I will be seventeen next birthday *and* my father has booked me some driving lessons.

This kind of clause connection is called *co-ordination* and words like 'and' are called *co–ordinating conjunctions*. They join clauses together but each clause retains its independece. A long sequence of written sentences consisting of co-ordinated clauses tends to become wearisome for the reader since it is never more than one thing after another. In speech long sequences of such sentences are common and less wearisome because by means of intonation, gesture and contextual cues we can signal more subtle connections between clauses. Consider, for example:

He had a rotten cold but he went to the meeting.

You should not have any difficulty saying that in an approving way which means 'Despite the fact that he had a rotten cold he did his duty and went to the meeting'.

You could also say it in a disapproving way, meaning, 'Knowing full well that he had a rotten cold, he stupidly went to the meeting'.

Intonation would convey the implied relationship between the clauses. If, however, we wish to state more explicitly one of several dependent relationships between clauses then we have to use *subordinating conjunctions* e.g.

a) *Although* I like novels, I'm not very keen on modern authors.
or
I'm not very keen on modern authors, *although* I like novels.

b) *If* you do it that way, you will regret it.
or
You will regret it, *if* you do it that way.

c) *When* you reach the steps, you must turn left.
or
You must turn left, *when* you reach the steps.

d) *Unless* you pay now, you will be asked to leave.
or
You will be asked to leave, *unless* you pay now.

Note that the structure of these sentences is so neat that you can invert the clauses without altering the meaning. Note also the usefulness of the comma in marking off each clause, but note equally that if the comma is left out the structure and the subordinating conjunction will still carry the meaning quite unambiguously.

Some of the relationships expressed by subordinating conjunctions are:
- causal (because)
- consequential (therefore)
- conditional (if)
- concessional (although)
- temporal (when)

The complexity of a sentence lies in the use of subordinating conjunctions to connect two or more clauses.

CLICHÉ

A cliché is an expression that is so frequently used that the idea behind it has become commonplace.
- It's a hard life if you don't weaken.
- Love makes the world go round.
- You can't buy happiness.
- Your health comes first.

There is no doubt that clichés can be tiresome if they occur too regularly. A common joke is that politicians' speech consists entirely of clichés. The trouble with clichés is not so much that they are well known expressions but that they can sound too easy and even insincere. They do not renew the language at all and if not used sincerely, they become bankrupt of meaning. On the other hand there are occasions when, sincerely meant, a cliché is just the right thing to say. What happens on such occasions is that the immediacy of the situation floods meaning back into the words:
- there's always somebody worse off
- put not your trust in Princes
- you never know what's round the corner.

Features of a language related to clichés are proverbs, aphorisms, sayings, mottoes. The whole area is an excellent quarry for language study projects. You could investigate literature as a source of clichés and classify their content and contexts.

The approach of a language student to any commonplace aspect of language use should not be one of finding obvious shortcomings to disapprove of, but rather of asking:
- What is the structure of such things?
- What are the functions?
- What variety is there in form or function?
- What are the social contexts of use?
- How do they compare in speech and writing?
- What are the origins? (Sometimes difficult to discover).
- What new 'clichés' or sayings have occurred in your own experiences?

CODE

The word code is used in a variety of ways in language study. Language itself may be described as a symbolic coding of experience far more advanced than animal signal systems appear to be.

Value systems (good/bad, right/wrong, us/them, male/female) are also encoded in a language so that the language we learn determines the way we think and behave (see **Sapir-Whorf hypothesis**). Consider for example the fact that the word 'right' always carries with it an approving moral judgement alongside a particular political persuasion. The word 'left' on the other hand is not only the opposite of 'right' but also associates 'leftist' political persuasions with the word 'wrong', a word of disapproval. Thus there is a built-in advantage to the word 'right' (i.e. right equals right) and a built-in disadvantage to the word 'left' (i.e. left equals wrong).

Gender coding is a very well known feature of English that disadvantages feminine or female concepts.

Code-mixing and *code switching* occur when two or more languages are in use (e.g. Punjabi and English). Users mix words and phrases from one language into the other or, on specific occasions switch completely from one language to the other. This makes an extremely good topic for a language study project because it tends to collect very interesting data and offers an opportunity to draw conclusions, with some objectivity, or personal experience.

The term code has also been used by Basil Bernstein to relate characteristics of language use to social class or community patterns of living: *restricted code* and *elaborated code*.

COHESION

Cohesion refers to syntactic links within sentences but more especially to links between sentences. Remember that it is not the same thing as *coherence*. The following passage is *cohesive*, it is hardly *coherent*:

> John plays cricket on Sunday. Cricketers from the West Indies are very famous. My father went to the West Indies once. He sailed in the Merchant Navy. Merchant seamen had a badge with MN on it and a crown on top. John collects badges.

COLLOCATION

Collocation refers to the way in which words habitually occur in the company of other words so that the use of one automatically invokes another. Popular examples are 'night and day', 'left and right', 'rights and wrongs', 'fish and chips'. Les Dawson's TV game *Blankety Blank* is based on the statistical probability with which words, especially compound nouns (see **nouns**), will collocate. In everyday language use, as well as in literature, it is always a pleasure to be surprised by an effective break in the expected patterns or an unusual collocation. It is also a cause of great laughter among young children (e.g. fish and Christmas cake; the Owl and the Copycat; the Frog Princess). These are all unexpected collocations.

COMEDY

In popular speech, this simply means something that is funny. In the theatre this is not always the case. Shakespeare's comedies, for example, are not always 'funny'. Instead, the word refers to a particular kind of play. Shakespearean comedy generally moves from confusion and uncertainty about identity and love to a conclusion in which confusions are resolved, lovers are united and there is a feeling of progression and resolution. *Comedy of Manners* is a general term for later seventeenth and eighteenth century plays which make their effect by satirising sophisticated behaviour, generally with a strong love interest; and *Social Comedy* is a term often used to describe later writing on a similar theme, such as the plays of Oscar Wilde.

COMIC

This has two meanings in the theatre: the usual, everyday sense of something funny, and the sense of 'referring to a comedy' in structure or tone. Because this can be confusing, it might be better to use the term 'comedic' when you mean the latter; it may sound a little fussy, but it makes the meaning absolutely clear.

COMPETENCE

Competence is a term that describes a persons fundamental knowledge of his or her own language. It is a term introduced by **Chomsky** and refers to the apparent nucleus of language knowledge that begins to unfold itself very early in life enabling humans to acquire their native language on their own, by an application of rules that nobody seems to have taught them. Chomsky distinguishes it from *performance* which refers to the variety of uses and abilities which competent language users display. Competence is apparently innate grammatical knowledge; performances are specific uses and learned behaviour. (See also **Saussure** on *language* and *parole*).

COMPLEX WORDS

Complex words are made up of at least two parts. There will be a main part (stem, core, head word) and one or more attachments (or affixes) which will affect how we understand the meaning of the core word. In morphological terms, a complex word is made up of one *free morpheme* together with one or more *bound morphemes*:

e.g. dogs	= dog+s
going	= go+ing
disabled	= dis+abl(e)+ed
playing	= play+ing
unstable	= un+stable
mismanagement	= mis+manage+ment.

Remember that a word cannot be 'more complex' or 'less complex'. It is either complex in structure or it is not. 'Dogs' and 'traditionalism' are equally complex words even though one is longer and contains two bound morphemes. Words that are not complex will be either *simple* or *compound*.

◄ Affixation, Morphology ►

COMPOUND WORDS

In much the same way that a compound locomotive is made up of more than one engine, or a chemical compound, more than one element, so a compound word is made up of two cores, or self-contained units. In morphological terms it is a word made up of two free morphemes. Sometimes the words are hyphenated, sometimes not. *Compounding* is a common feature of the English language and one of the ways in which **new words** are created. Well known compound words are – headrest, backache, toothbrush, greenhouse, into, moreover, policeman, catfish, doglead, strawberry, blackboard, overdrive.

The relationships between the two elements (or the free morphemes) of a compound word are varied but exact. A *blackboard* for example is a *board* that is *black* but a *greenhouse* is not a *house* that is *green*. It is the precision of the nuance and the economy of the strucuture that make compounds so useful in English. New compounds may seem odd at first: sometimes they are hyphenated, sometimes not; they seem like separate words and yet they are in process of becoming one word. The following are examples of new compounds in their original contexts, and in later metaphorical contexts:

a) i) The *sell by* date is 8 August 1989.
ii) I am long past my *sell by* date.
b) i) Batteries do not have a long *shelf life*.
ii) Government reports do have a long *shelf life*. They are not often taken off the shelf!

CONCEIT

Some idea of the meaning of this term may be gained by noting its similarity to the word concept, or idea. The conceit was a device in sixteenth and early seventeenth century poetry which often depended on an unlikely parallel being drawn between two very different entities. Often it is extended to very great lengths. In *A Valediction, Forbidding Mourning,* for example, John Donne compares himself and his lover to the twin legs of a compass to show how they are separate yet united when apart, and how a movement of one inspires movement in the other; the conceit even includes a note of bawdy which, in the poem, has an effect of great tenderness.

CONSONANT

◀ International phonetic alphabet, Phonology ▶

CONTEXT

Old style grammar books for schools contained hundreds and hundreds of sentences which pupils had to correct, alter, parse, fill in blanks, or explain. All of them were decontextualised sentences so that pupils had no knowledge of the social context in which they had been uttered. Most likely they had not been uttered by anybody but made up by a grammarian (see examples under parsing). Modern studies of language pay considerable attention to social context, recognising that context has a powerful influence on the interpretation of meaning. Often decontextualised sentences can be made to mean almost anything.

CONTRACTION

Contractions occur when the spelling or pronunciation of a word is shortened. By far the commonest examples are verb forms, and the negative form: e.g.

– *he'd*	for	*he would*	
– *I'll*	for	*I will*	
– *you're*	for	*you are*	(**not** 'your'!)
– *I'm*	for	*I am*	
– *they're*	for	*they are*	(**not** 'their'!)
– *haven't*	for	*have not*	
– *isn't*	for	*is not*	
– *who's*	for	*who is*	(**not** 'whose'!)
– *John's*	for	*John is*	(**not** 'John's' meaning possession!).

CONTRASTIVE PAIRS

This is a useful concept in language study because it permits so many comparisons. It is also surprising how frequently linguistic data comes in pairs.

In **phonology** we can contrast /pin/ and /bin/ in order to show that there is a meaningful difference between /p/ and /b/.

In **phonetics** we can contrast voiced and unvoiced sounds.

In **deictics** we can contrast here/there, then/now.

The contrastive approach is also helpful in stylistic analysis where the distinctive features of one kind of text can more readily be observed by contrasting and comparing them with the features of a different text.

COUPLET

A two-line unit of poetry. Shakespeare uses a couplet to end his sonnets with a statement of particular truth or originality; Alexander Pope wrote most of his poetry in the form of heroic couplets, and much of Chaucer's *Canterbury Tales* uses the same form. The following example is from Oliver Goldsmith:

Ill fares the land, to hastening ills a prey
Where wealth accumulates, and men decay.

COURTLY LOVE

A philosophy of love, and an attitude towards it, that influenced medieval literature. It flourished and was formalised in the royal courts of the South of France in the twelfth century. It dealt with aristocratic, extra-marital love conducted in secret. The male lover was totally subservient to his mistress, worshipped her as a goddess, and was completely at her mercy. Though the love affairs are often sexual and sensual, the physical side of the affair is treated with great dignity and decorum, and the love is a rarified spiritual experience as much as a physical one. Geoffrey Chaucer (?1345–1400) makes significant use of the courtly love mode of writing, but can also satirise it, as in *The Merchant's Tale*. By Chaucer's time middle-class morality was beginning to creep into courtly love tales, with an attempt to combine the idealism of courtly love with the morality of marriage, a very difficult balancing act as the two ways of looking at relationships view the relative dominance of man and woman quite differently. Chaucer's *The Franklin's Tale* is the best known example of such an attempt to combine the different outlooks on marriage and courtly love.

CREATIVE WRITING

Some syllabuses allow you to submit a collection of creative writing – poems, short stories, dramatic sketches or even radio or television scripts. This kind of work can be very stimulating and rewarding, but it can also be very time-consuming, so think carefully before taking it on.

Contrary to popular belief, you *can* teach yourself how to write *creatively* – poems and short stories are not things which just happen by spontaneous combustion, but need to be worked on.

The best preparation for such writing is careful thought and discussion – with yourself, with fellow-students, and with your teacher. Think carefully about those *ideas* which would make a good story or poem, or *structures* which might be interesting to pursue. Consider unlikely situations or ideas, or try to put yourself inside someone else's mind to record his or her feelings. These approaches will help you to get the *basic idea* – which you then need to hone carefully over a sustained period.

The only difference between creative writing for a language syllabus and that in a literature course is that, in the former, you are often asked to write a *commentary* on what you have written. This could:

- explain your aims;
- say how far you think you've achieved them;
- analyse the writing critically;
- suggest influences on the writing.

The commentary should *not* be a lengthy explanation of the circumstances under which you wrote the piece, as this does not discuss the writing itself. When writing this sort of exercise, try to be practical and specific. Avoid lengthy metaphysical speculations on how you were aiming to summarise 'the quintessential vacuity of the post-Freudian dilemma'; it may sound impressive, but it doesn't actually mean very much.

Comment instead on specific words, images or structures. A look at the entry under **questions** will help you here – and also read about the critical appreciation of **poetry**, **drama** and **prose** will help you to look at the work dispassionately. It's often a good idea to leave your work for a little while before writing a commentary about it – in this way, you'll see the whole thing much more clearly and be able to write about it with greater detachment and honesty.

CREOLE

A creole is a language based on two (sometimes more) languages which in time becomes the native language of its speakers. It can derive from a **pidgin** language created jointly by traders and a native population. Creoles are to be found in Jamaica and Haiti and were brought to England by West Indian immigrants.

CRITICAL APPRECIATION

Critical appreciation is one of the essential skills of literary study. It is the ability to read a text and understand both what it says and the techniques the writer has used in order to say it.

You may be doing a separate paper on this subject – check with your teacher or your syllabus to make sure. If you are you'll be given two or three passages – usually one of poetry, one of prose and one from a play. You'll then be asked to discuss them, showing what their main themes and ideas are, what techniques the writer has used to put them across, perhaps giving your own feelings about them.

Even if you're *not* doing a critical appreciation paper, the skills of critical reading are still important. In fact, they are the basic equipment of literary study: knowing how to read and understand a passage is the essence of the whole subject. So whether or not you're doing a paper of this sort, you need to master these skills.

◀ Drama, Poetry, Prose ▶

CRITICAL TEXTS

You may find it helpful to read what *other people* have to say about the texts you are studying. Certainly, there is no shortage of critical writing about most of the texts set at A-level. But be careful:

- Reading a critical text can be confusing, especially if you choose something that goes too deeply into an aspect of the text you're studying.
- Be selective – you can't read **all** that's been written on T.S. Eliot, let alone Shakespeare. Get advice from your teacher or lecturer on what to read.
- Try not to read material that is too old – a lot of libraries still have books which contain ideas and approaches which have now been superseded.

CRYSTAL, DAVID

A distinguished British linguist (b 1941) who was Professor of Linguistic Science at the University of Reading and is now Professional Fellow at the University College of North Wales. Through broadcasting, personal appearances and a range of stimulating books, he has done much to promote general interest in the field of modern linguistics. In particular he has engaged with the concerns of speech therapists and schoolteachers to make linguistics intelligible, and applicable to everyday life.

In books like *Who Cares About English Usage?* (Penguin 1984) and *The English Language* (Penguin 1988) he tackles many of the old grammatical prescriptions that many modern speakers are unsure about (e.g. not ending sentences with prepositions, or not splitting infinitives). He puts them in the cultural context of their origins and distinguishes between irrational advice derived from the prejudice that English ought to be like Latin, and the kind of practical advice which continues to make communicative as well as common sense.

Listen To Your Child (Penguin 1988) is written for parents but is an ideal introduction to language acquisition for A-level students.

His *Encyclopedia of Language* (Cambridge 1987) is monumental, fascinating, and indispensable to A-level students. See also reference to *Rediscover English Grammar* (1988) under **grammar**.

D

DACTYL

◀ Metre ▶

DEIXIS AND DEICTIC

Deixis is expressed in modest words like 'here', 'now', 'it', 'this', 'the above' but it is a vital concept if language users are to keep their bearings during conversation or reading. Deictic words are orientation words that locate precisely what is being talked about and where attention should be paid. 'This here' as opposed to 'that there', 'now' as opposed to 'then'. 'You on the one hand . . . while I on the other' – all of these are deictic references. If they are misused we become unsure about the meaning. The word 'this' is a very common deictic reference that is easily misused. Here is an example:

> 'Hamlet was cut off from his student past, digusted with the present, and pessimistic about the future. It was *this* that caused his anguish'.

In order to make unequivocal sense of this sentence we group three things together (references to past, present and future) so that the singular 'it' makes the best sense. The writer however has thought it important to itemise three causes and yet they came out as one thing at the end, 'It was *this* . . .'.

The sentence is not totally unacceptable but imprecise. Notice too the occurrence of another deictic word, 'it', which sets us off on the expectation of precision.

> 'It (was a combination of all these things) that caused his anguish'.

A similar sentence from a history essay:

> 'The barons made their own laws, levied taxes for themselves, refused to contribute to the King's army and were constantly fighting among themselves. Something had to be done about it'.

We can understand this sentence quite easily but notice that the final 'it' is imprecise. If it were changed to another deictic word 'them' we would know it meant the barons. If it were changed to 'these problems' we would know it referred to what the barons did. If it were changed to 'her' the effect on the reader would be quite disorientating to say the least. From this passage alone we can have no idea of the deictic references for 'her'.

If a story begins:

'He knew that it was something she had to do'.

We are intrigued, and that is a good way to begin a story: We have no idea who *he* is, what the *something* is, or who *she* is. We read on to find out. If the deictic questions are not answered we get annoyed.

Sometimes vagueness in the use of deictic words can be effective. Quite often nowadays we hear people say 'This is it ' with the intonation of a quite emphatic exclamation. Someone may be expressing a grievance about the college food, or the inconvenient timetable and end by saying:

'Nobody cares in this place'.

The response, 'I know. This is it.' is a lively way of expressing agreement but it also says 'You have put your finger on it' which is yet another deictic expression. Often though, in this sort of informal talk it is difficult to actually identify what 'it' was, even though at the time there was considerable feeling of agreement. Another good topic for a project.

DENOUEMENT

The final revelation of a key point or feature at the end of a novel or play. The most obvious example of a denouement is the revelation of 'whodunnit' at the end of a murder mystery, but there are others which are just as important in more serious literature – such as the revelation of the identity of Tom's mother in Fielding's *Tom Jones*, for example.

DENTAL

Consonant sounds made by the teeth and the tongue e.g. [d] and [t].

DESCRIPTIVE GRAMMAR

A descriptive grammar attempts to describe the structures of a language and the rules governing those structures. You could almost say that the term was tautologous since it is the business of grammar to identify and describe structure. Nevertheless the term descriptive grammar has become important because it makes a distinction between a scientific, linguistic approach to grammar and a non-scientific approach known as **prescriptive grammar**. Prescriptive grammar makes educational and cultural recommendations about what is correct use of English grammar, based largely on Greek and Latin models. Rules in descriptive grammar are observable regularities in the way language is used; rules in a prescriptive grammar state how people should talk and write. More often prescriptive grammars tell you what you should **not** do and for that reason are sometimes called *proscriptive*. (See also under **Crystal** for references to examples of prescriptivism).

A-level courses in language study are concerned with a descriptive approach to grammar. Prescriptive approaches are considered under attitudes toward language.

An extreme example of prescriptivism can be seen in the following excerpt taken from *A Manual of English Grammar* by the Rev. A.M. Trotter (1885):

Scotticisms

Instead of	*Say*
I cannot get into my box.	I cannot open my box.
Give me another one.	Give me another.
I am very dry.	I am very thirsty.
He feels afraid.	He is afraid.
Can you play cards?	Can you play at cards?
Did you drive across the bridge?	Did you drive along the bridge?
Who lives above you?	Who lives over you?

Prescriptive approaches at their best offer common sense, often they are pedantic and irrational, but at their worst they are deeply prejudiced and offensive. The very word 'Scotticisms' is an affront to millions of people who speak English with a Scottish accent. Notice too that there is no distinction between how a language is used in informal speech and how it is used in formal contexts.

DIACHRONIC

Diachronic literally means 'through time'. Thus a diachronic study shows the way that language and language use change over a period of time, whereas a synchronic study shows the variety of language at any single time.

DIACRITICS

For A-level, English language students should know the International Phonetic Alphabet so that they can transcribe accurately the 44 phonemes of British English when they need to transcribe them. Accuracy however is a relative term when we talk about phonemes but a phonemic transcription is better than phonetic spelling. The study of phonetics however requires an even more precise denotation of sounds and uses diacritical marks in addition to the symbols of IPA. Diacritics indicates such things as nuances of sound, points of articulation, stress and intonation. If you have studied French or

German you will know some of these marks:

´ indicates an acute accentuation in French
` indicates a grave accentuation in French
^ indicates a circumflex accentuation in French
¨ indicates an umlaut sound in German.

In phonetics there are many more (see p159 of *The Cambridge Encyclopedia of Language* (1987)).

DIALECT

Variety is in the nature of language just as it is in the nature of DNA to diversify itself into the myriad flora and fauna that exist in the world. We do not object to the variety of flowers in a garden, we enjoy it; but when diversity expresses itself in language we respond in equivocal ways. Dialect is just one of the ways in which a language will vary itself, and given the variety of needs which a common language serves, we should not be surprised by the range of that diversity. Even languages with less than a thousand speakers show evidence of dialectal variation, and the geographical distance between different dialects can be surprisingly small. Three years ago the writer of this guide was told by a Gloucestershire farmer that the folk on the other side of the hill 'talk different'. Despite living in Gloucestershire all their lives, they used different words and had 'funny sayings' so far as their neighbours were concerned.

It is important for A-level studies to have a concept of dialect which is not narrowly tied to the all too familiar regional variations. Yes, it is true that if you go to Suffolk you will find that quite a lot of very old dialect forms are still used. But it is equally true that new dialects have developed among modern townspeople and city dwellers whose lives have been as much formed by urban technology as ancient Suffolk lives were formed by agriculture.

When we talk about dialects in the context of the world's languages we are sometimes talking about differences that to all intents and purposes makes them seem like different languages. There are about 4,500 living languages in the world and they form the nuclei for about 20,000 dialects. A student from Singapore may well speak four dialects of Chinese and they will each sound very different. She may use one dialect when visiting grandparents, another at home, a third at school and a fourth at a factory where she has a part-time job. Somebody who only spoke the dialect called Mandarin Chinese would be unable to understand a speaker of the Pekingese dialect or a speaker of Cantonese. The fact that these dialects share the same writing system makes little or no difference to their intelligibility in spoken form.

To take another example, it is very easy to imagine that because we have one name for the first Australians, Aborigines, there will only be one Aboriginal language. In fact there are many: Tiwi, Walmatjari, Warlpiri, Aranda, Mabuyag are the names of just some of them.

Considering dialectal variety in a world context and remembering that more than half the population of the world **have** to speak two or more languages in order to live their daily lives, it makes the British preoccupation with regional variations seem rather insular at best and very small-minded at worst.

REGIONAL DIALECTS

The regional dialects of Britain exist for well know historical reasons. What we think of as English came to Britain in the form of a German dialect which in turn was derived from a descendent of what is now known as the Indo-European proto-language. Successive invasions brought other languages which co-existed with the languages of the Angles and the Saxons. The language of the Vikings is one familiar influence together with the Latin of the Church. Norman French later proved very influential on law and government after the Conquest.

There is a romantic fiction that portrays Anglo-Saxon, the language of Robin Hood, as living under successive iinguistic occupations, Norman French being the most oppressive, and finally attaining true sovereignty in the language of Chaucer and Shakespeare. There is some truth in this but insofar as it contributes to myths about Standard English (see below) it diverts our attention from the dialectal variety that has existed for a long time in Britain and which only began to diminish with the socio-cultural changes and developing communication networks of the 19th and 20th centuries.

Regional dialects are sustained by close community patterns, static geographical location, and strong oral traditions. Once significant changes occur in social life e.g. industrialisation, travel, an education system devoted to literacy, then changes take place in the language too. If you are interested in the geographical aspect of dialect you will find a dialect atlas worth consulting, e.g. *Word Maps: a dialect altas of England* by Clive Upton, Stewart Sanderson and John Widdowson (Croom Helm 1987)

Any study of a regional dialect will involve different aspects of linguistics: *phonology* (to describe the accent), *lexis* (to identify characteristic words), *grammar* (to describe consistently used features which may differ from other dialects), *semantics* (to explain the meanings of words and idioms).

SOCIAL DIALECT

The term dialect is also used in the sense of social dialect, that is to say, linguistic variations that can be perceived between different social classes. A pungently comic version of this perception is drawn by George Bernard Shaw in *Pygmalion*, a play which proved equally effective when translated by Lerner and Lowe into the musical, *My Fair Lady*. The study of social dialects, and of the interaction between social and regional dialects, is an important part of modern *sociolinguistics* (see *Sociolinguistics* by Peter Trudgill (Penguin 1975)). It is difficult to separate out questions of social dialect and regional dialect because of a predominant view that the less regional a dialect is, the closer it approximates to high social status, cultural propriety and economic success. One issue that illustrates the problem is the current promotion of *Standard English* by the Department of Education & Science in the National Curriculum for English: 5 to 16 (1989). 'Standard' has always been popularly interpreted as 'best' and given the association of Standard English with

Whitehall, the BBC, education and the professions, it is an understandable point of view determined by prestigious institutions.

Standard English is conceived by education and the professions as a norm drawn from different regional and cultural variations and suitable for mass communication, for teaching the native tongue, and for teaching English to second language learners. It is particularly suited to formal speech and to writing and is taught in schools, though it is acknowledged in the National Curriculum that Standard English can effectively be spoken with a regional accent. It has also become evident over the years that many people grow up *bi-dialectal*, that is, able to use Standard English in speech and writing, but also able to talk in a regional dialect which they, in fact, never wholly forget even if they hardly ever use it in adult life.

Once a concept of Standard English is established there is a danger that all other kinds of English will implicitly be regarded as *sub-standard* rather than simply *non-standard*. This seems to have happened in Britain at a time when new dialects of English have emerged in Asian and Afro-Caribbean urban communities. Variety has always been the spice of language because it spells growth and reflects a positive response to social change. Whatever the virtues and advantages of Standard English, it can only diminish if it does not possess the same kind of vitality. Many linguists would describe Standard English as a socio-cultural dialect (rather than a regional one) and have documented ways in which it has changed in response to innovation and trends in social and cultural life. (See *Learning Me Your Language* ed. by M. Jones and A. West (Mary Glasgow 1988), for discussion of some of the issues raised by the concept of Standard English).

OCCUPATIONAL DIALECT

So far, we have considered regional and social aspects of dialect. A third variety of dialect is occupational dialect, increasingly studied in recent years. In many respects occupational dialects (e.g. law, computer technology, medicine, sport, catering, entertainment, armed services, education, local government) may be regarded as *registers*. If you choose to undertake a language study project on an occupational dialect, decide for yourself which term you prefer to use.

DICTION

Diction refers simply to the *kind of language* that a text uses. Many modern poems, for example, use words which you would overhear in everyday conversation. Those from an earlier period might be much more formal; a sixteenth-century poem might use language influenced by a translation of the Bible into English, whereas an eighteenth-century one might use a diction full of references to Classical gods and heroes. Some poems might use a *specialist diction*, perhaps referring to a particular trade or way of life, to the language spoken in one part of the country, or in order to capture the character of a speaker through the words he or she uses. Being aware of a poem's diction plays an important part in deriving a full appreciation, because it tells you about the poet's attitude to the subject.

DICTION IN PLAYS

One of the key elements to look for in plays and dramatic passages in appreciation papers, is not only what the characters say but the words they use to say it. This tells you about:

a) the individual characters – for example, whether they are aristocratic or educated or speak in a popular dialect; whether they speak in a regional accent and so reveal their place of birth; if they use language related to a skill or profession; or whether they are serious or comic in the way they speak;
b) the setting of the play – the country or part of the country in which it is set, and the historical period;
c) the relationship between characters, which may be indicated by the way in which they address each other; formally or informally; using terms of endearment; coldly; with language suggesting a professional relationship; as old friends; or in any other way which reveals something about why they are together.

A close reading of the *kinds of words*, then, is just as important as noting what the characters actually say, in gaining an awareness of the situation and the overall significance of the passage.

DICTION IN PROSE

Just as the choice of words is important in poetry and drama, so it is in prose. The variety of possible kinds of diction is almost endless, and this is just as true of prose as it is of poetry. Try to focus on the diction of a piece of prose by concentrating on two related aspects:

1 The special nature of the diction – whether, for example, it is composed of the technical terms of a particular job or profession; whether it is formal and impersonal, or colloquial and intimate;
2 How this diction is appropriate to the purpose of the prose – to give importance to a public statement, for example, or to make a scene in a novel convincing by using words suitable to its main characters and historical and geographical setting.

In Elizabeth Gaskell's *Mary Barton*, for example, several characters speak in a north-country, working-class dialect. This is used to show the social divisions between rich and poor – the major theme of the novel.

DIMETER

◀ Metre ▶

DIPTHONG

A dipthong is frequently identified in writing as a *digraph*, that is to say, two vowels written together: e.g.

peace, piece, relief, oasis, said.

In each of the above cases the two letters represent one sound. Sometimes words used in English, but of foreign origins are written with *ligatures*; not only are the two vowel sounds blended into one, the letters are too: e.g.

œuvre, ægis, æon.

It is also possible to write these as oeuvre, aegis, aeon. You should remember that the term dipthong is esentially a phonological one referring in the first instance to any sound made by a blending of vowels. When they are spoken there is a perceptible shift in articulation and a perceptible auditory effect, however subtle. What we hear will depend very much on where, in Britain or the world, English is being spoken.

In England we recognise words like, 'foul', and 'foil' as dipthongs or glides because we can hear something like the beginning of a 'w' in 'foul' and we can hear something like the beginning of a 'y' in 'foil'. Words like 'loyal', 'royal', 'mayor' are all glides where the y sound is more pronouned. But there are words not spelt with two vowels which are nevertheless spoken as dipthongs: e.g.

fine, boy, cow.

If you can recollect how you have heard southern states American (e.g. Alabama) spoken in TV films you will know how some words are characteristically *dipthongized* by some American speakers of English:

said (sounds like 'say-yed')
all (sounds like 'owull')
boy (sounds like 'boh- we').

DISGUISE

◀ Elizabethan stage ▶

DRAMA

Generally this means a play or story, or even an event in real life, that is serious or sensational in some way. In its strict sense, it is simply a label for a type of art, like 'poetry' or 'prose', so try to avoid the popular sense.

▶ CRITICAL APPRECIATION

Many critical appreciation papers include a passage from a play as well as a poem and a piece of prose for you to write about. In such papers, you will be able to choose two of the three pieces offered but, as it's impossible to predict the nature of the passages, you need to be able to write about all three if you are to produce the best answer in the exam.

Writing about drama is in many ways similar to writing about **poetry**. There is a strong possibility that the passage set will be dramatic verse rather than prose and, even if it is in prose, you will still have to consider elements familiar from the critical process with poetry. **Diction, imagery**, situation and the nature of the speaker or speakers are, if anything, more important in dramatic writing than in poetry, and your experience in writing critical appreciation of poems will certainly help in your work on passages from plays. So, too, will the experience of reading closely, in the manner described under the heading **poetry**. Overall, then, there are many ways in which writing about unseen passages of drama is similar to writing about poetry.

There are also some new techniques to develop. They include looking for, and writing about the situation of the action and characters; how things change in the course of the passage; the nature of individual characters; what the characters contribute to the themes and ideas of the passage; dramatic interaction between characters; the importance of staging and physical action.

FEATURES TO NOTE

While you are studying a passage from a play, you need to look for a number of features. These are listed below. They aren't presented here in order of importance: you should try to be aware of them all as you read, gradually developing your own interpretation of the passage.

Meaning and situation

Sometimes, you will be given a brief note before the passage explaining something about the situation of the scene – who the characters are, what has just happened, and any other information essential to a grasp of the scene. More often, however, you will have to work this out from a careful reading of the passage itself.

Do this as you would with a passage of poetry – by making an initial interpretation which you will modify and confirm by careful and repeated reading, making your final interpretation only when you are sure that you have taken everything into account.

Setting

The actual, physical location where the scene takes place may not be of much importance to the action or main themes which the passage discusses, but you should look out for any clues which will help you establish where the scene is taking place. A close reading of the passage may give clues to this – look for:

- references to specific places;
- references or kinds of language which suggest a particular historical period;

- kinds of language which reveal a particular country or area.

Diction

One of the key elements to look for in dramatic passages is not only what the characters say but the words they use to say it. This tells you about:

- the individual characters – for example, whether they are aristocratic or educated or speak in a popular dialect; whether they speak in a regional accent and so reveal their place of birth; if they use language related to a skill or profession; or whether they are serious or comic in the way they speak;
- the setting of the play – the country or part of the country in which it is set, and the historical period;
- the relationship between characters, which may be indicated by the way in which they address each other; formally or informally; using terms of endearment; coldly; with language suggesting a professional relationship; as old friends; or in any other way which reveals something about why they are together.

A close reading of the *kinds of words*, then, is just as important as noting what the characters actually say, in gaining an awareness of the situation and the overall significance of the passage.

Tone

In poetry, the **tone** of voice in which the lines are spoken can often reveal as much as the words themselves. This is even more true in dramatic writing, since at its heart is the exchange of *ideas and feelings* between the characters. In everyday life, we communicate as much by the tone of our voices as by our words – so tone is of great importance in the theatre.

Mood

A dramatist will use language in the same way as a poet to create a **mood** or atmosphere. Read carefully therefore to work out, for example, whether the mood is tense or relaxed; uncertain or clear; reflective or dynamic – that is, whether it is concerned with thought or with movement and action. For example, many scenes of Peter Schaffer's *Equus* have a very great tension; O'Casey's plays about the Irish troubles show a dynamic mood, shifting rapidly from comic banter to tragic suffering; and Shaw's *Widowers' Houses* changes from romantic exchanges to moral discussion.

While reading to discover the mood of the scene, think about the rhythm and sound of the words to see if they are used to help convey the effect. This will not always be a part of the dramatist's technique, but it's worth asking yourself whether the choice and movement of the language is used to reflect the mood of the scene.

Action and movement

What is actually happening in a scene (check any stage directions), as well as indications of movement and development, are features to note.

Dramatic interaction

This involves the ways in which the dramatist allows the characters to exchange ideas and thoughts. (See the entry **dramatic interaction**).

Characters

Think carefully about the nature of each **character** who speaks or takes part in the scene you are considering.

Themes and ideas

Just as a poem may be concerned with one central theme or idea, so a scene of a play may wish to get across a particular concept. It might, for example, be a discussion of the nature of justice; or the futility of armed combat; or a point about the nature of love or human relationships. While reading, think carefully about this and keep asking yourself whether the passage does have a subject of this sort, or whether the action is its main concern.

This does not mean that you should seek to identify one theme for the passage. Shakespeare's *Measure for Measure* is concerned with justice, but that does not prevent it from having some very funny scenes of bawdy comedy: many of Shaw's plays contain debates about intellectual, social or moral issues, but they still contain striking scenes about personal relationships.

READING A DRAMATIC PASSAGE

While you are reading the passage, you will be looking for the above features and trying to assemble an overall interpretation in the manner suggested for reading **poetry**. To help you arrive at your interpretation, try the following approaches while reading:

Visualise the scene

Always try to *see* what is going on, as if it were being performed in the theatre in front of you. Visualise the actions of the characters and, if it helps, imagine the scene and costumes too. All this will make the passage real *as a theatrical event*, not just as a passage from a novel or a story. And this will help you become more aware of how the passage makes its effects *in the theatre*.

Imagine yourself as director

Pretend that you are directing the scene. How would *you* ask the cast to play it? What advice would you give your actors about speaking their lines, in terms of which words to emphasise, what gestures to make, where and when to move? Think of all these things as ways of making the scene clearer.

While you are doing this, you will be thinking about what the passage is fundamentally concerned with – a theme or idea, if there is one. And this will help you to understand how the passage works in putting across its main concerns, and what effects the dramatist is using to do this.

'Cast' the passage

If it helps to make the scene real, try giving the parts to individual actors whom you know. This can make a lot of difference – it can bring the scene to life for you and help you to understand its overall effect and significance. But don't get too carried away – an essay which tells the examiner who you think would play each part best, isn't going to do very well in the exam!

Try to respond as you would in the theatre

When you've imagined yourself as the director, think about how you'd react as a member of the audience if you saw the play for the first time. Would you be filled with anger, or moved to pity? Would you laugh and, if so, why and at what? Would you be caught up in the suspense of the scene, wanting to know what happens next? All of these are questions which are useful ways of evaluating the passage – thinking about how well it works in the theatre.

Look at the question

Many questions about dramatic passages ask you to consider a particular aspect of the scene. It might ask, for example, why it is funny, or how the dramatist builds suspense; how the poet uses language to convey ideas or emotions, or how a dramatic exchange develops and changes. Make sure, when you are reading the passage, that you have this firmly in your mind: it's easy to forget that the question has a specific target of this sort, and to write instead a general critical appreciation of the scene – especially if you have just done the same about a poem or piece of prose. Be sure, then, that you know *exactly what you're asked to do* in a question of this sort.

There is one more important point which you must bear in mind while reading a dramatic passage. Remember that the whole sequence of events has been created by one person – the writer of the play. It is *not* just a series of encounters or events which happened in real life and were then written down. Each speech and action has been prepared, corrected and revised as carefully as each word in a poem, so that they all come together to give the effect the dramatist desired. Your task as a critic – which is essentially what you become in this exercise – is to see what that effect is and to say how well the passage achieves it.

All of these points will be going through your mind while reading. As with a poem, try to relate the individual 'moment' – a line, or speech, or image – to the whole thing, and the expression – diction, tone and other elements – to the idea or emotion being put across. At the same time, try to relate this to the main topic raised by the question, unless you are being asked for a general appreciation of the passage.

Gradually, as you do this, you will find that your initial response or hypothesis will grow and clarify until you have a complete reading or interpretation of the passage and can set about writing your answer, using the techniques and the advice given under the heading **poetry**.

COMPARING PASSAGES

Sometimes a question will ask you to compare two passages of dramatic writing. When you are doing this, you need to read each passage closely using all the approaches suggested here. In addition, though, you need to *bring the two together*. Always think about one passage in the terms of the other. Ask yourself:

1 Which of the two is more effective on stage, and for what reasons?
2 Which has the more effective characterisations?
3 Which shows more complete interaction between characters?
4 How do the settings and situations of each differ?
5 What similarities and differencies are there of themes and ideas?
6 What similarities and differences are there in the kind of language the passages use?
7 How do all these similarities and differences change and develop in the course of the passages?

Make sure, too, that you cover:

a) any specific area which the question mentions;
b) your own response to the two passages, with reasons.

If you follow this advice, as well as the general points about comparing passages given under **poetry**, you should be able to produce clear passages of comparison about pieces of dramatic writing. Remember, too, that it's often easier to write about two passages than about one: as with two similar but contrasting colours, they are clearer when placed against each other.

MAKING NOTES

General or commentary notes

These are notes you can make during or just after the process of close reading. It's really a matter of going through and noting down points of importance in any of the areas mentioned above, and on any other topics or points which strike you as important or interesting.

In this way you'll produce a set of notes which are more or less a commentary on the scene, showing points of importance in various areas. As well as this, you can annotate your text in the way shown in Fig. N. 1 under **notes**. Be careful about this, though. If you're allowed to take the text into the exam with you, you may have to erase such marks. And notes in a text are often less clear than those you make on paper! Whatever method you use, make sure that your notes are clear – both in the sense of being well expressed and in the sense of being easy to read – you'll have to work from them later on when you come to revise, remember.

Duchess of Malfi

Act I 127 Conventional exposition, Antonio and Delio. Satire on court life (incidental)
"He rails at those things which he wants; / Would be as lecherons, covetous, or
Proud, / Bloody or envious, as any man, / if he had means to be so".
(Antonio on Bosola)
128 "He and his brother are like plum trees that grow crooked over standing pools; they
are rich and overladen with fruit, but none but cows, flies and caterpillers feed
upon them" (Bosola on Cardinal and Ferdinand)
129 Bosola feels cheated by Cardinal / Comparison of Court strata to hospital.
130 Obsequiousness of courtiers Rod and Chris.
131 Character of Cardinal: very jealous and vindictive
Character of Ferdinand: very perverse and turbulent
Animal imagery - spider - imagery of devils and gods etc.
Duchess: divine beauty and sweetness to wake the dead.
133 Beginning of plots of Card, & Ferd.
Imagery of plants - the oft shaking of the cedar tree fastens it more at root.
134 "Familiar-use of witchcraft imagery (devilishness) - hell etc.
135 Bosola should be "like a politic dormouse" -
Some classical imagery - "Subtler than Vulcan's net".
136 Hint of incest about persuasions to Duchess not to remarry
- later motive of money appears.
138 Imagery of death - making will etc.
140 "Tis not the figure cut in alabaster / Kneels at my husband's tomb".
141 Comparison of married bliss to harmony of the spheres.
142 Already Duchess described as mad - later madness imagery vital.

Act II 142 Satire on court behavior
143 Imagery of decay of human beings - a false façade presented to the
world. - also animal imagery.
144 "You would look up to Heaven, but I think / The devil, that
rules i 'the air, stands in your light."
(Antonio of Bosola)
146/147 Bosola's tricks to get her to eat the apricots show
she is pregnant.
148 Devil imagery " the devil takes delight to hug at
a womans girdle
149 Cover story of robbery to conceal the delivery
150 II/III - use of animal imagery - Ant. calls Bos a
mole who undermines him.

Fig. D.1

At the end of a session of detailed reading and note-taking, you'll end up with a sheet of general commentary notes like those shown in Fig. D.1. Keep them carefully and use them as a guide when reading through the text later on, and as the basis for revision and further notes.

Topic notes

Imgery of The Duchess of Malfi
Death, madness, witchcraft, sorcery, religion, animals, precious metals/jewels, (Classical)

Death, madness and illness
i) Scene where madmen play before the Duchess' murder
ii) When D. wants to marry A., he is summoned "to make a new will".
iii) "This is flesh and blood, sir;/ Tis not the figure cut in alabaster/ kneels at my husbands' tomb"
iv) D's marriage = a terrible illness (Ferd + Card) – treated with "desperate physic."
v) Constant references to death - create atmosphere
→ Used to build up atmosphere of gloom, underline final madness of Ferdinand, insane world etc.

Witchcraft, sorcery and superstition
i) Bosola = Ferdinand's "familiar"
ii) Ruined castle gives atmosphere (as does moonlit palace)
iii) Wolves digging up graves (cf Wasteland)
iv) Cariola dislikes disguise of flight to Antonio as a religious pilgrimage
→ Used to underline evil character of Ferd. + Card., gives atmosphere, textual 'thickening'.

Religion
i) References to heaven, hell and the devil
ii) "You would look up to heaven, but I think/The devil that rules i' the air, stands in your light."
iii) Movement of spheres, influence of heaven's rule on earth etc
iv) "What devil art thou that counterfeits Heaven's thunder?"
v) Used chapel of Loretto - shows power of religion with three characters.
vi) Character of priest is full of imagery, almost condoning and encouraging D. + Ant.
→ Atmosphere - char. of D. (v. religious), char of Ferd + Card. (irreligious).

Animals
i) Underlines baseness of character - B. = "a politic dormouse".
Shows insignificance and baseness of men's actions and motivations.

Precious Metals and Jewels
i) Opulence and greed - Ferd. + Card. shown in this light
ii) Also shows hypocrisy + deception of F. + C. "Why dost thou wrap thy poison pills/In Gold and sugar?" D. of M.

Classical
– "Subtler than Vulcan's net" – less important than others.

General
i) V. forceful in nature - an integral part of play + built up + used almost as 'leitmotif.'
ii) Without it D/M would be less interesting seen as tragedy
iii) Creation of atmosphere, including characters is main function of imagery.

Fig. D.2

Once you've made your commentary notes, you'll find that particular *topics* will emerge as important in the play. They could be:

a) themes or ideas;
b) particular kinds of language or imagery;
c) theatrical effects such as the use of suspense;
d) contributions of characters to the growth of the plot;
e) aspects of the theatrical nature of the play – the use made of sets, costumes, or action which is largely visual rather than verbal in nature.

One way of making these notes is to go through your commentary notes and to mark off each topic with a separate colour or number. You can then go back and write a separate sheet of notes on each topic. Fig. D.2 does this for *imagery* in *The Duchess of Malfi*. In this way you'll end up with a collection of single sheets which cover the main aspects of the play.

OTHER VIEWS

At this stage you can begin to *consolidate* and reinforce your work on the play by considering the views of *other people*. This might include:

- Reading critical interpretations of the play, including the introduction to your edition of the text. Don't be overwhelmed by critical readings, but instead try to absorb them into your own overall interpretation of the play.
- Discussing it with other people who have different interpretations. Once again, though, don't be too easily led into believing what they have to say – stand your ground and argue your own interpretation.
- Seeing productions. In an ideal world it would help to see two or more contrasting productions of each play you study, but in practice that's rarely possible. If you can see a single production, that's fine – it will bring together your work, and perhaps give you some new ideas. Once again, don't be led into thinking that this is the *only* way of interpreting the play – the way you have originally visualised it is just as valid, and might be a much sounder reading.

  By all means watch film or television adaptations of the play too, but be careful – vary often such **adaptations** change the action from the original. Remember, too, that the effect will be very different from that in the theatre; you'll be able to see the faces of the actors in close-up, so the director will be aiming your attention towards certain parts far more than in the theatre. The action, too, may well have been changed to allow for the greater potential of film: scenes may be cut or added, and material set indoors moved outside to give greater visual variety. So always make sure that you know just how closely the version you see is based on the play itself.

  If you can't see a production, don't worry. Thinking carefully about how you'd *like* to see it produced can often be just as valuable, if not more so. Consider the stage design, lighting, costumes, movement and any other aspects of the written text which are important. For example, if there are any particularly difficult scenes, ask yourself how you would make them 'work' on stage. If you're also studying art, try doing some designs.

Activities like these can be very rewarding, but make sure that they don't take over from the study of the play's text – as a blueprint for stage performance – which should always be the main focus of your attention.

- Read about the stage history of the play. Many editions of plays have a section on this, giving dates and brief descriptions of important productions. Knowing about its stage history can often help you to broaden your knowledge of how the play works in the theatre.

When you follow any of these approaches, make a few notes and keep them in your file with the commentary and topic notes. You may find that an aspect of a production will help to clarify a general point, and once again bring together the study and the stage. Always make a note of the date of the production, and who directed or mounted it – a useful detail which adds precision if you need to refer to it in support of a point in the exam.

WRITING ABOUT DRAMA

The business of writing about plays is similar to writing about poems or novels – it's the same process of defining the question, thinking of points which are related to it, and then supporting them with evidence from your knowledge of the text. See also the material under **essays**.

Questions on drama

Questions on drama will be of four main types.

1 Short questions on passages

Some papers may give you a passage from a play with a series of short questions on its expression, contribution to the play's themes and action and other aspects of its importance within the movement and growth of the play. These are most often set for Shakespeare's plays, but may also come up on other papers.

To find out whether such questions will appear in your exam, check your syllabus and past papers carefully.

2 Questions about a scene or part of a scene, which ask for comment on its place in the play as a whole

These questions usually appear in 'plain text' papers – those which allow you to take an unmarked copy of the play into the exam. Once again, you should check carefully with your syllabus to see if you can do this. You can practise referring to the text quickly and accurately. This is really the only difference between plain text papers and others; you can consult the text for quotations and references, instead of your memory.

3 Questions based on a quotation

These are just the same as those on a poetry paper, and will contain a quotation – generally specially created for the paper – which makes a statement about the play. Usually it will be a comment which is only partly true, and you will then be asked to discuss its validity.

When answering such questions, make sure that you understand the quotation, by looking carefully at the key words and trying to relate its judgement to the text itself. Next look at the question which follows it. It might simply be 'Discuss'; but it might be something longer, asking you to show how far the statement is true, to say whether or not you agree with it, or perhaps even to show that it is only a partial view of the text.

Once you have defined both quotation and question, you should *plan* your answer in the usual way by making a series of points which engage with the question, supporting each one with a quotation or close reference. It's quite acceptable to do this by referring to a scene by number – Act IV scene ii, or IV.ii – and then perhaps by adding a sentence to show the way in which what happens in it supports your point. When you're sure that all your points are relevant and in the best order, you can then go on and write the essay.

4 Questions about a particular aspect of the play

These need careful reading to make sure that you arrive at a precise understanding of the meaning of the key terms they use and the tasks they set you. Once you have done this you can make your plan, check it for relevance and order, and then write your essay.

Studying and writing about plays demands the skill of being able to see how the written text works on stage – just as a blueprint is the basis of a finished building, or a score for a symphony. You need to be able to write about literary elements when discussing a play – but you also need to be able to capture the life of the play as it grows and develops on stage. And you need to relate these two features to each other, and to the question, supporting your argument by close reference and quotation.

◀ Action, Adaptations, Character, Dramatic interaction, Essays, Poetry, Prose, Study skills, Tone ▶

DRAMATIC

In everyday conversation, we talk about 'dramatic events' as those which are surprising, or violent, or unexpected – like a sudden change of course in someone's life, or a bank robbery, or somebody making an announcement which comes as a shock to everyone who is listening. Used properly, this word is simply an adjective for drama – meaning 'to do with the drama or theatre'. If you use it, make sure you use it properly – expressions like 'Gwendolen then makes a very dramatic entrance' really say very little; as you're writing about a play, *every* entrance is dramatic. On the other hand, used properly it can be used to stress the nature of a scene as something which could only be done in the theatre, as opposed to in a novel or poem.

DRAMATIC INTERACTION

This is one of the most important ways in which writing about passages from plays differs from writing about poems or pieces of prose. You need to explore the ways in which the dramatist allows the characters to *exchange* ideas and thoughts, so that there is a genuine sense of people interacting with each other in a real, convincing situation. In *Look Back in Anger*, for example, the interaction between Jimmy Porter and his wife's friend Helena begins with violent abuse and ends in a passionate physical relationship; in Beckett's *Endgame*, the interaction between all the characters shifts in a repetitive, almost random way from tenderness to nostalgic remembrance to aggression and personal dislike.

Look especially for ways in which emotions, ideas and relationships change during a passage. Ask yourself questions like these:

- Are these two characters closer to each other at the end than at the beginning?
- Has an idea been developed or made clearer?
- Has a particular statement modified the actions or thoughts of another character?

When you find that something like this has happened, try to work out the reason *why*. Is it because of the use of a particular kind of language; the statement of a particular idea or feeling; or the announcement of some new information? Asking questions like these will help you understand the interaction between the characters and also the *movement* of the passage, which is one of the essential features of dramatic writing.

DRAMATIC IRONY

This is used to describe scenes when the audience knows something that the characters don't. It can be a very successful way of increasing suspense in a play and so making it intensely effective in the theatre.

◀ Irony ▶

DRAMATIC MONOLOGUE

A poem which conveys the inner thoughts of one person, as if spoken to himself or herself. Robert Browning wrote several such poems, the most famous of which is probably 'My Last Duchess'. Not to be confused with a **soliloquy**, which is a similar personal statement but made by a character alone on stage in a play.

DRAMATIS PERSONAE

Latin for 'persons of the play', this is simply a list of characters. It may also tell you something about their relationships, ages and perhaps something of their characters. If there isn't a separate list of characters, each one may be described on his or her first appearance. Read these details carefully: they're not part of the 'text' in the sense of being part of the dialogue, but they are just as important in the overall nature of the play. Careful reading will help you to understand the characters and to grasp the action and themes of the play more quickly.

E

ELEGY

A poem of mourning or lamentation, usually of a sad and reflective nature, though not always about a specific dead person. Gray's 'Elegy in a Country Churchyard', for example, is a very forceful political poem.

ELISION

In phrases like:

fish n' chips
cock o' the north
put wood i'th'ole (i.e. close the door).

a sound has been omitted in each case (two, in the last example). The sound is said to have been elided. An elision is an omission of a sound.

ELIZABETHAN STAGE

Reading a play by Shakespeare or another Elizabethan dramatist is made easier if you understand some of the conventions of the time – ways of acting or behaving which were taken for granted by both actors and audience.

Disguise In Elizabethan and Jacobean plays disguise is always inviolable. No matter how obvious it is that Cesario is really a woman, the characters will not penetrate the disguise until the dramatist wants this to happen. Don't fight it; that's just how it is.

Asides Characters often speak in asides – statements directed straight at the audience. These are taken to be thoughts going on in the speaker's mind, and thus are not audible to the other characters on stage.

Settings The Elizabethan theatre made minimal use of scenery and staging. The setting is thus conveyed by the action, or by clues in the speeches – 'This is Illyria, lady', for example. A modern setting may have very elaborate scenery, but in Shakespeare's day the actors and the words did almost everything to convey the scene – worth recalling in modern productions of *Lear* where wind machines and artificial rainstorms do their best to drown not only Lear's speeches but also the actor delivering them.

Music Music is immensely important in Shakespeare's plays. Its most common uses are as fanfares to introduce kings and important characters, and in songs. The songs of Feste, the fool in *Twelfth Night*, set the mood of exquisite melancholy; those of the Fool in *Lear* make serious and ironic comments about the situation of the king. Don't imagine that they are there by accident or as some kind of light relief: they are central to the dramatic movement of the plays.

Action There are often minimal stage directions in plays of this time. This doesn't mean that little action is taking place. Remember, while reading, that the opening entrace of Claudius, Gertrude and the courtiers in *Hamlet* would take several minutes, and reveals a great deal about the pomp of the court in stark contrast to the black robes of the prince.

Remember, too, that in Act IV scene iv of *The Winter's Tale*, the stage is full of characters of all social ranks celebrating the sheep-shearing festivities. No sheep, but a full cast of people acting out this celebration of a country process successfully completed, showing the place of order in nature which is so important in the play as a whole.

ELLIPSIS

Ellipses occur frequently in conversation. They are the omission of a word in a sentence for economy's sake. Users of English like economy, and changes in the English language frequently tend toward economy and simplicity.

The following conversation is highly elliptical:

A (bringing in a tea tray) Where shall I put it?
B Down there.
A Here?
B No. There.
A Two lumps?
B Mm.

If you were to re-write this replacing everything that has been elided it would sound a very elaborate and strange conversation, possibly even menacing, like a play by Harold Pinter, or absurd, like something out of an old fashioned reading book for young children:

A Where shall I put the tea tray?
B Put the tea tray down there.
A Put the tea tray down here?
B No. Put the tea tray down there.
A Would you like two lumps of sugar?
B I would like two lumps of sugar.

Elliptical sentences, verbless sentences, minor sentences, one word sentences are all very similar in function. They are a naturally occurring feature of interactive language. Much of their meaning is conveyed by intonation. Care must be taken when using ellipsis in writing.

EMBEDDING

Embedding is a feature of **grammar** whereby one statement or piece of information can be embedded in another structure. It is a process of insertion or *parenthesis*: e.g.

The car [that won the Monte Carlo Rally in 1952] was on display in Manchester.

or

Those of you [who are doing A-level] will need to be formally entered for the examination.

ENJAMBEMENT AND END-STOPPED LINES

An enjambement is the running-on of one poetic line into the next in both rhythm and meaning, in contrast to an end-stopped line which is complete in itself. The following passage contains both:

There she weaves by night and day
A magic web with colours gay.
She has heard a whisper say,
A curse is on her if she stay
To look down on Camelot.

There is an enjambement between the first and second lines, and also between the fourth and fifth, whereas the second is clearly end-stopped.

ENVIRONMENT

When attempting to look at, or listen more objectively to, language use, the term environment is useful for reminding us that language units occur in a continuum rather than as a succession of bolted on units. Organic, ecological metaphors are usually more helpful for describing language than mechanical ones. The environment of an individual phoneme will be the other phonemes that lie at either side of it. The way in which we pronounce a particular phoneme (see **phonology**) will be influenced by how we have had to pronounce the preceding phoneme and how we will need to pronounce the next. An extreme example of this can be observed in the way that we pause before deciding how to pronounce words that begin with uncommon combinations of consonants: e.g.

*pt*olemy, *pt*armigan, *ps*oriasis, *gn*u, *Dv*orak.

Yet if we look at the collocation of these same pairs of consonants in other environments the pronunciation presents no problem because it and the patterns are familiar ones in English:

op*t*ical, ine*pt*, co*ps*, i*gn*ite, a*dv*ert.

Environment, too, is a concept that can be used in stylistics when the location of a word or structure (e.g. a question or an exclamation) in a particular text is contrasted with, or related to, adjacent words or sentences.

EPIC

An epic poem is one of great length and elevated style which narrates a story of depth and seriousness centering on the deeds of a noble and brave hero. The two most famous examples are the *Iliad* and the *Odyssey* of Homer; in English, Milton's *Paradise Lost* places the story of the creation and fall of mankind within the epic tradition. See also **mock epic**.

EPIC SIMILE

An extended simile in which the parallels between the subject and the object to which it is compared – often known respectively as the tenor and the vehicle – are developed to very great lengths to show a whole series of parallels and resemblances. In *Paradise Lost*, for example, Milton compares the entry of devils into Pandaemonium to the swarming of bees, and the shape of the prostrate Satan to a great whale or sea monster.

EPIGRAM

A very brief statement, generally in one or two lines, with a moral significance and a wittily compressed expression. The poetry of Alexander Pope and the plays of Oscar Wilde are rich in epigrams – although the poetry of the former is far more than a series of such statements linked together. The Victorian poet Arthur Hugh Clough also produced some notable epigrams, especially in a poem called 'The Latest Decalogue':

Do not adultery commit
Advantage rarely comes of it.

EPISTLE

Verse or poetry, written as a letter. It may be in any form or style of verse.

EPITAPH

A short work, usually in verse, in memory of a dead person.

ESSAYS

Putting together the information and ideas you've gained from a critical reading is a vital component for success in literary studies, and this is almost always done in one way: *writing a critical essay*. In this sense, of course, the word 'critical' doesn't mean making a condemnation of what you've read; it means approaching with a sense of detached, objective analysis to make clear its ideas and themes and the ways in which the writer has chosen to express them. Not always objective, though: your own response to the text is important, too.

The critical essay is likely to form the backbone of your written work, in which you express your own ideas and responses to the texts you're studying. You will come across it in two, or perhaps three, ways:

1 Essays you write on your texts as part of your course, which will be read and assessed by your teacher or lecturer;
2 Essays you write on the texts in answer to exam questions, which will be read and assessed by the examiner;

and, in some cases

3 Longer essays which you will write during your course of studies, which will be graded by your teacher and then moderated by an examiner as a 'coursework' component of the examination.

Although you have far less time for exam essays than those you write while studying, there are still so many similarities between the two that the basic techniques hold good for them both. Here we look at the process involved in writing a critical essay, and suggest how you can do it more effectively both during your course and in the exam.

Writing an essay isn't just a matter of sitting down, starting at page one and going on until you get to the end. Doing it properly involves several separate *stages*, each of which needs to be completed with care and using a number of special skills. It's worth looking at the whole process before taking each stage in turn:

1 Defining your title
2 Defining your task
3 Doing the research
4 Brainstorming
5 Making a plan
6 Drafting
7 Checking and editing
8 The final version

Looked at in this way, the essay seems quite a task – and it's certainly not easy. Perhaps you need to look at the task rather as a science student would look at the process of conducting an experiment, with all the stages of designing and setting up the apparatus, observing the results, checking and analysing them, drawing diagrams, checking with other research, and then writing up the results. In your course, you'll probably be given several days in which to write an essay; when you realise what's involved, you'll understand why.

DEFINING YOUR TITLE

Unless you know *what* you are expected to write about, you'll be unable to do it. That doesn't just mean that you'll get a poor grade for the essay – it means that there'll be a gap in your notes and study material which you'll notice when you come to revise. This might mean that you're not fully prepared on the particular text and so are unable to answer a key question in the exam. Overall, then, knowing what the title *means* is an essential foundation for your larger success.

- Look at the *verb* to see what you're requested to do – discuss, analyse or compare, for example;
- study the *key words* of the question, to see what aspect of a text you're asked to approach.

DEFINING YOUR TASK

Once you know what the question is about, you need to decide what work is necessary for you to undertake in order to write it. This may include:

- deciding whether you need to read the whole text, or part of it – all of an anthology, for example, or just those poems on a particular theme;
- deciding what you need to consult amongst the notes you already have. These might include notes made in class or in your detailed textual readings;
- deciding what new notes you need to make. This might mean going through all or part of the text, looking for examples of a particular theme or for characteristic features of expression – and, in most cases, this is what the essay will involve;
- thinking about whether you may need to consult anything *other than* the text – a critical study, for example – and to take notes from it on the subject of the essay.

Taking a few moments to identify the nature and extent of your task will help you a great deal in completing it. It will also help you to decide how much time the various stages of the essay are going to take, and so prevent your running out of time at the last minute.

DOING THE RESEARCH

This is the stage which will probably take the longest. The most important task will be going through all or part of the text to find *evidence* of the way in which the writer covers the topic mentioned in the essay.

a) Using the text

The text should be your first and most important source for every critical essay. Go through it, constantly asking yourself what is relevant to the topic, and making *quick* notes of passages which are important, and why.

At the end of your critical reading, you will have a large number of references to the theme or topic under discussion. But don't imagine that you can use them as they stand; you'll need to edit and select from them, to arrange them in the best order, and perhaps to group them under related headings in order to make the series of points which are the basis of your essay. This happens at the planning stage of the essay.

b) Using your notes

Go through your *notes* to the text. They may point out things that you've missed while reading through the text and looking for relevant passages. Look, too, at any notes you've taken from class sessions – they may include relevant points, or spark off important ideas which you can develop in the essay.

c) Using critical texts

The advantages and disadvantages of using critical writings have already been discussed; remember, they need to be approached with caution and it's always better to think for yourself about a text than to accept someone else's view without question. If you *do* decide to read a critical text, do so with caution.

If you're reading a critical article, make sure that it's relevant to the topic by 'scanning' through it quickly, perhaps looking at the first and last paragraphs to get an idea of its subject.

If you're reading a book, don't start at the beginning and go all the way through. Instead:

– use the contents page to pick out the chapter or chapters which look the most relevant to your needs;

– use the index to look up words which are related to your topic of interest. This can often take you to the heart of the discussion and allow you to find quickly points which are relevant to your essay.

Once you've found the relevant parts, read the whole section through without notes – just *concentrate* on what's being said.

When you've done that, take notes, recording the relevant points. Follow the technique described in Fig. E.1 and use its layout – clear headings, sub-headings and numbered points, so that you can come back to the notes several months later and still understand them.

Only record what the writer says – or, if you add points of your own, make sure that you separate them. Put them in [square brackets], or put your initials after them, to show that they're your points, not the writer's.

If the critic says something briefly which you can't express better yourself, then write it down in quotation marks. But don't copy out whole paragraphs, either in your notes or in the essay. This will only show that you haven't understood the ideas fully enough to absorb them into your own writing.

A READING

1 Read the whole passage through without taking any notes.
2 Divide it into short sections

B FIRST DRAFT

1 Select the main points by:
   (a) deciding whether each point is relevant and including only those which are;
   (b) looking at beginning and ends of paragraphs for key points.
2 Use your own words as far as possible, BUT quote short phrases which you can't put better yourself.
3 Use sub-headings, number each point and start new points on a fresh line.

C CHECK

1 Check your draft against the original for:
   (a) inclusion of all relevant points;
   (b) accuracy of all points recorded.

D FINAL VERSION

1 Rearrange the order of the points if you think it could be clearer.
2 Present the points as clearly as possible.
3 Make sure that abbreviations are clear.

E REFERENCE

1 Give author, title, date and place of publication, page numbers of source.

Fig. E.1

Before you go on to *write* the essay, though, there are several more stages to go through. You need to go back to the notes, and to read them through carefully. Most essays contain between six and twelve key points, each supported by quotations or close references to the text. You need to begin thinking about what these points are, and how the material you've collected makes and supports them. While reading through your notes, you need also to be on the lookout for anything that isn't relevant to the essay title. These two processes will help enormously when you start planning.

BRAINSTORMING

Brainstorming is the process in which you take the essay title, sit down and just write down any points at all which you think are relevant to it. This *doesn't* mean writing a full essay. Instead, you should write each point as briefly as

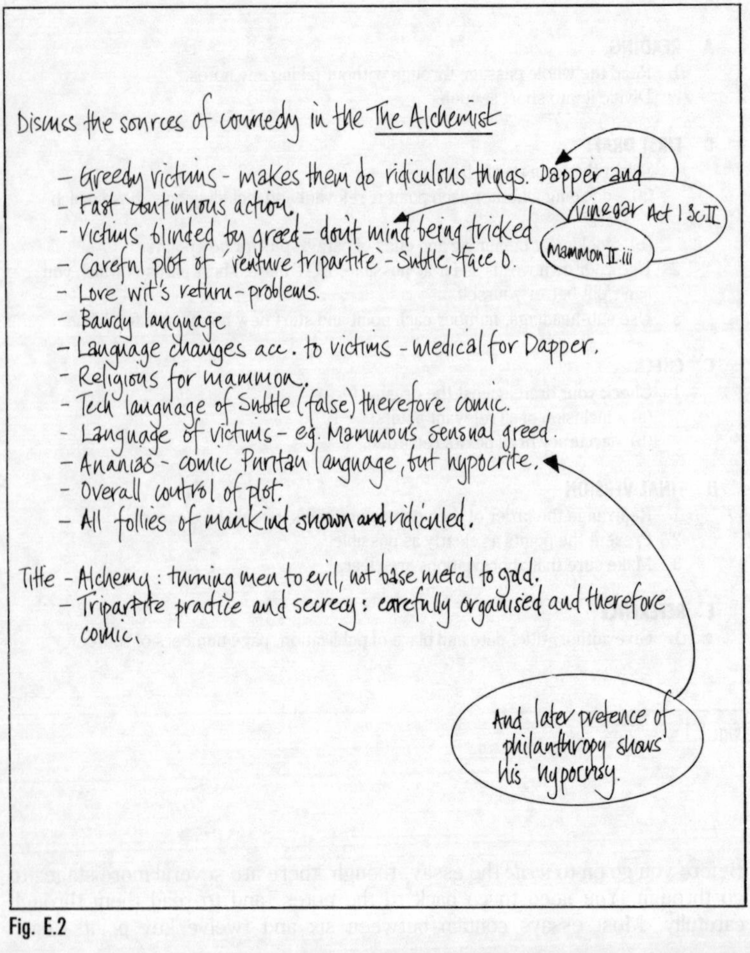

Discuss the sources of comedy in the The Alchemist
- Greedy victims - makes them do ridiculous things. Dapper and Vinegar Act I Sc II
- Fast continuous action.
- Victims blinded by greed - don't mind being tricked
- Careful plot of 'venture tripartite' - Subtle, Face D.
- Love wit's return - problems.
- Bawdy language
- Language changes acc. to victims - medical for Dapper.
- Religious for mammon.
- Tech language of Subtle (false) therefore comic.
- Language of victims - eg. Mammon's sensual greed
- Ananias - comic Puritan language, but hypocrite.
- Overall control of plot.
- All follies of mankind shown and ridiculed.
Mammon II.iii
Title - Alchemy: turning men to evil, not base metal to gold.
- Tripartite practice and secrecy: carefully organised and therefore comic.
And later pretence of philanthropy shows his hypocrisy.

Fig. E.2

you can, but clearly enough to express the idea; write each on a separate line, or in a different part of the page; leave plenty of space around each point – later you can go back and add related points to clarify it; don't worry yet about textual evidence – you can add that later.

Like most notes, you can produce 'brainstorms' in two ways – *linear* (Fig. E.2) (a list of points) or as a pattern or **spidergram** (Fig. E.3).

Your first brainstorm may include a lot of ideas that aren't relevant or are inaccurate. It doesn't matter – you can always cross them out later. The important thing here is to get all your ideas down quickly, to give you a working basis to build on later.

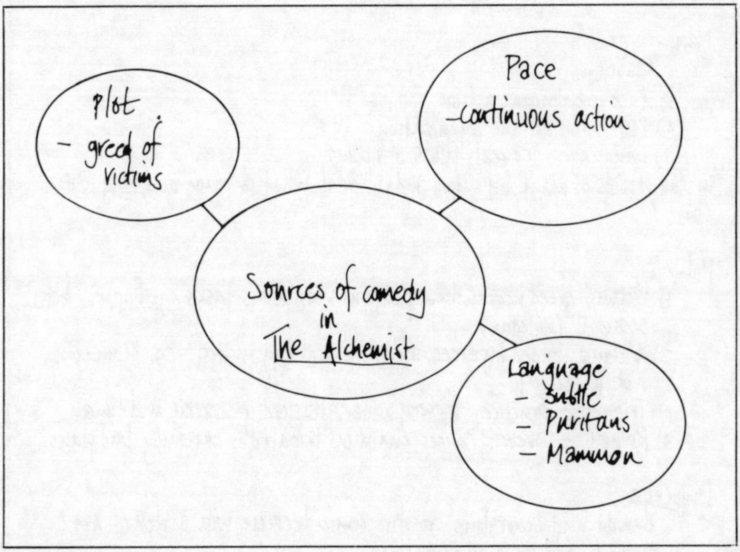

Fig. E.3

MAKING A PLAN

The plan is really the most important part of the essay. It will state in note form:

1 each of the key points you intend to make;
2 textual evidence for each one – not in full, but with line or chapter numbers.

In short, it will be a complete note-form answer to the question, and will look rather like the examples shown in Figs. E.2 and E.4. Don't expect to get the plan right first time – it may need several drafts which are halfway between a brainstorming session and a final plan. The plan shown in Fig. E.4 for example, was arrived at only *after* the rough plan shown in Fig. E.2.

Study the plan in Fig. E.4 and notice:

1 the way the introduction states the main ideas briefly and clearly;
2 the organisation into three main sections in answer to the question;
3 the way in which *points* are made *first*, and then supported by quotations or references to the text;
4 that the plan is complete in its own right – it conveys all the ideas needed to answer the question fully, on a single sheet of file paper.

The Sources of Comedy in The Alchemist.

Plan

Main sources are:
1) Pace - continuous action.
2) Plot - control and organization
3) Language - reveals follies of victims

In play - follies of mankind shown and ridiculed. What is comic and why is it comic?

Plot.

1) Victims' greed makes them perform ridiculous tasks eg. Dapper. Act I scene ii (Vinegar)
2) Victims blinded by greed therefore willingy gulled. eg. Mammon. Act II scene iii
3) Tripartite practice trickery under pressure of secrecy and time.
4) Return of Lovewit causes chaos in tripartite's carefully laid plans

Language

Bawdy and scurrilous crossfire comic because wits matched Act I scene I (add pace and vitality).
1) Changing language of Subtle: medical terms for Dapper; religious language for Mammon. (Change comic)
2) Overblown language of Mammon - clash reveals sensual greed. Later change to philanthropic attitude reveals his pretence. (Change comic)
3) Puritan Language of Ananias comic because of his hypocritical motive.
4) Highflown technical language of Subtle comic because of spurious logic

Subject of plot

Alchemy - usually metal → gold. here bad → to worse in men

Fig. E.4

Plans of this sort are essential to good essay writing because they allow you to arrange your material clearly and precisely; give you the chance to cross out irrelevant or inaccurate material *before* you've got half-way through a complete essay; and give you the essence of the essay in a single sheet, which is much easier to revise from than an essay of several pages.

For all these reasons, then, you should always make a plan of this kind when writing an essay. Many teachers will accept full plans of this kind instead of essays – not always, but perhaps on one occasion out of four. And remember that they will be of much more use than full essays when revising – it's much easier to take in ideas from a single sheet than from a full essay.

The way that the essay plan is organised is so important that it can't be stressed too often. It's organised around *ideas*, not around the chronological order of the play or novel you're writing about. You'll have to go through the work chronologically when researching for the essay: but you then need to change that, at the planning stage, into a sequence of points in a carefully grouped and logically arranged order. Only if you do this will you write a clear, logical and relevant essay.

DRAFTING

This is the process of actually writing the essay. Now that you know what you're going to say, it should be straightforward: all you have to do is to find the best words to use to say it.

1 Write in a simple, clear and direct style, aiming to make your points straightforwardly.
2 Follow the order of your plan – avoid 'introductions' which tell the story of the play or novel, or which give biographical information about the writer. If you have an introduction at all, it should summarise your main points very briefly, as suggested.
3 Each paragraph should have one major point as its basis. First use a 'topic sentence' to make the main point simply and clearly. Next, support it with a quotation or reference to the text to establish where this is shown. Then conclude with a brief reference to how the point is demonstrated elsewhere in the text.
4 If you can, use the words of the question quite often. This shows that you are really engaging with its ideas and it will stop you straying off the point into irrelevance.
5 At the end of the essay, summarize *briefly* what you have said so far and draw a conclusion which draws together your points, relates them to the question and rests firmly on a close reading of the text.

When you use quotations, follow the advice given under the heading **quotations** which reproduces part of a critical article. If you quote from a critic, do so briefly or, better still, express his or her idea in your own words, but acknowledge it by saying 'as Christopher Ricks has pointed out' or using a similar phrase. *Never* copy out whole sentences or paragraphs from critics and pass them off as your own work: apart from the moral implications of this, it just won't work in practice, as the difference in style will be obvious to an experienced reader. You'll lose marks and, most important, you won't have fully absorbed the ideas into your own writing.

CHECKING AND EDITING

At this stage, you need to go through and check your writing. Check for:

1 *accuracy of expression*. Do you say what you meant to, or is the expression ambiguous?
2 *accuracy of spelling*. Make sure that spelling is correct – especially that of the names of characters, as teachers and examiners get annoyed if it isn't!
3 *clarity of expression*. Make sure that you *don't* use long, winding sentences which get lost in the middle, or sentences without main verbs. Also avoid using syntax that's awkward and confusing to the reader.

When you've had a little practice at this kind of checking, you'll find that any changes can usually be made on your draft version. Cross out the incorrect expression and write the replacement clearly next to it. Don't bother with correction fluid – most exam boards won't allow its use, and it wastes time.

THE FINAL VERSION

If your draft version is so covered in corrections that it's hard to read, you may need to write it out again as a fair copy. But after a little practice you should be able to make most corrections to the draft so that the final version is legible and accurate.

Now you can give it in and wait for the comments. But, of course, it doesn't end there – read the comments carefully when you get the essay back, if necessary adding points to the plan so that you have a full coverage of the topic that you can then use for revision.

The process in practice

You might feel that the process outlined above is lengthy, complicated and time-consuming. It is – especially at first, when you're not used to working in such detail. But with practice, you'll find that you'll be able to produce essays much more quickly, but still following the same approach. Planning your time is one of the most important aspects – make sure that you work steadily on the essay through all the time available, building in a short break of a day or so in the middle between getting the information and starting the plan. In this way you'll produce something that is carefully thought out, rather than being hastily thrown together.

In an exam, you may feel there's no time for such an approach. Of course, you won't be able to consult the text or look at critical writings – but you will be able to consult your memory of the text, which by this time should be considerable. You'll also be able to go through the same stages, looking at the question, brainstorming, making a plan and then writing. All of this will take you probably five minutes at the start of the half-hour or 45 minutes you have for each question. A few moments at the end to check will complete the process. All this will help you to produce a better essay than you would if you'd just sat down and started writing straightaway.

Following this procedure in the exam also has one further advantage. It gives you a clear scaffolding to cling to at a time when you might not be feeling too happy or secure about things. This helps you get over nerves, and makes it easier for you to concentrate and perform at your best.

ETYMOLOGY

Etymology is the study of the origin of words and their historical development. Etymological dictionaries concern themselves with the origins of words as well as with their current meanings.

See for example the *Dictionary of Word Origins* in Longman Pocket Companion Series (Longman 1983).

Many words in English originated in other languages and have since become Anglicised. An etymological dictionary will give you some idea of the range of borrowings and assimilations that have taken place.

Etymology is possibly the oldest branch of linguistic study.

EUPHEMISM

This expresses something unpleasant in milder, inoffensive language.

EUPHONY

Pleasantly smooth and melodious language.

EXAMINATIONS

The best way to gain confidence for the exam is to have a thorough *knowledge of the text* and of the *techniques* you will need in order to write about the texts. Knowledge of the texts is something which you can acquire by careful and sustained study along the lines suggested under the headings **study skills** and **revising**; the techniques of answering questions in an exam are dealt with under the heading **questions**.

How to start

First of all, have a quick look at the paper. Make sure that it *is* in the format you'd expected – the same number of parts, with alternative sections or questions. In almost all cases it will be as you expected, but just occasionally it will be slightly different, perhaps because it is the first year of a new format or – in exceptional circumstances – because there has been an error in production.

If you find that something is wrong with the paper, keep calm. Go on and read through the rest of the paper quickly, then go back. It's easy to mis-read things in moments of stress, so check that what you thought was an error is really there. If it is, raise your hand and tell the invigilator. It's important to do this as soon as possible, because someone will have to call the Examining Board and get guidance on what to do. If it isn't a mistake, no harm will have been caused – it's far better to speak up and be proved wrong than not to say anything and have the wrong paper or some other mistake to contend with.

But it's very unlikely that this will happen. You'll probably be faced with a paper that is exactly what you thought. In your first quick reading of the paper, you should look at the sections which you are doing, getting a quick idea of the topics on which the questions are based. Look at all the paper – make sure that there isn't another question on the back page which you don't notice until you're running out of time. Think in general terms about which of the later questions you'll do, but don't make any firm decisions yet.

If your revision has gone well, you should at this stage be feeling comfortably reassured and confident that, though it won't be easy, you'll be able to write something on all of the questions you are required to answer. It's worth looking at the whole paper for this reason, as well as to check that it's what you'd expected in format: the reassurance is worth a good deal when you come to start writing.

Divide the time

Once you've read the paper, work out how much time you have for each question. Make sure that your watch is right, or that you can see the clock in the exam room. Now divide up the time fairly between the questions, remembering that 'fairly' doesn't mean 'evenly': you'll probably want to give slightly less time to the short-answer question, if there is one, than to the essay questions. If, as you should, you know the length and format of the paper, dividing the time should be straightforward. Before the exam, you will have worked out the timings of the questions with a calculation like this, leaving ten minutes at the end for a final check:

START 9.00am	(3 hour exam: 1 passage and 4 essays)
Question 1	30 mins
Other four questions	35 mins each = 140 mins
Checking time	10 mins
Total	180 mins = 3 hours

Once you've looked at the paper, write down the times on some spare paper that you can keep in front of you. Give a starting and finishing time for each question, so that you are constantly aware of how many minutes you have left for the question you're working on.

Question	1	2	3	4	5	Checking
START	9.00	9.30	10.05	10.40	11.15	11.50
FINISH	9.30	10.05	10.40	11.15	11.50	12.00

This may take a moment or two, but it will achieve a lot in organising the time you have available, especially if the times do not fall conveniently on hours and half-hours, as is the case here.

Remember that two brilliant answers and one that isn't started will not do as well as three competent ones – so don't get carried away with writing at excessive length. The answer is to stick to the time-plan as rigidly as you can as you are working through the paper. Look upon the final ten minutes' checking time as a 'crumple-zone' – it can go if you get held up in one of the questions, but it's useful to plan for it as it will give you time for a last-minute check and can be used as writing time if you need it.

◀ Essays, Questions, Revising, Syllabus, Study skills ▶

EXAMINERS' REPORTS

Most Examining Boards publish reports which say how candidates actually approached the exam in that year. These can be very useful, as they point out frequent errors and can suggest ways in which answers are more likely to gain good grades. Write to the 'Publications Department' of your Examining Board – but allow plenty of time for the reports to arrive.

EXEMPLUM

A term in medieval rhetoric for a story told to illustrate a moral point, or an 'example' of morality in action and practice. Chaucer's Pardoner includes in his tale a whole series of examples to demonstrate the basic idea of his tale.

EXISTENTIALISM

In existentialist philosophy, existence is the only thing we are certain of; man's life begins and ends in nothingness, and life is inexplicable, meaningless, and dangerous. The nature of our existence is decided by the choices we make to determine its nature. There are many variations of this philosophy, including even a Christian one, but its main appearance in literature is in the absurd theatre.

EXISTENTIAL PRONOUN

Once language students have acquired a confidence for analysing sentences into subject and main finite verb, they are sometimes thrown by the appearance of sentences beginning with the word 'there': e.g.

> There are several reasons why we should do it.
> There's a cold wind today.
> There's a lot of it about.
> There was a happy land somewhere.
> There is a problem with jogging.

Do not be confused by such sentences. When 'there' is used in this way followed by the verb 'to be' in the past or present tense it is referred to as an *existential pronoun* because the purpose of the sentence is simply to say that something exists.

EYE RHYME

Rhyme based on words which look similar but which are pronounced differently, as in 'how/bow' where 'bow' is pronounced as in 'bow and arrow'.

F

FABLE

A short tale or story conveying a clear moral lesson, as in the sixth-century Aesop's *Fables*.

FABLIAU

A short satirical or comic tale with a strong bawdy element; Chaucer's *The Miller's Tale* is one of the best-known examples.

FARCE

A very special kind of comedy which depends on mistaken identities, rapid entrances and exits, concealments and similar devices. It's unlikely that you'll study a farce – which is a pity, since writing them is an extremely skilled art which demands theatrecraft of a high order. Using the term simply about something which is very funny is imprecise and confusing: it's far better to use the word 'amusing' or 'comic' and then to go on and explain why the scene makes its effect.

FEET

◀ Foot, Metre ▶

FEMININE ENDING

A line of verse ending on a weak or unstressed syllable (see **metre**).

FIGURATIVE LANGUAGE

In its widest sense, this is any kind of language which departs from a commonly accepted standard or pattern of speech or writing. Its most frequent use, however, is to refer to language in which one thing is described in terms of another. The kinds of figurative language are **simile**, **metaphor**, **personification**, imagery and **symbols**.

FILMS OF NOVELS

◄ Adaptations ►

FIRST PERSON NARRATIVE

◄ Narrative voice ►

FLAT AND ROUNDED CHARACTERS

A flat character is one who is one-dimensional, often characterised through one feature or mannerism. He or she is a type, a caricature, or someone who behaves with little depth and complexity. A rounded character is more complex, can surprise the reader with his or her actions, and can change or grow over the course of a book or play. Often characters reveal themselves as rounded by being inconsistent; people are like that, too. In general, flat characters are simple, and rounded characters are complex. Thus in *Great Expectations* (1861) by Charles Dickens, Pip, the hero, is a rounded character, whilst Trabb's Boy (who has only the one feature of being cheeky) is a flat character.

FOOT

Each unit of regular metre is called a foot.

◄ Metre ►

FOOTNOTES

These can either be at the foot of each page, or at the end of an essay or book – in general it's easier to include these at the end. They will normally be concerned with giving the *source* of the passages which you have quoted. What they should contain, and how they might be presented, are shown under **bibliography**.

FORMULAIC LANGUAGE

There is an interesting area here for a language study project. Formulaic language is phraseology that has become fixed as part of a ritual or social routine. It is sometimes called *fossilised* because it is not subject to the same grammatical fluidity as other everyday language. Examples are:

> God save the Queen; Here beginneth (or endeth) the lesson; How are you?; Merry Christmas; Happy New Year; Take care; Mind how you go; I declare the motion carried; Yours faithfully; Yours sincerely; Cheers.

Language here is frozen into one form (or formula). Any modification would be immediately strange though not necessarily meaningless. Formulaic language eases relationships and interactions, it does not require you to stop and think. Compare the above with: How were you? Merry New Year; Give Care; Yours insincerely.

There are a number of social occasions when we use formulaic language and are grateful for it. It should not be criticised as **cliché** which is quite a different thing.

FREE VERSE

This is verse with no regularity in length of lines, metrical structure, or rhyme. Although much earlier prose has many of the characteristics of free verse – Coverdale's translation of the Psalms, for example, or Cranmer's Book of Common Prayer – free verse as it is now known was first used by writers such as Blake and Arnold in the nineteenth century. It became popular in the twentieth century with writers such as Walt Whitman, William Carlos Williams and T. S. Eliot. It should not be confused with **blank verse**.

FRICATIVES

If the tongue or lip is placed close to another part of the mouth so that there is a narrow space, the resultant speech sound will be fricative.

◀ Phonology ▶

FUNCTION

A-level English language syllabuses are as much concerned with the functions of language as with its structures. Traditionally structures have been the main concern both of school grammar books and of academic linguistics (e.g. the structuralist school of American linguists following Leonard **Bloomfield**). Knowledge about interconnected networks of language structures, and of how to describe them, has overshadowed the equally complex web of social functions that language serves. In recent years, however, through the work of linguists like **Halliday** and through the interdisciplinary approaches of **sociolinguistics** (including **pragmatics**), there has been a flood of knowledge about language functions. **Speech Acts** theory too, has contributed to that knowledge.

Whenever you are discussing a linguistic issue on an examination paper, or discussing data, or engaged in a stylistic analysis (all of these are required in Sections A, B or C of JMB Paper One, English Language A-level and are required in the London Board's Varieties of English and Aspects of English) you should have in your theoretical framework a repertoire of questions about social functions as well as language forms:

- how is language being used here?
- why is it being used?
- when and where is it used?

Be careful not to discuss function simply in terms of a speaker's or writer's intention. Ask yourself, 'If I took this construction away, what would be lost? What could be substituted?' There is an interesting experiment a class of students can carry out which demonstrates clearly how interconnected function and structure are and how equally extensive the function network is.

Students should work in fours: two are Martians, two are Earthlings. You will need some coloured shapes cut out of paper. Make at least:

- 4 red circles, 4 blue circles, 4 yellow circles, 4 green circles
- 4 red squares, 4 blue squares, 4 yellow squares, 4 green squares
- 4 red triangles, 4 blue triangles, 4 yellow triangles, 4 green triangles.

Any colours will do, it is the variety of shapes and colours that matters.

Martians float in the air. They cannot hear or speak but they can see and move coloured shapes on a tabletop. Students taking the part of Martians must never speak, and should try not to listen.

The two Earthlings have to invent a way of communicating via the coloured shapes. Find something that makes a breakthrough and develop it. Do not try to do too much. Earthlings may talk to each other. Devise your own method. This will not be an easy experiment but it is usually a fascinating one.

You will observe the importance of *interaction* and *feedback*. You will need to use the coloured shapes *consistently*. You will assign *arbitrary* meanings to each coloured shape. You will find *naming* things easy and expressing *grammatical relationships* difficult.

It is important to compare, in detail, your experiences with those of other groups, by explaining the grammatical rules of your new language to the other Earthlings. The Martians can now be converted to Earthlings so that they can talk about their experiences. If the class is large enough you will begin to see a glimpse of the many functions grammatical structures serve. Some groups will have started with greetings, names and pronouns. Some groups will have started with questions and answers. Some groups will have tried to communicate action e.g. making the Martians respond. Some groups will have tried to express time past and time present. Some groups will have tried to locate spatial relationships (e.g. you *there*, me *here*). Some groups may have tried several starting points and given up altogether. The important thing is to persevere with one starting point.

To some extent you have been put in the social situation of pre-linguistic humans and at the same time cut off from the prime source of language, namely speech. What you should have discovered is the overwhelming importance of having somebody to communicate to, of having something to communicate and of having a purpose for communicating it. If you used up all your coloured shapes in the first five minutes by associating each one with a person, place or thing you would simply have 'named' everything and a perfectly valid response would be the Martian equivalent of 'so what!'. If on the other hand you have tried to use the shapes to fulfil other functions, however modest, you will have begun to recognise the complexity of language functions.

Once again there is the possibility here for a project, or at least one piece of original writing in the informative mode.

G

GENITIVE

Genitive, in grammar, is a term used to denote possession:

– The head of the school.
– The school's head.

Both of these are examples of the genitive: the use of the word 'of', and the use of the apostrophe 's' in the second example. Do not think of the word 'genitive' as merely a label to stick on a structural feature, think of it as something referring to a necessary function in the deep structure of language. Without it, communication would be difficult.

GENRE (PLURAL GENRES)

The word genre has traditionally been used in literary studies to define different kinds of literature e.g. *novels*, *plays*, *poems*. Within these broad categories there have been sub-divisions of genres into, e.g. *social novels* and *science fiction novels; comic* and *tragic drama; lyric* and *narrative poetry*. In addition non-fictional literary genres have been recognised such as, *autobiography*, *travel writing*, *diaries*, *history*, *literary criticism*.

All genres can be seen as a combination of linguistic features that make the text the way it is and socio-cultural circumstances that determine both content and context of the texts. Two contributory developments to genre theory have been **structuralism** and *reader response* theory.

As a historical generalisation we can say that literary criticism (i.e. the ways in which we talk, think and write about literature) has moved from a writer focussed view of texts to a reader oriented view of texts. Writer focussed views (the oldest view) sees texts as the outpourings of inspired writers; reader oriented views stress the importance of the reader as a maker of meanings in the text. Between these two views is that of the New Critics and a number of eminent British academics (William Empson, F.R. Leavis) who emphasised the paramount importance of the text alone to convey meaning. Authors' intentions were unimportant, readers needed to learn critical disciplines according to established criteria of cultural value and literary excellence. Underlying this view is a conviction that it is the business of literary criticism to transmit cultural and moral values and to discipline reader response. In recent years both literary creativity and literary criticism have diversified in quite unanticipated ways. New genres in poetry, drama and fiction have appeared especially where there has been a mutual interaction between literature and other media. It is now said of Dennis Potter, for example (*Pennies from Heaven, The Singing Detective, Blackeyes*) that he does not just write for television, he writes and rewrites television itself. It is difficult to decide whether he has mixed existing genres in a highly original way or created a new genre.

In the literary experimentation of the past twenty five years the reader has acquired a new role and a new status. Variety in reader response has come to be regarded not as deviation from received critical opinion, but as an inevitable consequence of the reading process in which texts are as dependent upon their readers as they are upon their writers.

As young children we learn a range of genres which we reproduce in our own storytelling. *The Three Billy Goats Gruff, The Three Bears, The Three Little Pigs, The Tortoise and the Hare, Cinderella*, are all familiar tales that are encountered in a wide range of different versions. They provide us with a repertoire of powerful fictions that encode ideologies about power, wealth, good fortune, right behaviour, social justice, retribution, kinship ties, love and marriage, child rearing, rewards and punishment. (See **structuralism**). Genres are socio-cultural patterns and constructions that embody political or ideological values.

Sociologists have become increasingly interested in genres not only as literary variations but as ritual behaviour governed by social rules and encoded in language forms. In this sense, chidren, for example, have access to fewer genres than adults e.g. political processes, marriage. If we extend the sociolinguistic idea of genres to cover non-literary forms of writing we can see that whereas exclusion from literary genres (either as reader or writer) has socio-cultural consequences, exclusion from non-literary genres has personal and social disadvantages.

Non-literary genres express power in their form, content and context. Reports, records, business letters, official forms, legal documents, medical texts, technical instructions are all genres in which both the writing and the reading depend upon certain kinds of knowledge and shared interests that give personal and social power. Participation in the use of these genres means participation in their social functions. You could consider, for example, the social context of such genres as: a *curriculum vitae*, a school report, a solicitor's letter.

A current debate in education concerns the ways in which children implicitly learn literary and non-literary genres and how knowledge about them is explicitly taught and socially communicated by teachers. The movement in English examinations toward course work that demonstrates a variety of writing (for GCSE and A-level), is a sign of the interest in genres, but for A-level students of English language it is important to try and understand genre not as a matter of knowing the surface forms but of gaining greater insight, and more control over the kinds of language appropriate, so that it can be used effectively for the writer's own purposes. This includes command of the tone as well as of vocabulary.

The fact that when we write successfully in a genre (e.g. a short story or an item in a newsletter) we feel that we have largely been guided by intuition, is evidence of how completely the genre features have been internalised.

Even essay-type examination answers are a genre type. Every student should be aware that handling the genre in relation to the question, and the examiner, is as important to success as the content of the answer.

One way to begin to appreciate the diverse factors that contribute to the distinctiveness of a genre is to select an area where you detect varieties of genre and then classify them. The key questions will be about the criteria you use to distinguish one genre from another. You could start with obvious contrasts e.g. spy thrillers and detective stories; romantic fiction and family saga fiction; hi fi equipment test reports and performance car test drive reports. Once some broad distinctions have been drawn you will begin to discern sub-genres e.g. spy thrillers that concentrate on the intellectual game of spying as opposed to action packed adventure; romantic fiction in a medical setting as opposed to a 'Gothic' setting. Some features will be common to the main genre (e.g. fiction) others will be characteristic of your chosen sub-genre.

GLOTTIS AND GLOTTAL

The glottis is the space between the vocal cords (see **phonology**) which can be narrowed at will. When speakers omit the 't' sound in the middle of words like 'water', 'hotter', and 'butter' they are said to be producing a glottal stop by narrowing the glottis.

GRAMMAR

ATTITUDES

It is remarkable that something so harmless and helpful as grammar should have aroused so much controversy and ill feeling between different social groups. The old criticise the grammar of the young, teachers criticise pupils, parents criticise children, employers criticise employees, 'upper' social classes criticise 'lower' social classes, and even the Prince of Wales has criticised English teachers for not teaching proper English. The criticisms always emanate from positions of power, never *vice versa*; they are a familiar form of put-down. Insult or question other people's use of language and you intrude upon their personality, community background and self esteem, even when your intention is to be helpful.

Without even knowing much about linguistics, it is possible to hold very strong convictions about what is grammatically correct and what is not. Two very readable books by David Crystal discuss attitudes towards grammar:

Who Cares About English Usage? (Penguin 1984)
The English Language (Penguin 1988)

In the second, he lists the top ten complaints made about other people's misuse of grammar e.g.:

- you shouldn't say 'you and I' when you mean 'you and me'
- you shouldn't split infinitives i.e. not 'to quickly go' but 'to go quickly'
- you shouldn't say 'different to' but 'different from'.

Crystal goes on to demonstrate how these opinions, far from being absolute rules or laws, are often historical accidents, or popular misconceptions. You could investigate the complete list by asking a sample of, say twenty five, people to rank them in order of importance and to add any other misuses they can think of. This would make an interesting piece of original writing for course work e.g. a popular but informed article for a magazine or a five minute talk for Radio 2, or a ten minute talk for Radio 4. With more substance, attitudes toward grammar would also be a suitable project.

The *Longman Dictionary of the English Language* (1984) also discusses ten vexed points of English Grammar pp 1781–1784.

Fairly regularly people write to the press or the BBC about other people's faults of grammar. Here is a particularly offensive and snobbish example from a British tabloid (1985).

Consider the following sentence:

"He told them that he had stole the watch from a judge and that he stole the broach from his lawyer".

It is of course clumsy, ungrammatical and mis-spelled. I'm amazed to learn that education officials are recommending that such slipshod English should be given full marks in an examination paper. They say spelling and grammar are not important as long as the meaning is clear.

I'm glad that Chalky White, my old English master at the Henry Morton Grammar School did not permit such abuses of our mother tongue.

Uvverwise I wooden be able to rite proper like wot I do now.'

In fact, the sentence is not clumsy and is formed out of the speaker's accurate understanding of the grammatical rules for reporting speech. The words 'he had stole' may be ungrammatical (if 'he had stole' is what is meant) or mis-spelled ('stole' for 'stolen'). Apart from the mis-spelling of the word 'brooch', 'stole' is the only word in the piece that is questionable; if it is wrongly spelled then it cannot be ungrammatical, if it reflects the speaker's everyday grammatical usage, then it is spelled correctly. The writer of the item cannot have it both ways. It is quite possible that the piece is bogus anyway for apart from its curious content and uncertain context, the term 'lawyer' is not a usual one in British courts though common in the United States. In the final paragraph the writer resorts to making up stereotyped 'bad grammar' which convinces no one. Note too the moral indignation in 'permit such abuses of our mother tongue' and the vagueness, of the phrase, 'education officials'. All this indignation has been sparked off by one word ('stole') and reflects a great deal of prejudice and misrepresentation about modern English teaching as well as about the nature and functions of language. The underlying issue here concerns differences between spoken and written English though nothing is gained by the mockery and the prejudice demonstrated in newspaper items of this kind.

There is nothing at all wrong in wishing to make sure that your use of English grammar is conventional, correct and even elegant. These are wholly laudable aims. Advanced students of English, however, should be able to treat grammatical issues in a far more descriptive and knowledgeable way than the prescriptive, censorious attitude illustrated above. Words like 'clumsy' and 'slipshod' (also applied to personal appearance, dress and behaviour) are so often moral and aesthetic judgements with no basis whatever in grammatical or linguistic knowledge.

DEFINITIONS

Given the deeply felt attitudes that frequently accompany everyday uses of the term grammar, (including the ultra-permissive view that 'grammar doesn't matter so long as you can be understood' which is equally misguided), a concise definition of the word appears oddly clinical and not especially helpful. Moreover we need, not one, but two definitions to cover what Noam Chomsky refers to as the 'systematic ambiguity' with which we use the term. By that he means that the word can refer to our fundamental ability to use language at all (i.e. our *competence*), but it can also refer to the study of that competence.

Definition I

Grammar is the comprehensive description of all the elements that make up a language and of all the rules for combining those elements.

This definition adequately covers what we mean by 'a grammar book' or 'a grammar primer'. Such a book would help us to understand structural elements in a foreign language and would be a useful reference if we wanted to compare one language with another. It is possible to buy grammars of the English language but popular ones suffer from not being comprehensive enough so that descriptions given can seem at best, rather obvious, and at worst, incomprehensible.

A highly authoritative modern English grammar (all 1,779 pages of it) which you could consult in your local library is:

> *A Comprehensive Grammar of the English Language* (Longman 1985) by Randolph Quirk, Sidney Greenbaum, Geoffrey Leach and Jan Svartvik.

Your school library may possess a shorter version of the same basic approach:

A Grammar of Contemporary English (Longman 1972)
A University Grammar of English (Longman 1973) by Quirk and Greenbaum.

A shorter version still, and very lively to read is:

Rediscover English Grammar (Longman 1988) by David Crystal.

These four books are rather like a set of Russian dolls or Chinese boxes. Each one is identical in design but smaller, fitting comfortably inside the next size up.

In accordance with Definion I these books attempt to describe structural features of words, groups of words and sentences, and to identify grammatical and ungrammatical uses. A sentence such as 'Colourless, green ideas sleep furiously', is nonsensical but is nevertheless constructed according to recognisable rules of English grammar. 'Red helplessly one walker the for' is merely a string of words with no discernible principle of grammatical construction underlying it.

Grammar, in this sense of the word, describes and analyses the immediate constituent parts of any given stretch of language produced by a speaker or writer. It describes products and in doing so has created a body of knowledge which is usually divided by modern linguists into two fields: **morphology** and **syntax**.

Definition II

Grammar is the competence possessed by native speakers of a language in order to be able to use the language.

Grammar in this sense is something humans have in the brain. We seem to be programmed with grammar, which is the only reasonable explanation on offer considering how rapidly an infant learns its native language with little or no direct instruction from adults. When grammar is considered from the perspective of competence, far from being a matter of proper, or correct, linguistic manners, it becomes a matter of the deepest significance. It then has reference to fundamental ways in which humans think and map out the world in their minds. It encompasses (even defines) the dimensions of time and space in our minds, and in our communications. Much of the study of *verbs*, for example, is the study of tenses, or time indicators. *Prepositions* map out mental space (e.g. under, over, within, from, to) and define relationships (with, by, for). *Pronouns* help us to construct a clear 'who's who' in the mind. *Conjunctions* connect ideas together. Grammar is not the only way to map out the workings of the mind but it points our attention to the generative sources of language production, to those areas where thoughts and feelings begin to be put into the words that will eventually reach a spoken or written form outside the mind.

Definition I and Definition II are not unrelated but, as always with connections between products and creative processes, the relationship is complex.

GROUP

In Hallidayan grammar a group is a combination of two or more words but not including a finite verb. It comes between a word and a clause. An older grammatical term for it is a *phrase*. With the development of generative grammars (following **Chomsky**) the word phrase has additionally come to mean a unit such as a *noun phrase* or a *verb phrase*. Thus in a *phrase structure grammar* phrases can have verbs in them. For this reason it is a sensible idea to use the word group to avoid confusion.

◀ Halliday ▶

H

HALF RHYME

◀ Para-rhyme ▶

HALLIDAY, MICHAEL

M.A.K. Halliday (*b* 1925) has been a major influence on modern linguistics, especially in Britain and Australia. He has developed a descriptive grammar known as *systemic grammar* as distinct from, say, Chomsky's *transformational generative grammar*. Both grammars are systematic. They would have to be since language is by nature a system, but systemic in Hallidayan grammar refers to an interconnected series of systems that create the web or network known as a language. The systems operate within each other, and can be analysed at different levels.

The system of phonemes creates the system of words which in turn creates the system of word groups. Groups consist of two or more words and it is important to recognise that when two words work in conjunction with each other they are no longer just the sum total of the two words but will express a specific grammatical relationship.

The next system is the clause which is a group of words containing a verb. The clause system creates sentence systems while sentences are connected in cohesive ways that lead to the larger systemic units of paragraph and whole discourse.

Halliday's approach to grammar has always taken into account the functions served by language structures and his work is particularly relevant in the field of *pragmatics* which is concerned with what people do with language and how meanings are made. He has also drawn special attention to ways in which *cohesion* is achieved in texts (how one sentence links with another) and to ways in which *intonation* communicates meaning.

In the 1960s, based at the University of London, Halliday directed studies and projects to introduce sound linguistic principles to the teaching of reading and to English teaching in schools. The outcome was an approach to reading that has become known as *Breakthrough to Literacy*, and a programme of language study for secondary schools and colleges, *Language in Use* by Doughty, Thornton and Pearce (1971).

More recently, Halliday has stimulated investigations into how *theme* is introduced and maintained in the structure of a text. (See *A Functional Grammar* by Halliday (1975) and *Cohesion in English* by Halliday and Hasan (1976)).

HEPTAMETER

◀ Metre ▶

HESITATION

Hesitation phenomena, as they are sometimes called, should not be assumed to be signs of weakness, deficiency or inadequacy. There are clearly many reasons why people hesitate, or pause in speech and an investigative approach would first of all observe examples and then describe carefully the circumstances before deciding why the speaker had hesitated or paused. Note that hesitations can occur almost anywhere, though initial hesitation can have different effects from hesitation in the middle of words or utterances. When are they caused by reaction? When are they occasioned by the need to plan the next utterance? When do they convey emotional states? When and how are they used for rhetorical effects?

Notice, too, that hesitations can take the form of *silence*, or they can be expressed by *fillers*. If you are transcribing a silent pause, it can be indicated by a bracket with the number of seconds elapsed, like this: (3). Fillers are heard as 'ums and erms' and may be written as closely as possible to the way they sound.

HEXAMETER

◀ Metre ▶

HOLOPHRASE AND HOLOPHRASTIC

The term holophrase is used in child language acquisition studies to denote single word utterances which are functioning as more than one word in the context of utterance. They are in fact one word sentences. Well known examples are:

Teddy (meaning 'Give me my Teddy.')
Dada (meaning 'Pick me up please.')
More (meaning 'I want some more.')
Allgone (spoken as one word meaning not only 'I have drunk it all like a good girl.' but also, 'I want some more.').

There are many occasions when holophrases continue to be used in adult life quite acceptably, but there are others when we would regard habitual holophrastic speech as unsociable and even offensive.

HUBRIS

The pride that allows a tragic hero to ignore the warnings from the gods, and so bring about his **nemesis** (downfall).

HUMOURS

The four humours were originally thought of as four liquids existing in the human body, equivalents of the four elements from which the Universe was created. The balance of the humours dictated a person's personality and health. Much medieval and Elizabethan writing refers to this theory. Earlier references tend to refer to the basic fluids and the features they were meant to give people. A person with an excess of the humour *blood* in him was called *sanguine*, and was pleasure-loving, amourous, kind, and jovially good-natured; the Franklin in Chaucer's *The Canterbury Tales* is such a figure. Someone with an excess of *phlegm* in them was described as *phlegmatic* and was dull, cowardly, unresponsive, dour, and unexciting. An excess of *yellow bile* gave rise to a *choleric* person: vengeful, obstinate, impatient, intolerant, angry and quick to lose his temper. An excess of *black bile* produced a person who was *melancholic*: moody, brooding, sharp-tongued, liable to sudden changes of mood, and often lost in thought and contemplation. By the start of the seventeenth century the 'comedy of humours' had developed, in which people's behaviour was linked to one humour or feature – what we would now call a 'complex'. *Every Man in His Humour* by Ben Jonson (1572–1637) is a good example of such a play.

HYPERBOLE

A figure of speech using exaggeration.

I

IAMB

An unstressed and then a stressed syllable.

◀ Metre ▶

IAMBIC HEPTAMETER

◀ Metre ▶

IDIOLECT

With the interest and emphasis placed so extensively on dialectal aspects of English it is easy to neglect idiolect which is at least as important.

Idiolect is the language variety spoken by an individual person. It is made up of several personal and social elements: vocal timbre and pitch, sex, age, anatomy and physiology, regional dialect, social class, education, occupation, and a wide range of life experiences.

Idiolect is subject to change but has many permanent features. The best way to appreciate the uniqueness of a persons idiolect is to remember that a voice print is as effective as a finger print as a mode of identification. No matter how many English speakers are assembled in a room, they will all speak with perceptibly different voices. This is an aspect of variety always taken for granted, yet which is a remarkable differentiating feature of human beings speaking the same language or dialect.

IDIOM

Idiom is a term sometimes used to refer to a language or to a dialect, while literature has been described as the distinctly 'human idiom' to distinguish it from scientific, sociological, business or technological writing. Most frequently however the term denotes much smaller units.

Within a language idioms are expressions which seem to have their own rules and are difficult to translate. In other words, they mean something different from the sum total of their parts: e.g.

kick the bucket
throw a wobbler
three sheets to the wind
got out of bed on the wrong side.

Idioms are a richly fascinating area of language and many dictionaries exist which explain the origins of English idioms. (See for example *A Dictionary of Catchphrases* 2nd edition (RKP 1985), *Longman Dictionary of Phrasal Verbs* (1983), *Longman Dictionary of English Idioms* (1980)).

IMAGE

This is a word which is often used to describe an especially complex metaphor, one which may well involve comparison of the thing being described to a whole series of related other things. Most particularly, image can be used to refer to a whole series of metaphors which describe one thing repeatedly in terms of another. In such a sense, critics often talk of 'chains of imagery' or 'recurrent images'. Here, for example, is the opening of a Shakespeare sonnet which uses an image of this sort:

That time of year thou mayst in me behold
When yellow leaves, or none, or few, do hang
Upon those boughs which shake against the cold,
Bare ruin'd choirs, where once the sweet birds sang.

Here, the speaker is bringing together a whole series of parallels to the 'time of year' he is going through – his age. He mentions tree boughs almost devoid of leaves, those few that remain being yellow with age, and the boughs shaking in winter's cold. He then moves on to refer to ruined 'choirs', parts of a church or abbey, which continue the idea of age and desolation.

As before, you need both to *identify* the way an image works – by saying what it is that the writer is comparing the subject with – and to *comment on its effect*. Here, for instance, the effect is greatly to reinforce the idea of age by the stress on exposure and ruin: this is no rich old age, but rather a time of bleakness.

INTENSIFIER

Intensifiers are adverbs which intensify the meaning of a word:

He was *very* good.
I *really*, *really* like it.
He's *incredibly* good-looking.
I am *definitely* going.

INTERACTION

◀ Dramatic interaction ▶

INTERNAL RHYME

Rhyming words within a single line rather than at the ends of separate ones. For example:

And binding with briars my joys and desires.

INTERNATIONAL PHONETIC ALPHABET

The consonant sounds of English are:

/p/	as in ***part***	/f/	as in ***food***	/h/	as in ***has***
/b/	as in ***but***	/v/	as in ***voice***	/m/	as in ***mat***
/t/	as in ***too***	/θ/	as in ***thing***	/n/	as in ***not***
/d/	as in ***did***	/ð/	as in ***this***	/ŋ/	as in ***long***
/k/	as in ***kiss***	/s/	as in ***see***	/l/	as in ***let***
/g/	as in ***get***	/z/	as in ***zoo***	/r/	as in ***red***
/tʃ/	as in ***chin***	/ʃ/	as in ***she***	/j/	as in ***yes***
/dʒ/	as in ***joke***	/ʒ/	as in ***measure***	/w/	as in ***will***

The vowel sounds of English are:

(long vowels)		(short vowels)		(diphthongs*)	
/iː/	as in ***each***	/ɪ/	as in ***it***	/eɪ/	as in ***day***
/ɑː$^{(r)}$/	as in ***car***	/e/	as in ***then***	/aɪ/	as in ***by***
/ɔː$^{(r)}$/	as in ***more***	/æ/	as in ***back***	/ɔɪ/	as in ***boy***
/uː/	as in ***too***	/ʌ/	as in ***much***	/əʊ/	as in ***no***
/ɜː$^{(r)}$/	as in ***word***	/ɒ/	as in ***not***	/aʊ/	as in ***now***
		/ʊ/	as in ***put***	/ɪə$^{(r)}$/	as in ***near***
		/ə/	as in ***again***	/eə$^{(r)}$/	as in ***there***
				/ʊə$^{(r)}$/	as in ***truer***

Fig. I.1

INVOLVED NARRATOR

◀ Narrative voice ▶

IRONIC DETACHMENT

◀ Narrative stance ▶

IRONY

Irony is the use of language to express the exact opposite of what is actually said. In popular speech, the most familiar form of irony is sarcasm, when, for example, someone elaborately praises or thanks someone else for doing something inadequate or unkind.

In literature, irony is usually more subtle. In the general prologue of *The Canterbury Tales*, for example, Chaucer often ironically praises characters whom we know, by his tone and use of detail, to be morally corrupt, concluding the portrait of the Merchant with a couplet which appears to praise him but suggests that he is far from memorable:

> For sothe he was a worthy man with alle,
> But, sooth to seyu, I noot how men him calle.

Jane Austen, too, uses irony to powerful effect in revealing the niceties and pretensions of social behaviour. Of its essence, irony is a subtle mode; read carefully to make sure that you do not miss the ironic implications of a passage, and thus take at face value something which has a very different meaning from that which is instantly apparent.

◀ Dramatic irony ▶

L

LABIALS

Labials are consonant sounds made by the use of one or both lips.

The sound [b] is made by both lips. The sound [f] is called *labio-dental* because it requires the use of the teeth and the lower lip.

LAMENT

A poem expressing intense grief.

LANGUAGE PROJECTS

Projects have long been a feature of primary and secondary education (amusingly satirised in a novel by Jan Mark called *Thunder and Lightnings*). They remain very appropriate ways of investigating or researching a particular topic where data (or evidence) needs to be collected before conclusions can be drawn.

Local history, geography and cultural studies projects are by now familiar, but language study projects have also proved a very popular part of new A-level English Language syllabuses, and an increasing number of students are undertaking language study projects in English Literature syllabuses where course work is required, e.g. the language of Shakespeare's England; dialect in the novels of Thomas Hardy; regional dialect poetry; studies of ambiguity and metaphor; identifying linguistic features of a chosen writer's style.

As a general rule language projects are at their best when they report a small study full of interesting detail. Large scale studies require much more time than is available and many more words than examination boards prescribe. In the space of, say, 4000 words, large scale projects raise more questions than they can answer and have to resort to the kind of generalised comments that readers usually find unconvincing and uninteresting. A review of a large variety of magazines, or a comparison of extremely different radio programmes, are examples of projects that can become too diffuse. One candidate recently proposed to compare the language use of a Downs Syndrome child with the language use of a 'normal' child. On the face of it this seems a straightforward idea but it begs a number of questions and would require a large amount of data to make even one significant comparison. Better to concentrate on the Downs Syndrome child and to present the data as an interesting case study in its own right. Some normative reference points to begin with could easily be drawn from introductory books such as *Early Language* by de Villiers and de Villiers (Fontana 1979) or *Language Acquisition* by Fletcher and Garman (Cambridge Univ. Press 1979).

It is important in the first instance to choose a topic in which you are generally interested rather than one that seems easy. You do not have to prove a revelatory new theory in a tidy set of conclusions. Errors and problems encountered in the investigation are as interesting as the data itself and make good reading if they are recounted frankly and thoughtfully. A serious attempt to tackle something problematical, or a bit messy, is as likely to earn high marks as a safe topic, competently reported.

Some questions you should consider before writing a final draft are:

1 Does my title define precisely enough what I have investigated and reported?
2 Does the reader get a clear focus in the introduction on what the report is going to be about?
3 Have I explained to the reader how I went about defining my topic and collecting my data?
4 Have I presented the body of data in an objective, easy to read way?
5 Do the sections into which I have organised my project make sense? Are they appropriately sub-titled?
6 Is there a clearly stated linguistic idea, theory or principle to guide my investigation? If it has been drawn from a recognised text have I clearly acknowledged and described adequately the source of the idea?
7 Have I discussed the methods and procedures followed, and explained their strengths and any weaknesses?
8 Are the points made in the analysis and discussion of the data clearly itemised?
9 Have I kept closely enough to my original intentions? You are allowed to make occasional detours and you are not expected to prove in a heavy handed way any opening assertions. There should however be a discernible thread of theme or ideas running through your project.
10 Remember that you should be in control of your text. Signal to the reader where it is going. What is coming next? How one section relates to another? Why you are discussing a particular point?

Some things to remember when editing the final draft are:

1 It is usually better to leave the introduction until last of all. Remember, it makes the very first impact on the reader and needs careful thought.

2 A 'contents page' helps readers to find their way about.
3 Make sure that appendices are clearly identified.
4 Your bibliography should be accurate enough so that the reader can trace the books you refer to.
5 Titles, subtitles, sub-headings, page numbers, sections, sub-sections, footnotes, annotations, should all be consistent.
6 Data (e.g. transcripts, words and phrases used as examples, lists) should be clearly distinguished from your discussion of them. Be spacious, don't cram everything together so that it is difficult to read. Do use colour, varied layout etc.
7 Do write a one page **abstract** after the title page. It tells the reader what to expect and serves as a last minute check that you have got an overall shape to your project. If you find it difficult to write an abstract it could be that your project is not sufficiently well structured.

◀ Essays ▶

LEXICON

Lexicon is a Greek word used to refer to the vocabulary of a language. It may also be used as a synonym for dictionary.

Related words are:

lexis (words)
lexical (pertaining to words)
lexicology (the meaning of words)
lexicography (dictionary making).

LINE NUMBERS

If you're answering a question on a passage which appears on the exam paper, you will be able to refer to an expression by giving the number of the line on which it appears instead of quoting it in full. You might, for example, write 'the use of sea-faring imagery continues in lines 12–13 and recurs in line 24'. This can save a lot of time in the exam but still ensures that you support your points with close reference to the text.

LISTENING

One of the four language modes (*talking*, *listening*, *reading*, *writing*) though often linked with *talking* under the heading *oracy*. It is often referred to as the Cinderella of the language modes because of its general neglect as a research or educational topic.

It is easy to take listening for granted and aural evidence is by nature subjective, which is why it is important in A-level studies to learn to listen to what people really say and how they really say it. It is easy to hear what we want to hear.

Occasionally students undertake projects on how deaf people communicate. They may themselves have a deaf relative and some expertise in sign language.

LYRIC

Originally a song written for accompaniment by a lyre, the term is now used to refer to a poem which is short and is more concerned with an emotional state that with telling a story. A lyric poem may also explore a more complex state of mind: Matthew Arnold, for example, described his poem 'Dover Beach', which discusses the crisis of faith at the growth of the idea of evolution, as a 'Lyric Poem'.

◀ Ode ▶

M

MALAPROPISM

The use of a word which sounds like that which is intended but which has a comically different meaning – 'erogenised milk' instead of 'homogenised milk', for example. The term is derived from the name of Mrs Malaprop, a character in *The Rivals* by Richard Brinsley Sheridan, although this has been a source of comedy for centuries, being seen for example in the character of Dogberry in Shakespeare's *Much Ado About Nothing*.

MASCULINE ENDING

A line of verse ending on a stressed syllable.

MASQUE

A lavish form of dramatic entertainment relying heavily on song, dance, costumes, extravagant spectacle and special effects. The genre flourished in the first part of the seventeenth century, having been imported from Italy where it later developed into opera. Ben Jonson is sometimes seen as the greatest of masque writers. The masques produced to music by Henry Purcell represent a high point of English musical theatre. *Comus* by John Milton is a particularly famous masque.

MELODRAMA

Originally, in the ancient Greek theatre, melodrama was a special kind of play in which spoken words were accompanied by music which created atmosphere. It then became associated with eighteenth and nineteenth-century popular plays which did the same, often dealing with sensational crimes or highly emotional themes. As these developed and the music was omitted, the word came to be given to any highly sensational action. Nevertheless, it is a weak use of the term to describe events in a play as melodramatic, and you'll do far better to describe simply the effect that is being created in the audience.

METALANGUAGE

A problem with language is that we only have language with which to talk about it. It is also true that when we think, we have only language to think with, plus whatever kind of non-linguistic thinking we are able to detect or express. Thus thinking about language is itself a linguistic activity.

Reflection on language takes many forms. We can talk or write about books we have read; we can read books on how to write better, or about how conversation works; and we can listen to a lecture on reading or writing. There is a considerable range of interactions between the language modes of reading, writing, listening and talking and over the centuries the common vocabulary for talking about language has been used in a variety of effective ways. We apply terms like 'tone of voice' to writing. We say things like 'let me see what you have said', and there are many metaphors to describe language and human behaviour in terms of each other:

- I can read you like a book.
- In today's game he rewrote the history of cricket.
- His singing speaks to me in a personal way.
- His tenor saxophone speaks with a voice all its own.
- I'm tongue tied.

A metalanguage is a set of descriptive terms that we can use to talk about language in as precise and verifiable a way as possible. This book is a guide to metalanguage in that it explains linguistic terms such as verb, noun, subject, phoneme, morpheme etc.

It is not uncommon to hear the complaint that there are too many metalanguages and that linguists cannot agree on terminology. This is not true – linguists agree on a great deal, and where there are differences it is usually because the topic itself needs more research or has been approached from a variety of viewpoints which need not be mutually exclusive. Already there are signs of interaction between systemic grammar approaches and generative grammar approaches. (See **Halliday** and **Chomsky**).

For A-level English language it is important to make a start on a metalanguage and develop it slowly in practical ways. Rote learning of terminology without practical investigation offers little or no insight into language. Labelling is not at all the same thing as identifying a feature, recognising its significance and being able to say something interesting about it.

Set out below is a suggested nucleus for a metalanguage that will help you to further your understanding about the nature and functions of language and which will 'attract' new terminology as the need arises in specific contexts of study. Remember, again, that a metalanguage is a better way of talking and writing about language it should not be a baffling code.

1 Phonetics – phonology (phonemes, intonation, stress, voiced/unvoiced, articulation).
2 Morphology (morpheme, affixation, derivation, inflection).
3 Word classes (noun, verb, adverb, adjective, preposition, conjunction, pronoun, determiner, interjection, grammatical words, lexical words).
4 Syntax (group, clause, sentence, subject, object, indirect object, main verb, prediction, adjunct, agreement (or concord), noun phrase, verb phrase).
5 Discourse (text, cohesion).

The suggestions here are concerned with language structures, that part of metalanguage that seems to cause most anxiety. If you get into the habit of using these terms, it will not be long before you are wondering what all the fuss was about. Do not be put off by the large number of subdivisions in each category. The important thing is to know why the category exists. If you read something about the difference between finite and non-finite verbs, think of it as a new distinction you can file away under 'verb'. Similarly with distinctions between adverbial and relative clauses, or between compound and complex sentences, so long as you understand the relationship between a clause and a sentence you will be able to make sense of these distinctions.

When you are studying a grammatical distinction, learn it as well as you can and test it out on examples of your own. Do not worry about all the other things lurking in the linguist's metalanguage that you have not learnt yet. Concentrate on learning a little bit very well so that you can use it confidently. Remember, it is a linguistic fact that language is systematic, so if you learn one bit well it will interconnect with other bits of the system as you go on. Babies learn their native language in a similar way and can do so because of the systematicity of the language. If you are learning a second language or are already bilingual you will have a grammatical advantage so far as other students are concerned. The comparative method is a good way of learning about grammar.

Whilst curiosity alone will sometimes be enough to make you want to know more about the structures of language it is important to have a reason for grammatical description or analysis. If you feel you are doing it for the sake of it, something has gone wrong and you will be better employed studying functions of language. Once you begin to see that differences in function relate to differences in structure, the point should become clear again and your use of terminology more purposeful.

METAPHOR

This is a comparison which is stated by *implication*: there is no particular word of comparison – 'like' or 'as' for example – to reveal a metaphor. Here, for example, is John Donne using the idea of a woman as the true Church – Christ's 'Spouse' or bride:

> Show me, dear Christ, thy Spouse, so bright and clear.
> What! Is it She, which on the other shore
> Goes richly painted? or which rob'd and tore
> Laments and mourns in Germany and here?

Here, Donne is asking whether the true church is the Catholic church of Rome 'which on the other shore (continental Europe) Goes richly painted', a reference to the richly coloured statues of saints used by the Catholic Church. Or is the true church the 'rob'd and tore' figure lamenting in Germany and Britain – the Protestant church with its much starker rituals?

Identifying the metaphor is not enough; you have to explain the effect. In Donne's poem, the metaphor is very striking because it makes the Church like a person, and helps Donne attach to a religious poem something of the passion of a love poem – a drawing together of different areas of experience which is very powerful.

The best metaphors work in exactly this way. They link things together which most people would never think of linking, and so offer us a startling new insight. Your writing about metaphor should always aim to make clear *what* this insight is, and the impact it makes on you, the reader.

METRE

All **verse** – and, indeed, all prose and dramatic writing – has a rhythm, or pattern of stressed and unstressed syllables. If this pattern is regular or recurrent, it is called metre: each unit of regular metre is called a **foot**. Strictly speaking, poetry which is written in a regular metre is called verse. Even though the poetry is written in such a pattern, however, it does not have to be regular and repetitive in rhythm – otherwise it would be mere doggerel. Many of the finest effects in English poetry come from the tensions between the regular metre and the irregular rhythm – creating effects rather like syncopation in music, where the strong beats fall where we do not expect them and the whole piece is given much greater energy as a result. The study of metre is a very specialised area and it is unlikely that you will ever need to analyse the metrical structure of a passage. There is certainly no point in going through a poem and marking it out into regular units of metre – what is more important is to be aware of the way the poet uses the metrical structure and the rhythm, perhaps in conflict with each other, to create effects which add further layers of significance to the poem or underline those already there.

Metrical poetry is written in various combinations of standard feet, all composed of various combinations of stressed syllables, written as — and unstressed syllables written as ˘ . The four most common feet in English poetry are as follows:

Iamb: an unstressed and then a stressed syllable.

Ĭ weep | for Ad | ona | is – he | is dead! (Shelley)

Anapaest: two unstressed and one stressed.

The Ăs sy | rian came down | like the wolf | on the fold | (Byron)

Trochee: a stressed and an unstressed. Most often, the last foot in a line of this sort has only a single, stressed syllable, as here:

Here a | lit – tle | child Ĭ | stand | (Herrick)

Dactyl: a stressed and two unstressed syllables. A whole line of this foot is rare – most often a spondaic foot is added at the end, as here:

Just for a | handful of | silver he | left us (Browning)

There are, in addition, three other kinds of metric feet, rarely used in English verse:

Spondee: two stressed syllables, as in the first four feet of this line:

What is | beauty | saith my | sufferings | then? (Marlowe)

Pyrrhic: two unstressed syllables:

Ă slum | bĕr dĭd | my spĭ | rĭt sĕal | (Wordsworth)

Many writers feel, however, that there are no true pyrrhic feet in English, since one syllable is always stronger and the form inevitably changes into an iamb. You must reach your own conclusion on this, as in so many other issues of pressing controversy.

Amphibrach: two unstressed syllables separated by a stressed.

Ăs Chlo e | came in to | the room t'ŏ | ther day (Prior)

As the pyrrhic lapses into the iamb, so the Amphibrach shifts into the anapaest; there are few really convincing uses of this foot in English.

A line of metric verse may have different numbers of feet, and is named according to its length:

Monometers have one foot
Dimeter, two feet
Trimeter, three feet
Tetrameter, four feet
Pentameter, five feet
Hexameter, six feet
Heptameter, seven feet
Octameter, eight feet.

Of these, the most frequently encountered are the following:

Iambic pentameter, a five-foot line of iambs, used by Shakespeare, Milton and many other poets.
Alexandrine, an iambic hexameter, used by Pope and other eighteenth-century writers.
A **fourteener**, or line of fourteen syllables, which is another name for an **iambic heptameter**.

Scanning a poem – going through it to work out the nature of each foot and the length of the lines – is an approach which can be taken to poetry, but in many ways it achieves little unless it is undertaken along with an analysis of the rhythm, pace, sound and other qualities of the writing, and an enquiry into how they assist in conveying the essential idea, mood or other basic significance of the writing. At A-level, there is often little to be gained by metrical analysis and a lot to be lost, since it takes up time better spent on looking at the other qualities which go to make up the overall effects of poetry. An an exercise in analysing **structure**, and in comparing English literature to classical writing, an approach based on scansion can be very valuable, but it is highly specialised and, unless undertaken with care, can be misleading about the rhythmic and other effects of the poem in question.

◀ Enjambement and end-stopped lines ▶

MIDDLE ENGLISH

This is the historical term for the form of the language from the middle of the twelfth century to about 1500. It is thus the language used by Gower, the Gawayne-poet and, most important, Geoffrey Chaucer. The language has many similarities to modern English but also several differences. These lie not only in the meaning of individual words – many of which, though apparently similar to modern ones, are very different in meaning – but also in grammar and syntax.

SPELLING

This is not always consistent – that is, the same word may well be spelled differently. Since language was largely spoken and not written, there was no standard spelling. Remembering this will help you to recognise words which look the same but are spelled differently. For example, both 'mone' and 'moone' mean 'moon'; 'wrought' and 'wroughte' mean made, did or produced, according to the context in which they are used.

PARTS OF SPEECH

Plural nouns

These are usually formed by adding -es, as in 'knightes' for 'knights' – not too different from present-day forms.

Others take -en in the plural, to give 'eyen', or simply -n, giving 'shoon'. Some of these plurals remain today; 'children', for instance, is the plural of the Middle English 'childe'.

Possessive forms

Generally formed by the addition of an s or -es, these are often the same words as plurals. The context decides their function. There is no possessive apostrophe in ME – it writes 'the kinges peyne', not 'the king's sorrow', for example.

Pronouns

Middle English often uses 'thee' and 'thou', and not 'you', when the person addressed is a close friend or relative – like the French 'tu' and German 'du'. The word 'thee' can be spelt with one e or two – a point to remember, as this can lead to serious misunderstandings.

For personal pronouns, ME is splendidly non-sexist. Instead of 'his', 'hers', and 'theirs', the one word 'hir' or 'hire' was used. This can cause problems, since there is no indication of the gender of the people or things referred to, which can sometimes make it hard to see exactly which group is in question.

'Hem' is used instead of the modern 'them'; and 'his' instead of 'its'.

Verbs

Infinitives end with '-e' or '-en', as in 'to werke' or 'to werken'.

Present participles will usually end in -ing or -ynge; in Middle English i and y are often interchangeable.

Past participles often begin with a y – 'ywroghte' for 'did' or 'made', for example. If you need to check such words in a dictionary or Chaucer glossary, look for them under their **second** letter as well as under y in the glossary.

SYNTAX

There are some important differences between Middle English and the modern syntax.

Order of verb and subject

Often the verb comes after the object and not before, as it would in modern English. Here are some lines from Chaucer's *Franklin's Tale:*

And many a labour, many a greet emprise
He for his lady wroghte, er she were wonne.

Modern English would say 'He did many a labour and many a great undertaking for his lady, before she was won over', instead of 'Many a labour...he...did'.

Negatives

ME will use a double or even a treble negative of the sort which today would be looked on as 'wrong'. It might, for instance, say 'There nas never noone', – literally 'there was not never none'.

Auxilary verbs

The verb 'gan' is used to convey a past tense – for example, in 'gan wepe', meaning 'began to weep'. Alternatively, 'did' may be used for the same purpose, without the added emphasis it has now – 'he dide wepe' meaning simply 'he wept' rather than the emphatic 'he *did* weep'.
When you're studying Chaucer or any other text in ME, make sure that you have an edition which gives the text in the original language and has a good glossary. **Don't** read it in a modern 'translation': if you do, you'll lose all the richness of sound, association and other elements which are as rich in ME poetry as in that of any other period.

MOCK EPIC

Writing of this style uses the elaborate and ceremonial style of epic writing to describe events and feelings of little consequence. The finest example in English is Pope's *The Rape of the Lock*, which describes the stealing of a lock of hair in terms of an Homeric conflict. This kind of writing is also known as mock heroic.

MOCK-HEROIC

◀ Mock epic ▶

MONOMETER

◀ Metre ▶

MOOD

◄ Drama ►

MORPHEMES

Words may be split into different components. They may be split into their constituent letters:

e.g. underground = u+n+d+e+r+g+r+o+u+n+d.

They may be split into syllables:

e.g. underground = un+der+gr+ou+nd or un+der+ground.

Neither of these sets of units adequately describe the structure of the word's meaning. The first is purely alphabetic but useful insofar as it is consistent. The second represents an attempt to write down spoken units of a word, something which can vary according to the different ways in which a word can be spoken and heard. (See **syllable**).

Morphemes are minimal units of meaning that cannot be reduced further without destroying a word's meaning. There are two kinds. First there are *free morphemes* which consist of many thousands of words in English which stand on their own. The following passage is made up entirely of *free morphemes*:

> John sat on the chair over by the window. He drew a pen from his pocket and gave it to the woman.
> 'Sign', he said.
> 'But will I be a success?'
> 'Sure', came the reply.
> 'Leave me to fix the whole trip'.

The other kind of morphemes are called *bound morphemes* because their meaning potential can only be realised when they are bound to free morphemes.

The following is a re-write of the earlier passage with bound morphemes underlined:

> John was sitting on the chair by the windows. He drew a pen from one of his pockets and gave it to the woman.
> 'Sign', he said.
> 'But will I be a success?'she asked.
> 'Sure', he replied.
> 'Leave the organisation of the whole trip in my hands'.

Bound morphemes add extra meaning to words:

e.g.	-ing	= continuous present tense
	-s	= plural
	-ed	= puts a verb in the past tense
	-ation	= changes an action (a verb) into a thing (a noun).

Occasional adjustments have to be made for spelling (as in *reply/replied* and *organise/organisation*) but these are easily recognised. The important factor is that the meaning remains intact and comprehensible to any user of English. The changing of a 'y' to an 'i', and the dropping of an 'e' are spelling conventions only.

The range of observable morphemic combinations in English words is as follows:

a) Free morpheme + bound morpheme(s).
b) Bound morpheme(s) + free morpheme.
c) Free morpheme + free morpheme (e.g. headrest, backache).

The combination of two bound morphemes is hardly likely to occur though some students have argued that *anti-ism* could be used to mean 'a disposition to be against anything and everything'! It's a nice idea but an exception that proves the rule.

Free morphemes are said to have *content meaning* in that they refer to something outside themselves. Bound morphemes, on the other hand, are said to have *grammatical meaning*. This means that they can be used to alter the grammatical function of a word e.g. change its tense, change it to plural, turn it into a negative, change it from an action to a thing.

Sometimes bound morphemes are described as either *inflexional* or *derivational*. Inflexional morphemes change the function of a word by adding a different tense ending or a plural -s. When learning a second language it is sometimes necessary to learn how to *decline* nouns and *conjugate* verbs, both inflectional processes. In every case the words never change their class, they remain nouns or verbs.

Derivational morphemes on the other hand change the class of a word. From the word 'nation', for example, we can derive:

nationalisation (noun)
de-nationalise (verb)
national (adjective)
nationwide (adverb)
nationality (noun)
nationally (adverb)
nationalised (adjective).

MORPHOLOGY

is that branch of grammar which deals with the structure of words. The word morphology is derived from Greek 'morphe', meaning shape or form. This meaning is reflected in the children's television character Morph, a lump of plasticine that can be changed into any shape or form by his creator. Originally the word was used in English to name the branch of biology that deals with living forms. Later it came to be used in grammar. Words are not quite as malleable as a lump of plasticine but their shape or structure is frequently changed in everyday use. Morphology studies these changes and attempts to discover the rules that govern them. It is wise, though, to remember the original biological use of the word and to think of words more as living things than as inanimate, mechanical objects.

It you took any English word and listed all the ways in which that word could be changed according to use, you would in fact unerringly apply a series of morphological rules:

e.g. walks, walker, walkers, walking, walkway, walkman, walked, walk

e.g. organise, disorganise, reorganise, organisation, organiser, organisable, organising, organised.

The extent and the variety of alterations that can be made to English words permit a wide range of meanings.

◀ Morpheme, Allomorph, Syllable, Affixation ▶

MORPHOPHONEMICS

The relationship between **morphology** and **phonology** is sometimes straightforward, but sometimes complicated. The study of that relationship is called morphophonology and the relationship between morphemes and phonemes is referred to as morphophonemic.

A very common morpheme for forming the past tense is '-ed' as in happen/happened, stop/stopped, waste/wasted. All these examples look consistent when written down but each one is pronounced differently. 'Happened' ends with a /d/ sound, 'stopped' ends with a /t/ sound, and 'wasted' ends with an /id/ sound.

Similarly there are phonological variations in the use of the plural '-s' morpheme:

cats (which sounds like an /s/)
dogs (which sounds like a /z/
houses (which sounds like an /iz/).

In the cases of the past tense '-ed' and the plural '-s', the morphophonemic relationship is not constant, but varies. The meaning however remains the same. The fact that the phonological variations do the same job makes them **allophones**. (Related words: morphophonology, morphophonemic).

MULTIVALENCE

◀ Ambivalence ▶

MYTH

An anonymous or traditional story which tells of mysterious and strange events far back in history. *Mythology* is a collection of such stories. Myths often deal with elemental situations such as the creation of the world or the actions of gods, and are associated with primitive societies. These stories are often basic to the nature of human existence, and as such exert lasting appeal. In literary writing, 'myth' does not suggest untruth – it is quite acceptable to talk of 'the Christian myth' without suggesting that the story is untrue. Instead it suggests action on a symbolic rather than a literal level.

N

NARRATOR

The character who presents the actions and feelings in a novel or short story. It may or may not be the same as the actual writer.

◀ Narrative stance, Narrative voice ▶

NARRATIVE STANCE

This is the *attitude* of the narrator or story-teller in a novel, to the narrative or story itself. In many novels, this attitude is not openly stated – it is simply an account of the events as they occur, apparently without comment (see realism). But this is usually found only in more straightforward novels, and a novelist may well use a different or more sophisticated stance.

1 Self-conscious narrator

Here, the narrator will often speak directly to the reader, either in separate parts of the novel or while the action is actually taking place. Henry Fielding, for example, begins each book of *Tom Jones* with a chapter in which he addresses the reader directly, and often makes similarly direct comments in the course of the novel's events.

More recently, John Fowles, in *The French Lieutenant's Woman*, has used similarly direct address, to ask questions of the reader, and break through the pretence of realism of the traditional popular novel. Such direct statements can be very effective, as they force the reader to think about the nature of the novel, and focus his or her mind on issues or themes being discussed.

2 Involved narrator

Often the narrator will be someone who is involved with the events going on. A well-known example of this would be the character of Jane in *Jane Eyre*, who knows only what she herself sees and learns about other characters, or Pip in *Great Expectations*.

This narrative stance has a considerable influence on the nature of the book. As the story is told by someone who *doesn't* know all that is going on, it makes things more exciting for the reader, and an element of suspense is introduced. It also means that we come close to experiencing things directly ourselves when we read the novel. The 'I' of the narrator becomes the 'I' of each reader, and so we are drawn closely into what is happening.

Sometimes a writer will split the narration between a number of characters. In *Bleak House*, for example, Dickens uses both an omniscient narrator and one of the main characters in chapters headed 'Esther's Narrative'; in *The Moonstone*, Wilkie Collins changes the narration from one character to another as the novel progresses. These are exceptions, however, generally the narrator remains constant, and involved with the action throughout.

3 Ironic detachment

If a book is being narrated by an omniscient narrator, very often a tone of ironic detachment may be used. Perhaps the most celebrated example of this is found in the works of Jane Austen, whose style is one of considerable irony in terms of her approach to the characters and the action. Read carefully to be aware of such an approach: if you fail to notice the ironic voice, your grasp of the novel will be severely limited and you will reach misleading conclusions about the writer's attitude and also even about the sequence of events and the characters' feelings being presented.

Narrative stances like these have a very considerable impact on the nature of the novel. As a result, one of the first things you need to do when reading is work out both the narrative voice and the narrative stance. Until you do this, you will not appreciate the full meaning and resonance of the writing.

NARRATIVE VOICE

Who is telling a story has a considerable effect on what the story is like. If you see a traffic accident, for example, your account of it will be very different from the account by the person driving the car, or the man on the bicycle who was knocked over.

The same is true of a novel. If the story is told by someone who is involved, you need to be aware of that, and to think about how his or her character influences the selection of incidents, the language used, and the general nature and movement of the story. If, on the other hand, the story is told by someone outside the action, the whole presentation will be different.

An omniscient narrator

Here, the story is told by a figure who is not identified – the writer simply writes the story, deciding what to put in and what to leave out, and assuming complete knowledge of all the characters' thoughts and actions. This is the most common technique in the popular novel, where the reader never stops to think who is writing and what attitudes he or she brings to the events and characters.

An identified story-teller

Some novels are actually 'told' by a figure who is identified as the narrator, who tells the story in a clearly-defined situation. Conrad, for example, has most of his stories told by someone of this kind: *Heart of Darkness* begins with a group of characters gathered on the deck of a boat moored on the Thames, one of whom then tells the story. This changes the relationship between writer and reader, by putting in a clearly-identified 'character' between the two.

First-person narrative

This is named after the grammatical term 'first-person', meaning 'I'. It is used when the person tells the story as if events happened to him or her. Its advantages are that it allows a direct involvement in the story; its disadvantages, perhaps, are that the narrative is coloured by this character's knowledge and attitudes to events. Sometimes it can be difficult to sort things out. The narrator in *The Great Gatsby*, for example, is involved with the action and tells the story to reveal his own feelings.

When you are reading, you should always make sure that you know *who* is telling the story, and what effect this has on the novel as a whole in terms of the view we are given of events, the tone of voice that is used, and the attitudes that are presented.

NATURALISM AND REALISM

Two specific terms used in the modern theatre in ways which are not quite what you might expect. 'Naturalism' refers to a play which is concerned with re-creating external, everyday life in great detail – for example, a scene in Terence Rattigan's *Flarepath* which calls for a reproduction Lancaster bomber to be produced on stage.

'Realism' is rather different: it concentrates on issues of life and death which are fundamental to human existence – the purpose of life, the reality of God, or similar large philosophical matters. Make sure that you know the difference between these two and use them correctly if you are writing about a twentieth-century play, or wish to use the terms to describe an aspect of an earlier work.

NEMESIS

The fate that overtakes the tragic hero, or the punishment that he deserves and cannot escape.

◀ Hubris ▶

NEGATION

Negation is the capacity of a language to generate negative forms:

not, never, non–, no, nowhere, neither.

NEW WORDS (NEOLOGISMS)

It is a feature of the English language that it creates new words and phrases continuously. Sometimes the term 'coining' is used to describe the process: neologisms is a word used in linguistics to refer to 'new words'.

New words can be formed by a variety of processes. Words may be '*borrowed*' from other languages (e.g. anorak from Eskimo); they may be constructed from *acronyms* (e.g. nylon comes from New York–London Company, the name of the firm that discovered nylon); they may be *eponyms*, taken from somebody's name (e.g. Wellingtons, Hoover); they may be complete inventions (e.g. yuk).

There are also *morphological* processes whereby new words are made:

blendings: e.g. brunch = breakfast plus lunch; Victorian plus Edwardian = Vicwardian

compounding: e.g. in + put = input; green + peace = greenpeace.

New words are also formed by *derivation* from existing words. The word 'pedestrian' for example is the source for words like 'pedestrianised' and 'pedestrianisation'.

Another process is known as *functional shift*. Here there is no morphological change in the word itself but the grammatical function is shifted. The noun 'video' for example has become a verb in such sentences as, 'Will you video *Brookside* for me tonight?' The nouns 'tape', 'record' and 'photograph' can be used in similar ways. A recent example of functional shift is the word 'access' used as a verb in such sentences as, 'Show me how to access the information'. Usually 'access' is a noun or occasionally, an adjective.

Occasionally new words are formed by shortening an existing noun, to produce a new verb:

hawker – to hawk
stoker – to stoke
editor – to edit

This process is called *back formation*, the shorter verb form refers to the longer noun.

You need historical evidence in order to determine in a particular instance whether the process was one of derivation or back formation.

NOMINAL AND NOMINALISATION

These words occur in a variety of contexts in modern linguistics and can cause some confusion. They should always be understood in the light of what we know about nouns. Sometimes the word 'nominal' is used as a noun and means 'noun'. Sometimes it is used as an adjective e.g. *nominal group*. A nominal group in Hallidayan linguistics is what would be meant by a 'noun phrase' in traditional terminology. Occasionally it is used to describe words which we would normally regard as adjectives but which may be used as nouns: e.g.

- the *idle* need not apply
- the *successful* will be rewarded
- the *rich* are always with us
- the *helpless* will give up altogether
- the *rejected* should not despair
- how are the *mighty* fallen.

Fundamental to the meaning of these terms is the idea of *naming* or *identifying*. This is reflected in familiar uses of the word as in, 'He's only the nominal head' (i.e. in name only); 'She has been nominated' (i.e. named); 'They paid her a nominal sum' (i.e. something that could be called a sum but not reflecting true worth). Norminalisation, is the process of creating nouns (by morphological means), and has the great advantage of making it possible for us to conceive the 'thing' a speaker or writer wishes to talk about. There follow some examples of nouns formed from verbs:

> her *awareness* (to be aware), the *opening* (to open), their *quarrelling* (to quarrel), in the *running* (to run).

The word 'nominalisation' is itself an example of the process it describes.

Indeed '-isation' and '-ification' are common suffixes used in nominalisation: e.g.

> nationalisation, rationalisation, naturalisation, colonisation, conceptualisation, unification, yuppification, modification, edification, notification, signification, magnification.

In a TV documentary (January 1990) the following remark was made in a pub.

> 'All the breweries have gone in for this Vicwardianisation now. Why don't they ask the locals first. We don't want it'.

'Vicwardianisation' is a nominalisation made out of 'Victorian' and 'Edwardian' and refers to the nostalgic conversion of pub interiors. Notice the use of the determiner 'this' preceding 'Vicwardianisation'. It is often used in front of nominalisations to draw special attention and to convey a degree of proximity to it:

– all this guzumping that's going on
– I didn't think we'd have all this aggravation
– this decimalisation will never catch on
– this pedestrianisation's come not before time.

'That' is also used to express a degree of distance:

– all that mugging going on
– I don't agree with that immunisation
– that privatisation will make everything dearer in the end.

Note that the word 'nominative' is not used in English grammar though you will find it used in Latin, for example. It refers to the subject of a verb. The school of philosophy known as 'nominalism' asserts that things exist in name only.

NOTES

Organising your notes

Over the time that you're studying, you will amass a large volume of notes. Keep them clear and well organised.

If you make quick notes in classes, write them up clearly afterwards.

Put the points in the best order, use headings, sub-headings and numbered points.

As your notes increase, keep those for each text in a separate folder, or separate part of a loose-leaf binder.

Make an index of your notes, so that you know where your notes on each topic are. If you have a lot of notes, make a separate card-index, with a summary of topics on each card.

Keeping your notes organised right from the start will save you a lot of time searching for the right piece of paper when it comes to revising. And writing them out clearly and precisely will help you remember the ideas – so it will make revising a lot easier because the ideas will be that much fresher in your mind.

Diagrammatic notes

These are useful for giving an instant overview of a set of ideas.
Use them when:

planning **essays**;
listing topics for **revising**;
making notes on individual concepts.

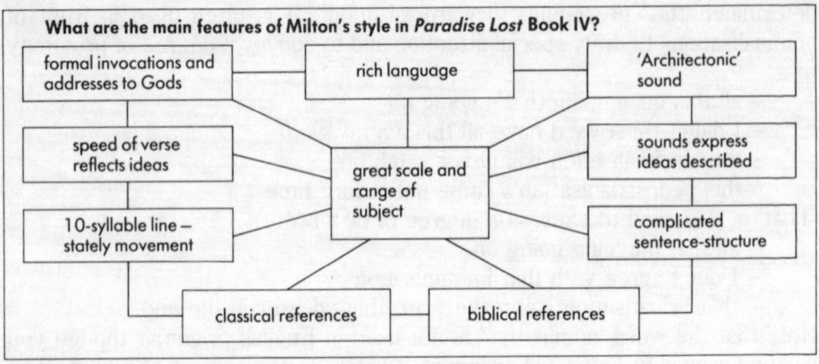

Fig. N.1

They are particularly useful when you don't want to put ideas in any specific order – when all your ideas are of equal importance.

◀ Drama, Revising, Study skills ▶

NOUN

A noun is commonly regarded as the name of a person, place or thing. In other words it identifies what we want to talk about. *Naming* is an important function of language though it is by no means the only function.

'Persons' and 'places' do not present a great problem so far as recognising nouns is concerned. Where the noun is the name of a person, or a country, or a company, or a river it is called a *proper noun* and is usually written with an initial capital letter. The rest of the nouns are called *common nouns* and make up a sizeable proportion of the vocabulary of any language.

'Things' present problems. If we are talking about common, concrete objects – chairs, tables, food, compact discs, make-up, books, a college, a school, dogs, cats – the appropriateness of the term is fairly obvious. *Abstract nouns* (e.g. love, truth, beauty, happiness, justice, freedom, goodness, security, faith, honesty) are not perhaps immediately obvious but can easily be identified as abstract nouns with a little practice.

It is important to remember that the term noun defines a class of words put to work in a particular way. It is the way they are functioning in a grammatical structure that makes them nouns. Consider the following examples:

Seeing is believing.
Sight is a precious faculty.
The *unseen* can be unnerving.
Looking is a more positive act than *seeing*.
Walking is enjoyable exercise.
Let us go for a *walk*.
There is a pleasant *walk* alongside the canal.
The *walkers* came down the High Street three abreast.

All the italicised *words* function as *nouns* yet *they* are all derived from familiar *actions* that might normally be considered **verbs**. A *number of nouns* are derived from *verbs* in this *way*. *They* have not lost their *information content* in the *process*. They still refer to '*seeing*' and '*walking*', but *they* are functioning as *nouns* because a *speaker* or *writer* has made *them* the '*thing*' *he* wants to say *something* about, or wants to identify. (Note that in the last paragraph every noun has been italicised. Note, too, that pronouns have also been italicised because they substitute for nouns. Note also that whilst 'to see' is not so obviously an action as 'to walk', it still requires somebody or something to *do* it, and is therefore a verb).

Nouns are often surrounded by other words that modify, amplify, qualify them. They then become *noun phrases*. The definite article and the indefinite article ('the' and 'a') frequently occur in company with nouns:

> The house.
> A book.

Nouns are frequently combined with adjectives:

> The redbrick house.
> A paperback book.

Often two or more adjectives are used:

> The large, detached, redbrick house.
> A fat, illustrated, paperback book.

Noun phrases can be expanded by connection with other nouns:

> *The large, detached, redbrick house* at *the end of the lane.*
> *A fat, illustrated, paperback book* on *the coffee table.*

For the purposes of analysis it is much more useful to be able to identify a noun phrase however long it is than simply to identify individual nouns. A noun phrase is an important unit of meaning as well as a major grammatical unit.

When a noun phrase (sometimes signified as NP) is functioning as the subject of a sentence it can be replaced by a pronoun (e.g. 'it', 'he', 'she', 'they'), a helpful way of identifying the grammatical subject which will always be a noun, a noun phrase or a pronoun.

NOVEL

The word used to describe any extended work of fiction longer than a short story. In most exam papers, one or more novels will be set for detailed study, as an opportunity for students to see how writers make use of *prose* to show the development of themes and relationships within a *plot* or sequence of events or feelings told by a *narrator*.

THEMES

Novels discuss themes and ideas just as poems or plays do. They may not always be present in quite such an explicit way, but very often they will be of major philosophical or human significance. Read the text closely to try to work out what issues, if any, the novelist is attempting to address. Discuss your ideas with fellow-students, or with your teacher; when you are familiar with the novel, you might like to supplement your ideas by reading a critical study of the novel, being careful *not* to accept all the views it gives without reservation.

As you go through the book, make notes on the changing ways in which the theme or idea is treated, so that you can then assemble your notes on the topic in preparation for the exam.

Attitudes

Look, too, at the attitudes to particular topics presented in the novel. Be aware, of course, that the attitudes of the narrator may not be those of the writer, or that the novelist's ideas may emerge only when you compare the views of *several* of the characters. You may well have a question on this topic, so it's worth thinking carefully about it while you are reading the novel in detail and taking notes on any passages which seem to suggest a particular attitude.

HUMAN NATURE AND RELATIONSHIPS

Many novels are concerned not so much with individual people from a particular historical period but with aspects of people which are common at all times. Jane Austen, for example, is concerned with human characteristics such as pride and humility; Dickens is often concerned with the nature of love, greed or evil among humankind.

Other novelists are more concerned with the interaction between people. D. H. Lawrence explores the range and extent of relationships between men and women in his novels, as well as that between humankind and the natural world – a topic which he shares with Thomas Hardy, although the two approach it in very different ways.

Once again, you need to think carefully not only to see the importance of such topics, but also to work out what you think the writer's attitude towards them might be.

CONTEMPORARY REFERENCES

Many novelists are concerned to make points about topics and events which they see as being of major significance to the time about which they are writing. George Orwell's *Animal Farm* is an extended allegory in which every event of the story is a precise parallel to an event in the Russian revolution, and is used to make a critical comment about Communism. Elizabeth Gaskell's *North and South* is a sustained criticism of attitudes and material conditions in industrial towns in the 1830s and 40s.

These topics are often of major importance, so that you need to understand the contemporary references the novel makes. Usually this can be done by reading notes in your edition, or perhaps by consulting a historical dictionary or history text book. Be careful, though, that you don't get so interested in the period that the novel becomes less important than the history. You need to know only enough about the times being written about to allow you to understand the novel and its themes fully: you will not be asked questions which will demand a detailed historical knowledge, and the text itself must always be your main concern.

USE OF THE SETTING

In many novels the physical circumstances in which the action takes place will be almost as important as one of the characters. Hardy, for example, uses the bleak setting of Egdon Heath in *The Return of the Native* to create an atmosphere of desolation; E.M.Forster makes India itself a major force in *A Passage to India*. Other novelists will use a setting for symbolic purposes; in *Bleak House*, for example, Dickens uses the foggy streets of London as a symbol of the obscurity and lack of direction of the lawsuit which is a major aspect of the plot.

Always think carefully about the setting of a novel and make sure that you are aware of what it contributes to the work as a whole on both a literal and a symbolic level.

OBJECTIVITY

An impersonal and detached style of writing in which the author treats a subject as far as possible without personal bias. It is doubtful whether any book is truly objective; some appear to be more so than others.

OBJECTS (DIRECT AND INDIRECT)

The *direct object* is the name given to that part of a **clause** or **sentence** which 'receives' the action of the main verb. It is usually a noun or a noun phrase and normally follows the verb. The pattern constructed is usually described as Subject-Verb-Object or SVO.

The direct objects are the words in italic, below:

The dog ate *the bone*.
The boy kicked *the ball*.
The girl rode *a bicycle*.

Notice that the direct object can usually be transformed into the subject of a matching clause in the passive voice:

The bone was eaten by the dog.
The ball was kicked by the boy.
The bicycle was ridden by the girl.

Indirect objects are connected to the subject in an indirect way. The following examples illustrate indirect objects:

They gave *Sarah* a present.
She bought *her mother* a hair dryer.
He made *them* a slap up dinner.
They gave *him* a kiss.

In each case the direct object of the verb has been displaced by an indirect object.

There are a number of English verbs that take indirect objects. They usually need the preposition 'to' inserting before the indirect object, or else the preposition is implied; e.g.

bring, hand, owe, write, throw, give, tell, show.

Others require the preposition 'for', or else it is implied, e.g.

buy, save, find, reserve, get, cook.

OCTAMETER

◀ Metre ▶

OCTAVE/OCTET

The first eight lines of a sonnet.

ODE

A long poem, lyric in style and serious in subject, following a clear structure. It is written in a series of stanzas each of which has three parts, strophe, antistrophe and epode, each having lines of different length. The regular ode of this sort is best exemplified by Gray's *Progress of Poesy*. Later writers have used a much freer structure but retained the idea of combining lyricism and seriousness in, for example, Wordsworth's *Ode: Intimations of Immortality* and the odes of Keats.
◀ Lyric ▶

OMNISCIENT NARRATOR

◀ Narrative voice ▶

ONOMATOPOEIA

The use of words which recreate the sound of the noise they name:

crash, clunk, thud, splash and so on.

OPEN-BOOK EXAMINATIONS

Some boards give you the chance to take the texts into the exam room with you. In some ways this may seem to make the exam easier, but in practice it makes little difference. In general, you will be asked to write in detail about one passage of the text – a chapter from a novel, or a scene from a play, say. You will probably be asked to say how the passage is typical of a particular aspect of the writer's style, or how it contributes to a particular theme or concept.

The point to remember here is that while you need to refer closely to this passage and to other parts of the book to show how the two are related, you should *not* spend a great deal of time looking through the text to find examples. It is very easy to lose a great deal of time in this way – so make sure that you *know* the text thoroughly and can find examples you need without spending a lot of time looking for them in your text.

Remember, too, that the text will have to be 'clean' – without any notes or comments which you have added during the year. If you have a heavily-annotated edition, you may well be refused permission to take the exam – so do make absolutely sure of your Examining Board's policy by checking the syllabus well in advance and, if necessary, buying another, plain copy of the text to use in the exam.

ORACY

Oracy is a term used to cover speaking (see **speech**) and listening. The word *orality* is sometimes used but usually with the special sense of *oral tradition*.

Institutional education tends to devalue oracy in favour of literacy yet language has its origins in speech and there is considerable evidence that pupils can learn as much through talk (not just listening) as they can from reading and writing.

The National Oracy Project in schools throughout England exists to promote better understanding of the nature and functions of oracy both in learning and in life.

Investigating the ways in which people talk to each other in given contexts is one of the most popular areas for language study projects.

ORAL WORK

This is something which is best prepared for by working closely with your teacher. Remember that you'll be assessed on:

1 *Clarity of speech* – including volume and audibility, and quality of diction (sounding ts and ds, for example).

2 *Quality of speech* – matching your intonation (the pitch of your speech) to what you are saying, and avoiding speaking always at one level, which is dull and fails to convey the nature of what you're saying.

3 *Understanding* – the degree to which your expression shows that you understand what you're reading, in the sense of pausing in the right places, emphasising important words, and pronouncing unusual words correctly.

Apart from getting advice, the best way to prepare for this is to *practise*. If you can, do it before an audience, to get used to speaking in front of others. At first, or if you find talking in public difficult, do it in private – try a dramatised reading of Anthony Burgess in the bathroom!

OXYMORON

A rhetorical figure in which two opposite meanings are combined for special effect, as in 'burning ice' or 'holy sinner'. The main value of such a figure is to present a startlingly new concept or way of seeing.

P

PARADOX

An apparently self-contradictory statement that on closer examination is shown to have some basis of truth. As well as illustrating a truth, a paradox concentrates the reader's attention on what is being said, through the initial shock of an apparently nonsensical statement.

PARAPHRASE

To paraphrase a text is to say the same thing in other words. Converting passive sentences into their active form (or vice versa) is the simplest form of paraphrase:

> The man was hit by the car. (The car hit the man).
> The woman gave him a quid. (He received a quid from the woman).

Paraphrasing on a more extended scale raises the question of how can the alternative be the same in meaning when nuances have been removed? One measure of the difference between prose and poetry is that prose can be paraphrased reasonably well whereas it is impossible to paraphrase poetry without destroying its effect as poetry.

Paraphrasing is most useful for making a difficult, specialist text, more accessible to a general reader.

PARA-RHYME

Also known as half-rhyme or consonantal rhyme, this occurs when two words have the same consonants but not the same vowel sound: bone and bane, fall and fail, drown and drain, for example.

Its most extensive use occurs in the poetry of Wilfred Owen, where the sense of incompleteness it gives perfectly matches the desolation of his subject matter – the waste and senseless suffering of the trenches in the First World War, as in these lines:

> I am the enemy you killed, my friend.
> I knew you in this dark; for so you frowned
> Yesterday through me as you jabbed and killed.
> I parried; but my hands were loath and cold.
> Let us sleep now . . .

PARATAXIS

Paratactic construction, though linear, are in effect listings. Nouns may be linked without conjunctions in the following way:

> He packed a torch, a map, a compass, a groundsheet and a gun.
> He ordered soup, fish and chips, bread, Eccles cakes and tea.

Clauses can also be linked in this way:

> She opened the door, stepped inside, looked around, and gave a whoop of delight.
> He removed the fuse box cover, scanned the fuses, stopped at one with scorch marks, and removed it for closer inspection.

Note how a connecting word, 'and' is usually used at the last item.

PARODY

◀ Burlesque ▶

PARSING

Parsing is a descriptive analysis of sentences in which constituent parts are named according to their functions and their structural relationships. A simple example follows:

The dog bit the man.

This consists of a *definite article* introducing a *common noun* which serves as the *subject* of the sentence, followed by a *transitive verb* in the *past tense* which *acts directly* on the *object* of the sentence, another *common noun* preceded by the *definite article*.

Occasionally, parsing is a helpful way of explaining a grammatical point to someone learning a new language. Some years ago it used to be a regular activity in schools as part of the English curriculum, but this kind of grammar teaching has largely been discontinued in English schools. If language were not systematic and rule governed, parsing would be impossible. The knowledge that can be demonstrated by parsing is valid and worthwhile, and the activity of parsing should be carried out accurately. There are however two things to be borne in mind:

1 *You need to know why you are doing it.*
2 *You should beware decontextualised sentences*. They may look as if they stand alone grammatically but in everyday acts of interpersonal communication, and in written texts, sentences are generated in company with other sentences which will influence the way in which we comprehend their meaning. Often sentences are much more difficult to parse than the example given above, especially in spoken English.

Noam Chomsky compared the following sentences in order to demonstrate the limitations of parsing.

a) John is eager to please.
b) John is easy to please.

On the surface they look identical but at the level of deep structure they are quite different. (a) is an active construction while (b) is a passive construction.

PAST PAPERS

One of the best sources of help when you're revising is the actual exam paper.

However detailed the syllabus, it's only past question papers which tell you exactly what the questions look like and the kind of topics that come up. Look at:

The layout of the paper. If there are alternative sections, make sure you know which you are preparing for. In the exam it's easy to get a little flustered and to mis-read the instructions, so keep the chance of a mistake to a minimum by knowing what you're expected to do in advance.

The number of questions and the time allowed. This will help you to revise by allowing you to write answers in the time you'll have in the exam – generally it works out at between 30 and 45 minutes for each question, but there are exceptions.

The nature of the questions. Find out whether you're more likely to be given an excerpt from a text as the basis of a question, or a quotation for discussion. Don't waste time trying to 'spot' questions and predict what's going to come up and base your revision on that: there's little chance that you'll be right. Instead, get a general idea of the topics and the wording used.

PASTICHE

◀ Burlesque ▶

PASTORAL

Derived from the Latin *Pastor*, shepherd, this is a strand of writing that presents life in the country as the ideal form of existence. It is often concerned with shepherds and shepherdesses living a perfect life of love, song and delight in a natural world which is perfect and idyllic. Shakespearean pastoral – for example, *As You Like It* or *The Winter's Tale*, takes the elements of classical pastoral – *Daphnis and Chloe* by Longus, for example – and adds to it a sense of order attained by achieving the proper relationship between man, woman and the natural world.

A related strand of English literature sees the natural landscape as a symbol and representative of the celestial, an idea strong in such writers as Thomas Traherne and Henry Vaughan. Other related terms are Georgic (from the Greek word for plough) and Piscatorial (about fishing or fishermen).

PARTICIPLES

Because verbs have a great deal to do in English they consist of many parts (or forms). The word participle denotes two forms of the verb:

1 *the present participle* ending in -ing (saying, loving, eating, walking)
2 *the past participle* ending in -ed if the verbs are regular verbs, and in a variety of other ways, if the verbs are irregular.
Regular: loved, walked, lacked, jumped, baked, painted, played.
Irregular: are, found, bought, wrote, read, said, sang.

Notice that many participles function as **adjectives** (a singing teacher, a lost cause, a walking stick, a proven case).

PARTS OF SPEECH

This is the traditional term for naming different types of words used in a language. The notion of 'parts' is useful insofar as it suggests a systematic whole to which individual parts contribute. The names of the principal parts in English are: nouns, verbs, pronouns, adverbs, conjunctions, adjectives, prepositions, articles. A problem arises however if these names are applied to individual words out of the context of the sentence in which they are being used. For example the word 'fire' could be used as a noun (He built a *fire*), a verb (*Fire* him if his work is unsatisfactory), or as an adjective (She checked the *fire* equipment).

Statistically a word like 'chair' is most likely to be used as a noun but it can also be used as a verb (I will chair the meeting) and it can be used adjectivally to describe something e.g. a chair leg, a chair lift, a chair manufacturer.

It is best to think of the traditionally called 'parts of speech' as names for *classes of words*. The criterion for deciding which class a word belongs to is one of use i.e. how is the word being used by a speaker or writer at a given time.

We use language essentially to make meanings, and a vital resource in that meaning-making process, is the words themselves. You will also find it helpful, however, to think of a language as a network of empty or wordless structures that enables us to put words in meaningful patterns and combinations. As well as a *vocabulary of English words* we also have in our minds *a repertoire of grammatical structures* in which to put words. This is well illustrated by the experience of being lost for words. Here are some examples:

a) We need to . . . to . . . (ah yes!) to galvanise the whole school, to get everybody really whizzing along, if we want to . . . to . . . to change our image.

Notice here that the overarching grammatical framework for this sentence is marked by 'We need to . . . if we want . . . '. This structure is so reliable that we can invert it without altering the meaning, 'If we want . . . we need to . . . '. There is no doubt about the class of word needed in each case, the hesitations indicate that the speaker is searching for an appropriate word in each case.

b) All you have to do is fasten the thingamajig to the whatyoumacallit and you will have your own er . . . er . . . whatever.

This is a highly unsatisfactory sentence so far as explicit definition is concerned and is not likely to help someone wishing to make a 'whatever'. The empty word classes here are the nouns for 'thingamajig', 'whatyoumacallit' and 'whatever'. The grammatical structure (i.e. the interrelation of word classes) is perfectly adequate but virtually empty.

c) She is a very er, pigheaded . . . er, stubborn . . . er, determined young woman.

In this example the grammatical structure is a straightforward statement 'She is . . . '. It is just the sort of thing that might be in the mind of someone writing a reference, trying hard not to introduce a note of personal criticism by using an adjective that carries disapproval. Eventually 'determined' has been decided upon as an appropriate description for a reference.

PASSIVE VOICE

The passive voice denotes that the subject of a finite verb is the receiver of the action:

He was buffeted by the winds.
She is loved by everybody.
I am overwhelmed by them.

The passive voice is contrasted with the active voice whereby it is denoted that the subject performs the action of the verb:

> The winds buffeted him.
> Everybody loved her.
> They overwhelmed me.

PATHOS

Literary writing which evokes strong and genuine emotions, often of pity and sorrow.

PENTAMETER

◀ Metre ▶

PERSONIFICATION

A particular kind of **metaphor** in which an object, often a part of the natural world, is addressed as a person. For example:

> With how sad steps, O Moon thou climb'st the skies!
> How silently, and with how wan a face!

PHATIC COMMUNION

Phatic Communion is a notion derived from the work of an anthropologist, Bronislaw Malinowski (1884–1942).

In an urban, technological society there is a tendency to concentrate on those aspects of language that transact information and get things done. Language however serves other functions than message communication and direct action, and one of these functions is *phatic communion*. This occurs when people use language to pass the time of day without any specific purpose in mind beyond establishing human contact. Greetings, remarks about the weather, questions like 'How are you?', comments on the news that don't invite extended discussion, are all examples of the sort of phatic communion that goes on at bus stops, in waiting rooms and on any occasion when people have to pass the time of day without having chosen to be together. Total silence seems unbearable to most people; some sort of communication is necessary to acknowledge one another's existence.

PHILOLOGY

Philology is the study of the history of languages. Modern *historical linguistics* and *comparative linguistics* derive a good deal from philology which is an ancient study. Before the invention of recorded sound philology inevitably took most of its data from documentary evidence though corroborations have been sought in fieldwork which is one of the reasons why it is important for linguists to know more than one language.

The tape recorder has revolutionised field research by making it possible to record language and dialects for posterity. Our knowledge of the Indo-European language connection, and of the ancestry of English within that connection, has been gained by the piecing together of a variety of philological and etymological evidence.

PHONETICS

The speech sounds humans all over the world are able to produce are many and varied. Some languages include sounds that are notably distinctive (e.g. the 'click' sounds of the Kalahari bushmen). Many use sets of sounds that are common throughout the world. The study, or the science, of these speech sounds is known as *phonetics* and people who specialise in this area of linguistics are known as *phoneticians*.

Students in English schools, when they study French and German, soon become aware of phonetic differences:

The French vowel in a word like 'plume' (pen), produced by shaping the mouth to produce the vowel in a word like 'loop' but saying instead the vowel sound in a word like 'leap';

The resonant French nasal sound in words like 'chanson' (song) or Anglais (English) which might be written phonetically as 'shongsong' and 'Onglay';

The German umlaut over vowels, as in 'öfnen' (open) indicating a sound like the English 'ur' as in 'hurt' but only like it, not identical;

The German 'z' which sounds like the 'ts' at the end of the English word 'cats' and causes difficulty for English speakers when it occurs at the beginning of a word e.g. 'zeit' (time) pronounced 'tsite'.

Not only individual speech sounds but combinations and patterns of speech sounds can be unfamiliar and difficult for a second language learner.

As an area of study, phonetics consists of three branches:

1 *Articulatory phonetics* – a science which studies how speech sounds are produced and seeks to measure and describe them accurately. It draws upon knowledge of anatomy and physiology (e.g. breathing and the diaphragm, the vocal folds, lips, teeth, tongue, palate, nasal cavities, throat).

2 *Acoustic phonetics* – a science which studies the physical properties of speech sounds. Very much akin to physical science, it uses sophisticated instrumentation for recording, measuring and analysing data.
3 *Auditory phonetics* – a science which studies how we hear speech sounds. It is concerned with physiological factors like the ossicles in the inner ear, and with neurological factors in the brain itself.

Each of these branches is concerned with a stage in what may be called the soundstream of speech which begins with a column of air pushed up by the diaphragm muscle which is then squeezed and shaped via the articulatory organs, emitted as voice into the atmosphere, (where its acoustic properties may be observed), and which ends in auditory perception in the mind of a listener via the outer, middle and inner ear.

In phonetics the characteristics of speech sounds may be studied without any reference to their meaning in a given language. The main concern is an accurate understanding of their physical properties. The knowledge gained is of considerable value to speech therapists, voice and singing teachers, and teachers of modern languages. Phoneticians have also served as expert witnesses in cases where tape recordings, voice prints and accents have featured as forensic evidence.

◀ Etymology ▶

International Phonetic Alphabet

Because phoneticians are concerned with the scientific description of speech sounds, no matter what language those sounds express, they have recourse to the International Phonetic Alphabet (IPA) which is an agreed system of notation for recording speech. Thus it is possible for an international gathering to understand any data presented by a phonetician from anywhere in the world. When speech is written down using IPA it is called a *phonetic transcription* and will contain not only symbols for the individual sounds (or *phones*) but also *diacritical* marks to indicate the specific details of voice production that account for differences in accent, intonation, articulation, timbre, and which indicate vocal impediments, or unusual features.

Terminology

Phonetics also employs a set of basic terms with which to locate the origin of a speech sound, to describe the manner in which it is produced, and to define accurately one sound as distinct from any other.

Speech depends upon breath. One linguist, Charlton Laird, has even defined language as 'educated breath'. Consequently most speech sounds are described as *pulmonic* in character because they use air from the lungs. Since they depend upon air breathed out they are also called *egressive*. The clicks of the Kalahari bushmen mentioned earlier, depend upon air sucked into the mouth and are therefore *non pulmonic* speech sounds.

Once the air is on its way up the *trachea*, pushed by the *diaphragm*, it

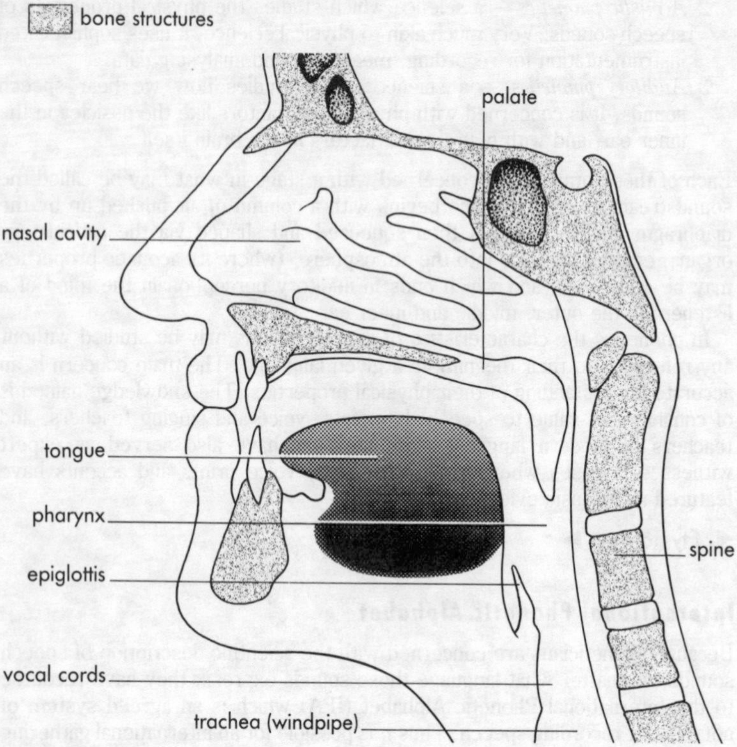

Fig. P.1

passes over folds of tissue in the *larynx* (sometimes called *vocal cords* or *vocal folds*) which may or may not vibrate according to the intention of the speaker. If the vocal cords are apart, offering no resistance to the airstream, the sounds produced are referred to as *voiceless*. Sounds in English such as 'p', 't', 'k' and 's' are all voiceless. If however the vocal cords are close together the airstream is forced to push its way through, causing them to vibrate. The sounds produced by vibration are called *voiced* sounds. In English 'b', 'd', 'g' and 'z' are voiced sounds. Note how they may be paired with the unvoiced sounds:

Unvoiced	**Voiced**
*p*it	*b*it
*t*ip	*d*ip
*k*ot (i.e.cot)	*g*ot
*s*ip	*z*ip

Say them to yourself and note how close they are i.e. how little physical change is necessary to say each pair. But note also how unvoiced sounds emit more air. Put your hand about an inch away from your mouth as you say each pair. Notice how much more forcefully the expelled air hits your hand on unvoiced sounds.

Vowels and consonants

A further distinction usually made at this point is the distinction between *vowels* and *consonants*. When a new born baby utters its first cry it utters what might be considered the prime vowel, confirming that the lungs work, that the nervous system is in order and that the vocal cords are intact. The sound is open, unimpeded and distinctly audible. Voice, like life, depends upon breath. The counterpart to the first cry is possibly the last scream in the face of sudden death, often written in comic books as aaaaagh! It's the same vowel though uttered in quite different circumstances. All the *vowels* are uttered in a relatively unrestricted way through the mouth or the nose.

Consonants, on the other hand, are sounds caused by restricting the free flow of air resulting in friction as the air continues to push its way through.

The term *nasal* is useful because it describes the fact that some consonants (e.g. 'm' and 'n') sound the way they do because air escapes through the nose. When air passes through the mouth it produces what are called *oral* sounds.

Physicality of language

Phonetics reminds us constantly of the sheer physicality of human language by emphasising the dependence of speech upon *breath* and upon articulatory *organs*. If you had any cause to doubt the significance of this consider:

a) how difficult it is to speak when you are short of breath;
b) what difference a bad cold in the head makes to your pronunciation of consonants e.g. 'a bad code id de head';
c) how self consciously you speak when you have burned or bitten your tongue;
d) how odd it feels to speak with half your face anaesthetised after a visit to the dentist, and how easy it is to bite your tongue or the inside of your cheek;
e) how missing teeth can affect speech sounds;
f) how emotions can affect voice production;
g) how easy it is (and embarrassing) to spit unintentionally while speaking;
h) how much effort is required to learn the pronunciation of a second language, especially one with very unfamiliar sounds.

Other terms which identify and define later stages in the production of speech sounds are:

a) *Place of articulation* (see diagram)
The significant point of narrowing in the vocal tract e.g. the hard palate (*alveolars*), the tongue and soft palate (*velars*), the lips (*labials*), the teeth (*interdentals*), the hard palate (*palatals*);

b) *Manner of articulation* (see diagram)
The way in which narrowing or constriction of the airstream takes place e.g. stopping the air completely when it reaches the mouth (*stops*); stopping the air, then releasing it slowly (*affricates*); partial obstruction and friction (*fricatives*); partial obstruction but no friction (*liquids*); no obstruction but rapid gliding of tongue (*glides*); producing a hissing sound (*sibilants*); vibrating the uvula (*uvular*); closure or friction at the glottis (*glottals*).

The term **dipthong** is also used in phonetics to describe a sequence of two sounds. Usually the two sounds are a vowel plus a glide.

Aspirated sounds

Aspirated sounds occur when some words are pronounced because of the position of a sound in relation to other sounds. The word 'pot', for example, begins with an aspirated sound. You can feel the puff of air on your hand when you say it. If however you say the word 'spot' you will not feel the strong puff of air.

Because of its new position in the word the 'p' in 'spot' is said to be *unaspirated*.

Variations

Finally, phonetics is also concerned with what are usually referred to as *prosodic features* of speech sounds. These are variations which can occur in the following ways:

Duration of a sound	(i.e. long or short);
Vocal pitch	(i.e. high = fast vibration of vocal cords low = slow vibration of vocal cords);
stress	(i.e. a change in pitch, volume or length of sound);
amplitude	(i.e. loudness or softness of voice).

Amplitude is a term also used in physics and acoustics. Pitch is sometimes referred to as *frequency range* in physics and acoustics.

Even after the briefest consideration of all the phonetic variables that come into operation when a person speaks, it is not surprising that each speaker has a distinctly personal voice which we can soon learn to recognise even over the telephone. In addition to all the factors of voice production, phonetic and prosodic, there are also wide anatomical variations in the articulatory organs themselves. All manner of shapes and sizes, are present in any sample of human beings, (male and female, young and old), which explains why voice prints are as reliable for identification purposes, as finger prints. It also illustrates why phonetics must proceed scientifically if it is to construct a body of knowledge that is verifiable and useful.

PHONETIC SPELLING

This is a device in which the letters of the alphabet are used not to spell a word in its conventional orthography (spelling) but to give an idea of how it sounds. It is helpful if you are communicating with people who do not know the International Phonetic Alphabet but it is at best only an approximation and often requires a degree of originality. Here are some comic but pretty accurate examples. If you can understand them then the usefulness of phonetic spelling is vindicated:

wivgorragerrusimbux (We have got to get our hymn books).
purremineer (Put them in here).

Both occurred in a Warrington primary school. You could no doubt produce examples of your own. Their effectiveness however will be limited and they depend upon readers supplying a great deal of information themselves. Warringtonians would recognise them easily but would people from other parts of the British Isles?

PHONOLOGY

PHONEMES

All languages draw upon the repertoire of human speech sounds to form their own distinctive sound systems in which a selection of sounds is combined in ways that give a language its individual character. The study of all the possible human speech sounds, and how they are made, is called **phonetics**. *Phonology* is the study of the sound system of any one particular language: English, Norwegian, Hindi, Mandarin Chinese, Arabic, Italian or whichever. Naturally, phonology will draw upon phonetics and the International Phonetic Alphabet but it is concerned with not just the physical properties of the sounds themselves but with the rules of use that enable the sounds in a phonological system (i.e. a language) to have meaning.

If you can imagine coming to the English language for the first time ever, the immediate problem would be to make sense of the continuum of sound that you would hear. In writing, words are normally separated by empty spaces, but in speech there are no automatic pauses between words. Indeed, the pauses usually occur for rhetorical effect, or to gain breathing space, rather than to separate the words. What sort of segments or units make up the sound system of a language then? The alphabetic letters of the spelling system do not help nor is there any consistency in the **syllables** of English. Consider the variations illustrated in the following examples in which alphabetic spelling has been represented phonetically:

bough	=	bow
although	=	altho
trough	=	troff
ought	=	ort
through	=	threw
Oughtrington	=	Ootrington

Despite the recurrence of identical letters, 'ough', there are six distinctly different sounds in the above examples.

A generally accepted approach in modern linguistics is to analyse the sound system into the minimal sound units that are used to convey different meanings. These minimal sound units of meaning consist of vowels, consonants and dipthongs drawn from the world's repertoire of speech sounds and represented in the International Phonetic Alphabet. The individual units are called *phonemes* and the English system is generally considered to use the forty four phonemes set out below in IPA symbols each with an example alongside:

The sounds of English

The sounds of English are shown in Fig. I.1 on page 88.
When using IPA symbols, listen very carefully to the sounds you are transcribing. **Beware** English spelling. Note that phonemic transcriptions are written between slanted brackets. Note also that the sign : after an IPA symbol indicates a long vowel.

Note for example that a word like 'tear' can be pronounced in different ways:

tear /eə / as a noun to rhyme with 'rare'
tear /ɪ/ as a noun to rhyme with 'fear' or 'tier'.

Note also how vowels like /a/ /c/ / / and /3/ are r controlled, that is to say they seem to be followed by an inevitable r sound.
The same is true of the following dipthongs:
/ɪə//eə//ʊə/
Phonemes are used by linguists to identify recurring, meaningful sounds in the continuum of spoken English. When a sound change causes a change of meaning the change is said to be *phonemic*. In the following examples the second and third sounds remain constant but the first sound (or phoneme) has been changed, in each case, causing a change of meaning:

e.g. /nɪt/
/sɪt/
/bɪt/
/pɪt/
/hɪt/
/lɪt/
/wɪt/
/fɪt/

If the final sound is changed the meanings are changed once again:

e.g. /nɪn/
/sɪn/
/bɪn/
/pɪn/
/hɪn/
/lɪn/
/wɪn/
/fɪn/

You will have noticed however that 'nɪn', 'hɪn' and 'lɪn' are not normally considered to be English words, which illustrates another characteristic of the phonology of a language, namely that phonemes occur in familiar patterns and combinations. The three examples here are not, on their own, recognisable, meaningful combinations but they may occur in a meaningful way in longer words:

e.g. hinder, nincompoop, lintel.

If the vowel phoneme is changed, yet another change of meaning occurs:

e.g. /sæn/
/bæn/
/pæn/
/hæn/
/næn/ **not** /na:n/ as in Nan bread (Indian baking)
/læn/
/wæn/ **not** /w ɒ n/ meaning 'sickly' or 'pallid'
/fæn/

Again, there are some words that do not have recognisable meanings in English: 'san', 'han', 'lan' and 'wan'. The word 'nan' can of course mean 'grandmother' or 'childminder' and is therefore acceptable, but whilst there is an English word spelled 'wan', it is pronounced in a way that rhymes with 'one' rather than with the other example given. This demonstrates, once again, how the sound system (the phonemes) of English do not correspond with the alphabetic or written symbols. It is a simple arithmetical fact that 44 phonemes won't go into 26 letters. When you are attempting to transcribe spoken English into phonemic symbols it takes a little practice to blot out of your mind the familiar English spelling and transcribe what you hear, not what you see. Careful, critical listening is an essential skill in the study of language and often it is necessary to compare what you think you hear with what other students hear in order to arrive at the most accurate transcription. There is always room for disagreement because listening can be a very subjective response, but there is no doubt that phoneme theory is of considerable help to students beginning linguistics and it continues to be useful to linguists in a variety of ways. Phonemes may be defined as minimal units of meaning in a speech sound system.

PICARESQUE

In Spanish the *picaro* was a rogue or villain. The term 'picaresque' traditionally refers to a novel with a central figure or picaro who is a low-born rogue or knave, and goes on a journey which involves him in a sequence of adventures, frequently unconnected, and which are comic or satirical. Thomas Nashe's *The Unfortunate Traveller* is a true picaresque; Fielding's *Joseph Andrews* and *Tom Jones* develop the form into much more sophisticated fiction.

PIDGIN

A pidgin is a language devised by traders who speak different native languages. It is used for the purposes of trade and will develop into a **creole** only if its use becomes socially extended.

PLANS

◀ Essays, Study skills ▶

PLAY

Remember to use this word when you are writing about a play. If you frequently refer, as many students do, to 'the book', then you will suggest to the examiner that you have no understanding of how the play works *on the stage*. This may or may not be true – but don't give the impression of ignorance by a mistake which can so easily be avoided.

PLOT AND SUB-PLOT

The 'plot' is the main line of action of a play, novel or short story. This doesn't mean that it is everything which happens – plot and story are not necessarily the same. It is the main force which drives the play along; for example the spiritual and physical struggle of Joan of Arc in Shaw's *Saint Joan*. The 'sub-plot' is a secondary level of motivation – in *Saint Joan*, for example, the struggle between the English and French. It could also be a series of events which happen to some minor characters, which reflect the actions of the major figures – the relationship when Maria and Sir Toby Belch in *Twelfth Night*, for example, which reflects that between Orsino and Viola/Cesario.

The terms are used in the same way about novels. Beware of becoming too interested in the simple sequence of events, though – just telling the story isn't something you'll be asked to do in the exam.

◀ Prose ▶

POETRY

The skills of **critical reading** are the basic equipment of literary study; knowing how to read and understand a passage is the essence of the whole process. (See 'The Reading Process' below).

Looking at *poetry* in this way is particularly important. Poetry often uses language in a much more imaginative, inventive or unorthodox way than prose does. This means not only that the possibilities of the readers getting it wrong are greater – but also that there are more *clues* to what's going on: for example, why one word is used rather than another, why the order of words is reversed, or why a particular rhythm is there.

Many people worry about answering questions on poems they don't know. If you haven't *seen* the poem before, they say, how can you prepare for it? In one sense, of course, you can't – there's certainly no way of telling which poem is going to appear on the paper. But in other ways, you can prepare for the exam by developing certain *techniques* of reading.

You can learn how to:

a) read a poem in detail;
b) discover who is 'speaking', and what the situation is;
c) work out its 'meaning';
d) identify particular ways in which language is used – metaphor, simile, imagery;
e) recognise how the sound of the words add to the effect;
f) recognise the role of rhythm in creating effect;
g) see how the structure of a poem adds to the overall impact;
h) think about your own response to the poem;

– and, as important as all of these

i) write clearly, concisely and quickly to express all these points.

This section gives you help and guidance on these techniques so that you can read and respond to a poem, and write an appreciation of the sort you'll need to produce in coursework or in the exam. But remember that this is a process which takes time to develop: you need to get lots of practice in reading, discussing and thinking about poems, so make a point of testing and developing what you learn here by using your skills as often as you can.

FEATURES OF POEMS (TECHNIQUES AND DEVICES)

There are several features that you need to look for when you're reading a poem. Some will be more important than others according to the nature of the poem. The features given here obviously won't all appear in every poem – and they certainly aren't given in order of importance. In most poems, several of these features will work together to produce the effect, but, for ease of discussion, they need to be teased out so that you'll be able to recognise them when you see – and hear – them.

Meaning

Even though you may think that poetry works in a very imprecise way, and can be interpreted in different ways by different readers, for the great majority of poems one can still say that there is a clear meaning. Sorting out this meaning is a major priority when tackling appreciation exercises. Some poets will use words for their sounds, or rhythms, or for the general associations they create; but, in most poems, each word will have a *specific meaning* which you need to identify. This *doesn't* mean that you have to write a prose translation of the poem; but it *does* mean that you need to have a very clear idea of the meanings of the words used in the poem before you can begin to write sensibly and clearly about it.

Words can have difficult meanings, for several reasons. A poet may deliberately use an unfamiliar word to make the reader think hard. A word which is familiar now could have had a quite different meaning in the time when the poet was writing. 'Punk' is an interesting example: to the Elizabethans it meant 'prostitute'; in America earlier this century it was a term of abuse, rather like 'heel'; today it refers to a particular type of social attitude amongst young people! A poem may contain a word which you haven't encountered before. A poet may use a word which has a very specific meaning in order to convey a particular area of experience – the tools of a particular trade, for example, or a word in the dialect of a particular region.

Knowing how to deal with such words does not depend on a standard routine, but it is certainly not always easy. Here are some suggestions:

Do all you can to develop your own vocabulary. Read as widely as you can, and use a dictionary – not a pocket or compact one, but the full *Oxford English Dictionary*. This will give you a whole range of different meanings for a word, and show you how they have changed down the years.

Try to tease out a meaning by its *context*. You may not be able to get it completely right, but you can probably have a good stab at it. Think, for example, about the last word in the first line of this passage:

> Turning and turning in the widening gyre
> The falcon cannot hear the falconer

There is no reason why you should know the word 'gyre', which Yeats uses to mean a whirling circular motion; but you could perhaps work out that it means motion of some sort and, if you've ever seen a falconer control a falcon, might know that the bird often flies in a circle around its master.

In most cases this mixture of research and intuition will be successful. In an exam it's very unlikely that you'll be able to use a dictionary. A very difficult or uncommon word may be explained in a footnote – so make sure that you look to see if there *are* any notes of this kind. If there aren't, do the best you can from the context, using your common sense to tell you whether your reading is roughly accurate.

Allusion

Some unfamiliar words occur because the poet is making an **allusion** – a reference to someone or something which brings in a series of associations which extend the meaning of the poem and enrich its significance.

Diction and tone

Diction refers to the kind of language that a poem uses, informal, formal, specialist (particular region, trade, etc.) and so on.

Tone really means the tone of *voice* in which the poem is written. Is it, for example, tender, gentle, angry, vigorous, comic or self-mocking?

Situation and speaker

Many poems take place within a particular *situation*. Although you should not spend a long time exploring this – you will end up giving a paraphrase of the poem – you should try to understand what the situation is and be able to express it briefly in your answer.

Sometimes you will be able to do this from an early line or lines, as in this poem by Hardy:

> I leant upon a coppice gate
> When frost was spectre-grey

where we learn straight away that the speaker is talking about an occasion in winter where he is leaning against the gate of a small clearing in a wood.

In other poems, you will need to piece together the situation by looking closely at details. Look closely for signs which will tell you:

- who is speaking;
- who is being spoken to;
- how many people are speaking – the poem may well be a conversation between two or more 'voices', which you can tell apart because they use different diction and tone;
- where and when this is happening;
- any information about what has happened before which we need to know.

Of course, not all poems contain a situation of this sort. Many are more meditative, the poet thinking aloud about ideas or feelings:

> Even such is Time, that takes in trust
> Our youth, our joys, our all we have,
> And pays us but with earth and dust

or

> Well then; I now do plainly see,
> This busy world and I shall ne'er agree;

for instance.

Grammar and syntax

Grammar and syntax are 'rules' of writing – the first is about parts of speech, using the right form of a verb, and other 'rules' of language; the second is about getting words in the right order. You might think that these two rules have nothing to do with the freer elements of writing that you associate with poetry. In a way you'd be right – poets and other writers often break the rules to create a particular effect. But the rules are important when you come to read a poem – because they help you to work out exactly what the poem is saying.

When you're reading a poem for the first time, it helps to make sure that you know what each word is doing, and you can do this by thinking about its *grammatical role*. Is it a verb, a noun or an adjective? Is it the subject or object of the sentence? These are questions which can be very useful in sorting out what's going on in a poem at a very basic level, especially when you're just finding your way around it.

Sometimes this can work at a straightforward level.

> The sparrow's chirrup on the roof
> The slow clock ticking, and the sound
> Which to the wooing wind aloof
> The poplar made, did all confound
> Her sense;

Here the poet is using several different effects of sound, rhythm and imaginative language; but we will not get far in grasping any of them until we know how the lines work in a simple grammatical way. Looking at it *grammatically*, we can separate the elements like this;

The sparrow's chirrup on the roof	*Subject 1*
The slow clock ticking, and the sound	*Subject 2*
Which to the wooing wind aloof	*Subject 3*
The poplar made, did all confound	*Verb*
Her sense;	*Object*

We know, then, that these three sounds all worked to 'confound her sense'. Now that we know this, we can think about how they did it, what sort of sounds they were, and how the poet uses them to create atmosphere and other effects as part of the whole poem from which this excerpt comes. But unless we appreciate this simple structural form, a deeper reading is very difficult.

In this example, the poet has used a conventional order of words – subject, verb, object. But sometimes a poet can change the order and, unless you can work this out quickly, you can get the meaning quite wrong.

Here's an example.

> A cold coming we had of it,
> Just the worst time of the year
> For a journey, and such a journey

At first reading this can be confusing, but thinking about grammar helps us to disentangle the first line:

> 'We' is the subject;
> 'had' is the verb;
> 'a cold coming' is the object

– so, in everyday language, what the poem is saying is 'We had a cold coming – it was cold when we came'.

This sorts out the meaning of the first line, but it doesn't tell you much more. You need to ask *why* the poet has written it in such a way – why has he turned round, or inverted, the usual word order or syntax? The answer is simple – to make 'cold' the most striking word in the line by putting it at the start.

Changing the order of words, so that more emphasis is given to a word which is particularly important, is a technique which poets can use to create an effect. It's not something that happens all the time, of course, and it's not the only way to give emphasis – but it's one of several techniques which are available for a poet to use. A knowledge of syntax and grammar will therefore help you to recognise this, when you see it.

Notice that it is important not only to explain the effect of a particular technique: but also to explain *why* it is used. This is a key principle in critical appreciation: don't just write about what the poet has done, but go on to say *why*, and *what it adds to the poem's effect*.

So: a knowledge of the basic principles of syntax and grammar will help you to sort out the basic meaning of a poem, and can sometimes allow you to recognise a particular effect and understand why it is being used.

Figurative language

This is the term used for language which describes one thing in terms of another – the kind of comparison which is frequent in poetry of all kinds. As with the other features we've discussed so far, your aim should be first, to identify such use of language; then to say what it achieves – how it adds to the poem as a whole.

Figurative language can be divided into various kinds, those listed below are most commonly found in poetry and are described more fully under their separate entries.

Sound

Language doesn't only communicate through meaning: it conveys a lot of things through sound. Read the sections on **metre, rhythm** and **rhyme**.

Structure

Many poems make their effects in part by their *structure*. This could be:

a) by having a refrain or repeated line at the end of each stanza, in order to convey a sense of order;
b) by subtly changing the refrain in the last stanza, to show a departure from a pattern;
c) by having a pattern which in some way reinforces the meaning of the poem – perhaps changing from order to disorder to mirror such a change in a dramatic situation, for example, or changing in just the opposite way to show a sudden resolution.

Once again, you should look out for these things. They will not *always* be there but, when they are, comment on them and say why they are important in the poem's overall effect.

Conclusion

Very few poems will use all of these devices, but most will use one or more to get across their ideas and feelings. And, of course, they don't use them in isolation: poems make their effect through complex combinations of all the things mentioned here, and also through the nature of the ideas and feelings they are concerned with.

How to go about putting together the aspects we've discussed here to show how they contribute to the poem's idea, impression or significance, is the subject of the next section.

OVERALL CRITICAL APPRECIATION

Finding individual examples of the use of devices such as *sound, rhythm, metaphor*, etc. is an essential stage in reading and appreciating poetry. But how do you take this a stage further, to gain an overall grasp of a whole poem? And, once you have that, how do you write about it?

Making the move from spotting and analysing individual features of a poem to writing a coherent, overall critical *appreciation* of it is the subject of this section. It's particularly relevant to the critical appreciation paper in the exam, but it's also important for many other parts of your study. What it has to say will help you to read, understand and enjoy poetry texts you're studying for other papers and to answer questions on set texts of poetry which give you a passage of poetry as an example, and ask you to use it as the basis of general comments about the poet or the anthology studied.

This section begins by looking at how you read a poem, by studying each individaul part to develop an awareness of how each 'moment' fits into the whole text. Secondly, it looks at how you should consider and develop your own response to the poem – what you think and feel about it. It then gives some advice about how to write about poems in the critical appreciation paper, with plenty of examples for you to work on.

Sometimes, appreciation questions ask you to compare two poems on a related theme. A section of this entry looks at how to approach such questions, and how to make sure that you really *compare* the two texts rather than discussing first one and then the other.

THE READING PROCESS

Whenever you're confronted with something to write about in an exam, there's a temptation to feel that you're not *working* unless you're *writing*. But when you are tackling a critical appreciation question nothing is further from the truth. The *real* work is done when you are reading and thinking about the poem or other text, so that, when you come to write, you know what you are going to say and can relax and concentrate only on *expressing* your ideas – not on *finding* them. Ideally, you should spend at least half of the available time in reading and thinking about the text, jotting down notes and planning out ideas, and only the second half in actually writing.

What do you *do* during this reading, thinking and note-making time? For much of it you will be looking for and trying to understand the various *devices* we've looked at under their separate headings. But it may help if you divide the reading process into several clear stages.

1 First reading

When you read through the poem for the first time, try to do so fairly quickly and smoothly, at a regular pace so that you can begin to feel the rhythm and general movement it has. Don't worry about particular details – words, allusions or metaphors that you can't understand at once. Instead, go for an overall idea.

While you are doing this, try very hard **not** to form any firm impressions about what the poem is actually concerned with, or what it says. At the same time, try very hard to read what is *actually there* and not what you *think* is there. If you misread something the very first time you read it, you will probably continue this misreading and never realise the mistake – a point recognised by perceptual psychologists as a major obstacle in learning. So: read carefully, but keep an open mind as to the text's overall significance.

2 Read it aloud

This isn't something that you can do in the exam, of course – but you can do it while practising. Having the poet's words in your mouth is the best way of getting to know them – their feel and movement as well as their 'meaning'. By doing this you will:

- Feel the rhythm of the piece and know which words are given stresses to bring out their importance;
- Understand whether the rhythm is being used to create an effect or reinforce a meaning;
- Hear the sounds of the words and tell if it reinforces their meaning;
- Sense the tone of the speaker's 'voice' and judge how it fits in with the poem's significance.

Although you can't actually read the poem aloud in the exam, you can still go through the motions of reading it – actually shape the words with your mouth so that you *feel* what it's like to read. This may sound crazy and be embarassing at first, but you'll soon get used to it; you'll also realise that it does help you form an awareness of the poem in the ways listed above. But while you're doing this you should still try to keep an open mind about what the poem says – resist the temptation to come to conclusions about what it's concerned with too soon.

3 Read in detail

This is the stage where most of the work is done. Once you've read the poem to yourself and aloud, you need to go through it more slowly. Try to break the poem into *sections*. Each one could be:

a stanza;
a sentence within a stanza;
a single line containing a complex use of language;
a paragraph within a poem in one long stanza.

It doesn't matter how you divide the poem, as long as each part is a *complete unit of thought and expression* – don't, for example, stop at the end of a stanza if the sense goes on to the next one, or start at the beginning of a line if a new sentence has started at the end of the line before.

The most important thing to do here is to *ask questions* about every stage of the poem. Here are some that will be useful:

First – and most important – *questions about uses of language* which strike you as important.

Why are they there?
What do they do?
How do they make their effect?
Why do I respond to them as I do?

Then, when you've thought about these points, try some more down-to-earth approaches:

Questions on meaning
Is this meant literally – just what it says – or is it a metaphor of some kind?
Does this word mean what I think it does, or is there another meaning I've missed?
Questions on structure
Why is the poem arranged into lines or stanzas in the way it is?
What does the sound contribute to the line I'm reading?
What does the rhythm add?
Questions on grammar
What's the main verb of this sentence?
Which is the subject and which is the object?
Is this an inversion of syntax?

Asking questions like these will help you to *recognise* the various features of the poem; gradually you will assemble a series of clues as to what the poem is concerned with and how it works.

FORM A WORKING HYPOTHESIS

From what you've read of the poem, you'll be able at this stage to work out a hypothesis – a rough idea of your interpretation of it. This will cover:

- An idea of the poem's *subject* – the point that it is making, the situation it records, the idea that it advances, or any combination of these or other significances;
- An idea of the *techniques* it uses to get its message across;
- An idea of your own response to it.

I've described this as a *working hypothesis* because, once you have a rough idea about these two aspects of the poem, you should always be *reviewing* and *modifying* your overall idea in the light of the answers you get to your questions about individual passages of the poem. Don't reach a final interpretation of the poem too soon – always be prepared to change it in the light of what you're reading.

As you go through this process, you'll find that your hypothesis gradually becomes clearer, and you arrive at a final interpretation of the poem. It may help to think of the reading process in the way suggested by Fig. P.2. the interpretation gradually develops in the centre as you try to bring together ideas and their expression, individual passages and of course the whole poem.

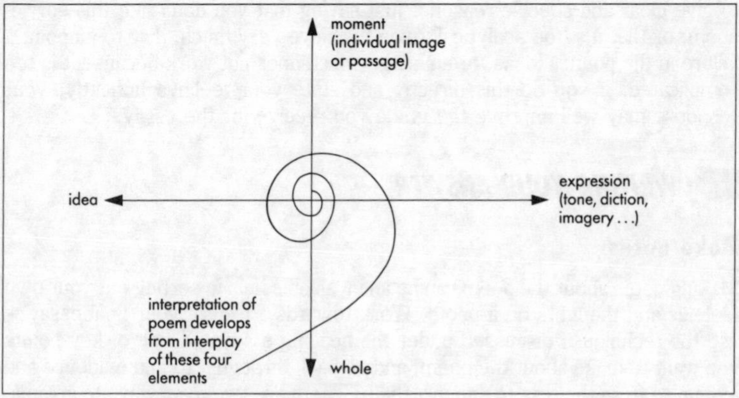

Fig. P.2

INDIVIDUAL RESPONSE

Writing an appreciation isn't just a matter of saying what the poem is about and how it works. It's also about making clear your *response* – your own feelings and thoughts about the poem. This is an important part of the process, although it clearly shouldn't overwhelm the essay. A long, gushing statement of how much you like the poem and how moving you find it will not achieve a very good grade; instead you should *demonstrate* those qualities in the poem which you admire or find effective.

By all means make comments on your response while you are talking about *particular features* – you might, for example, say that you find an image particularly effective because it looks at a topic in a new way, or is unexpectedly witty about it. At the end of the essay, write a brief paragraph which draws together your response to the poem. In it, say:

a) what features of the poem you like or don't like;
b) why you respond as you do.

In doing this, be sure that your response rests on features of the poem itself, not on quite unrelated, personal, factors. Do *not*, for example, say:

> I like this poem because it is about horses, and I am very fond of horses.

Instead, say;

> I like this poem because it offers a new way of seeing the relationship between the human and the animal world, showing how arrogant people are in controlling animals in the ironic tone it adopts.

You don't, of course, have to *like* the poem. If you dislike it, though, you have to give clear and specific reasons. Just saying that you don't like this sort of poem, or that it's 'too analytical', won't achieve very much. Try to pinpoint a failure in the poem's ideas, or an image which does not work because it is too complicated: if you do this directly and state your feelings honestly, your response may well improve the grade you receive for the essay.

WRITING YOUR ANSWER

Make notes

Making notes about the poem can be an invaluable help in sorting out your own feelings and thoughts on a peom. Work towards a plan of your final essay – use the techniques discussed under the heading **essays**. Think of key points you want to make about the poem, and go back through it to find evidence and examples from the text to support them. There are two main ways to arrange an essay of this sort. You can structure it according to a series of points – eight or ten features which you consider to be the most important aspects of the poem, arranged in the best logical order, and supported by appropriate quotation or reference.

Alternatively, you can go through the poem from beginning to end, pointing out important aspects such as ideas or features of expression as you do so.

In practice, the best way is often a combination of the two. You might organise your answer like this:

a) short statement of the poem's main ideas and techniques – a paragraph should be enough;

b) body of essay working through the poem, showing how the ideas are developed and expressed, noting changes of tone, diction, development of situation, and growth of argument as appropriate to the individual text, supported by quotation and reference;
c) concluding statement giving your response, based on specific features of the poem.

Your plan should outline your approach, making clear the points and the order in which you make them. When you come to write the essay, you will only have to think about expressing yourself clearly, as the ideas will already be there for you in your plan.

Final essay

An essay in a critical appreciation paper should follow the same approaches and principles as an essay in any other paper. (**Essays**). But there are some additional points.

Don't paraphrase. Your task is to explain what the poem is about and how it makes its effect, not to paraphrase it in prose. Give a short account of the poem's situation and its main concern, but don't just write down all that happens: analysis and comment are needed instead.
Identify then explain. When you are talking about an important feature of the poem, make sure that you follow a pattern in your approach. First identify the feature – say what it is and where it occurs, by line number or brief quotation. Then say what it contributes to the poem's overall effect.
Support your points. By all means begin a paragraph or section with a clear statement of a point, or an assertion about the poem's concerns or techniques. When you do this, though, you must go on to explain where you see it and how it functions in the poem – otherwise it will be just an unsupported assertion, lacking the detailed evidence and analytical argument you need to do the job properly.
Quotations. Keep them short – there's no point in copying out the poem that's in front of you. Refer to specific individual words or short phrases, but when you mention longer passages use line numbers, which will normally be given in the paper.
Style. Keep the style simple, straightforward and clear. Don't go in for pretentious-sounding words or phrases – just say what you mean in a direct fashion.

COMPARING POEMS

Appreciation papers quite often ask you to *compare* two poems on a similar theme. Although this may at first sight seem to involve twice the work, it is often actually more straightforward – especially if the poems are very different in style or in the way in which they approach the topic, since each one can help to clarify the other.

There are many ways in which writing a comparison is similar to writing about one poem. For example, you need to read both poems in the way suggested earlier in this entry and the general points about planning and writing your answer also hold good. But there are some important new points to be aware of.

Compare features while reading

Instead of spending a lot of time on one poem and then moving on to the next, try to move rapidly from one to the other. Read the first one and then go to the second; while you are asking questions about the first, think about how you'd answer them with reference to the second. Keep glancing from one to the other – in this way you'll find that not only will you notice features of each one, but the *difference* will help to clarify your interpretation of both as individual poems.

While you're doing this, remember the various categories in which differences might occur; in meaning; figurative language – metaphor, for example; rhythm; sound; grammar and syntax; structure; the overall impact it has on you.

Think, too, about the attitude that each poem has to its subject. The two will be similar in some ways, but will contain differences in meaning and approach – so try to define these while you are developing your working hypothesis.

Your response

You may or may not be asked directly for your own response. If you are, it will be just as important in a comparison as when you are writing about a single poem. Here you will need to say which of the two poems you prefer, and *why*. As before, your opinions should be supported by *reasons* – the poems' techniques, structures or the ways in which they approach their subject.

Planning your answer

Structure your plan so that you *compare* the poems – bring them together to show similarities and differences, perhaps like this:

POEM A	POEM B
Has regular rhythm	Irregular rhythm following flow of action
Uses very formal diction	Uses freer, conversational diction
Classical allusions	No allusions

Making a *table* like this can be very helpful – you may not use all the points that you record, but the discipline of writing notes like this can help to get your mind working to reveal the points of likeness and difference between the two poems. Your response, too, can be added to the plan, so that you are aware of every point you will make in the essay *before* you come to write it.

Writing your answer

Make sure that you bring the poems together, and do not discuss first one and then the other. The best way of doing this is by using sentence structures which bring the two together, like these:

> The first poem makes a very personal statement, whereas the second is far more objective . . .
>
> In place of the first poem's rich natural imagery, the second uses a more detached descriptive style . . .
>
> The first poem lacks the urgent tone of the second . . .
>
> Both poems treat the subject with considerable restraint . . .

Keeping this technique in mind will certainly help you to achieve the aim of the question and genuinely compare the texts: make a point of using similar structures when you are writing to make sure that the comparisons you have made when reading and planning receive proper expression.

Questions on poetry

Questions on poetry will usually be of three main types.

1 Questions which give you a complete poem, with an accompanying question.
Generally, this will ask you to comment on the features of the poem which are typical of the poet's work, or of an aspect of the anthology's nature if it comes from a collection by many poets.

Tackle these by reading the given text carefully, identifying its representative features and then finding examples of these elements elsewhere in the collection. Always make sure that you *relate* the poem to the whole collection in this way, otherwise you will end up writing a study of just one poem.

2 Questions based on a quotation.
In most cases, the quotation will be specially invented for the question, and will be a statement which is partially true about the poetry.

Your first task here is to look carefully at both the quotation and the question itself. Make sure that you know what the question means, perhaps by concentrating on key words and concepts. You should then marshal your ideas by writing a *plan* which makes a series of relevant points, supporting each one with a textual reference or quotation. Having done this, you can write the essay.

3 Questions which ask you to discuss a particular aspect of the poetry.
These are generally more straightforward than quotation questions, but still demand close reading to define precisely the task they set you to complete.

Once again, you should make a plan with a series of points, each supported by a quotation or reference, making sure all the time that you are *relating* your knowledge to the question. When you are sure that you have done this in the plan, write the essay.

◀ Allusion, Diction, Essays, Figurative language, Metre, Poetry (collections), Rhythm, Sound, Tone ▶

POETRY: COLLECTIONS

When you are studying a text which is a collection of poems, either by one poet or by several from the same period, there are special difficulties to be met and special techniques to be mastered.

The basis of the process is, of course, **critical reading**. This helps you to understand individual poems. But how do you get beyond a careful grasp of one poem, and progress to an understanding of the *whole collection*? How do the themes and ideas come together, and how do you get to know the poet's techniques and approaches? If you're studying an anthology, how do you gain an overall view of a group of poems which may be widely different?

When you have solved these problems, you need to know how to write about poems. How do you know which ones to select as examples? How do you quote from poems in an essay? And how do you organise your points about a collection of pieces of writing which may each be very different from the others?

These are the problems fundamental to studying poetry which this section addresses. It gives advice on:

- Reading individual poems in a collection;
- Knowing how to group poems;
- Bringing together your work to give a view of the collection;
- Sorting out important themes;
- Sorting out important techniques;
- Selecting poems for detailed reference to the exam;
- Dealing with anthologies from different periods;
- Separating the 'background' of the poet's life and times from the 'foreground' – the text which is the principal focus of study;
- Writing about poetry collections – getting to know how to see them as a whole, and which poems to refer to in essays.

Reading and studying a collection of poems is a demanding, as well as a fulfilling, task. Yet, because it depends on a close knowledge of individual texts, it builds on the foundations laid in your study of separate poems for critical appreciation (see poetry). This section aims to help you make the difficult transition in literary studies from a close reading of a short text to a larger awareness of a complete volume.

▶ *APPRAISING A COLLECTION*

Before you get down to careful study of individual poems, it's worth just having a quick look at the collection as a whole. For most people, the hardest thing at A-level or equivalent examinations is moving from close study of one short passage to a knowledge of a whole book – so it's worth going quickly through the collection to see if there's anything that will help you to make this move.

a) Look at the contents page. Are the poems arranged in any particular way? They could, for example:
   be grouped under periods;
   be arranged in themes;
   consist of various sequences of poems, which could be regarded almost as separate texts in their own right.
b) Glance at the introduction to see if particular ideas are suggested. This doesn't mean that you should read the introduction before you read the poems: instead, it means that you should look quickly to see if there are any hints about how the poems might be grouped together according to subject or theme.

'Mariana'

1 M. is waiting for her lover, in a deserted, decaying house.

2 Narrator speaks to set scene, with refrain spoken by M. herself.

3 No reason given for scene or events; instead poem concentrates on creating desolate atmosphere through description of house and its surroundings.

4 Narrator seems sympathetic, in creating setting to reflect M's loneliness.

5 Makes effect through v. rich, full sounds ;

With blackest moss the flower-plots
Were thickly crusted, one and all

6 Recurrent refrain stresses the Stillness – M. is not ever, it seems, to leave the house.

She said, 'I am aweary, aweary,
I would that I were dead!'

NB repetition emphasises boredom and stillness.

Fig. P.3 Making notes on record cards

When you've done this, you may have some idea about how the collection is put together. Now try to glance quickly through the poems, reading some quickly to yourself to get a very rapid, general idea of subject and treatment. Don't worry at this stage if you don't understand a great deal – later reading will put that right. Instead, just try to gain an overall idea of the main topics, attitudes and structures used by the poet or poets.

This will give you a few ideas to think about while reading the poems in more detail. But don't make up your mind too firmly about anything yet – such as the poet's main preoccupations or the themes about which he or she writes. Keep an open mind, as you would while developing a working hypothesis about a poem or other text in the earlier stages of critical reading.

While you are working through the volume of poems, you should be building up a collection ofsets of **notes** (Fig. P.3). Writing them on small record-cards has the advantage that you can read them easily to refresh your memory of individual poems. This will also help you at the next stage – where you arrange them in different orders, grouping the poems together in different ways.

Grouping the poems

Each poem in a collection or anthology exists as a complete work in its own right. But when you are studying a *collection*, it helps to group poems together, since this allows you to see the volume as a whole, as more than a gathering of separate texts.

When you have completed notes on several poems, start thinking about what they have in common, in any of the aspects mentioned above. Once you've looked at all the poems, of course, you'll be in a better position to group them together – but thinking about *shared features* and contrasts even while you are still reading each one critically in detail, will help you in two ways:

1 It may reveal aspects of the individual poem you're currently reading;
2 It will help you to be more aware of those poems which do, or do not, share common features.

There are usually several different ways in which the poems in a collection can be grouped together. Think in particular about:

Subject. Do several of the poems discuss the same theme – for example, a particular aspect of love, the idea of suffering, old age, humankind's relationship with the natural world?
Attitude. Does the poet's attitude remain the same in several poems, or does it develop? Are there similarities in outlook in poems which have different themes?
Style. Often the poems in collection will have similarities in the way they are written. These might be characteristic features of the poet's style in a collection by one writer; or similarities of style in a particular period of poetry; or ways in which a series of different styles may be seen in a period anthology. Under the heading of 'style' come all features of the expression of poetry – its form, tone, diction, imagery and structure.

Other striking features. Don't restrict your grouping to these areas. If any other aspects strike you repeatedly in the poems, then think about grouping them under that particular heading.

The way to approach the grouping of poems is simply to think about an aspect or feature which you have *seen* several times in the various poems. You can then list the poems which share it under a clear, descriptive heading. This should give you a series of themes or features, each with a number of poems beneath it.

When you are thinking of themes or features, remember any points that have been made in class about the main features and themes of the poet's work. The introduction to the edition you're using may have some suggestions to make, too. Use these as a way of getting ideas – think for yourself, but be willing to take suggestions from other sources. Try **brainstorming**, too – sitting down and just making a list of as many characteristic features as you can (see Fig. P.4). You'll be surprised how many you can find in just a few minutes.

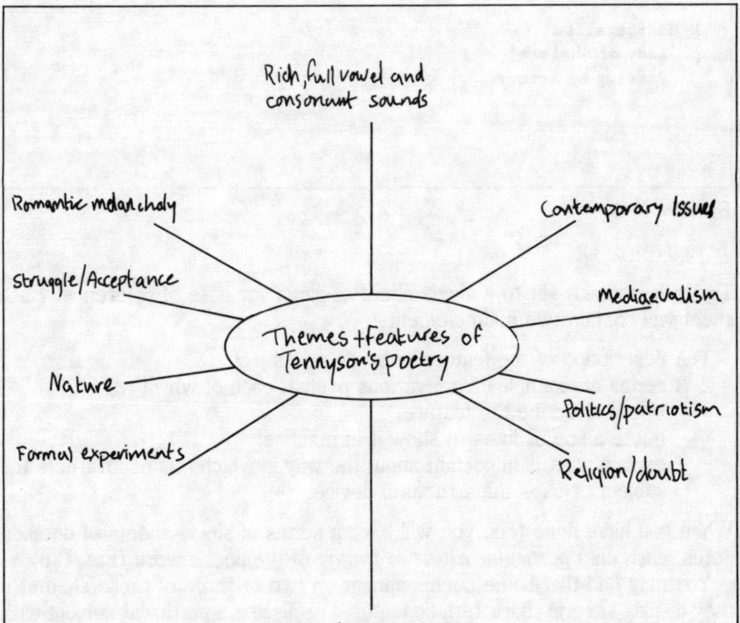

Fig. P.4

Now take each feature and list the poems which demonstrate it. This will give you a sheet like the one in Fig. P.5.

You can now go on to develop this into *more detailed notes* on each feature.

Features of Tennyson's poetry

1 Rich vowel and consonant sounds
'Mariana'
'Claribel'
'The splendour falls ...'
'Ulysses' (ending)
In Memoriam ('Ring out wild bells')

2 Formal experiments
'Locksley Hall'
'The Two Voices'
In Memoriam
'Maud'
'Rizpah'
'Vastness'

3 Mediaevalism
'Lady of Shalott'
'Passing of Arthur'

4 Religion and Doubt
In Memoriam
'St. Simeon Stylites'

5 Contemporary Issues
'Passing of Arthur'
'Locksley Hall'
'D. of Wellington'
'Charge of Light Brigade'

Fig. P.5

Try to keep each set to a single sheet of paper for ease of reference. Each sheet will contain two main elements:

1 A description of the feature, attitude or subject;
2 A series of examples from various poems, each of which will:
   – briefly describe the feature;
   – quote a line or lines to show it in practice;
   – explain what is important about the way in which this poem treats the subject or uses the structural device.

When you have done this, you will have a series of single sheets of detailed notes, each on a *particular aspect or feature* of the poet's work (Fig. P.6).

You may find that some poems appear on two or three of these sheets, if they display several characteristic features or discuss a particular subject with a particular attitude. You may also find that you can *select* poems on each sheet, as the best examples of the particular feature, to avoid giving endless examples where one or two would be enough.

In this way you will build up a set of notes on the anthology or collection as a whole, which rests firmly on your detailed reading of the individual texts.

A word of warning: don't assume that the groupings you have are the only ones, or that examiners will set questions based on them. They may well have different ideas, so be prepared to think quickly in the exam and to 're-group' the poems according to a topic, theme or idea that may form the basis of an exam question.

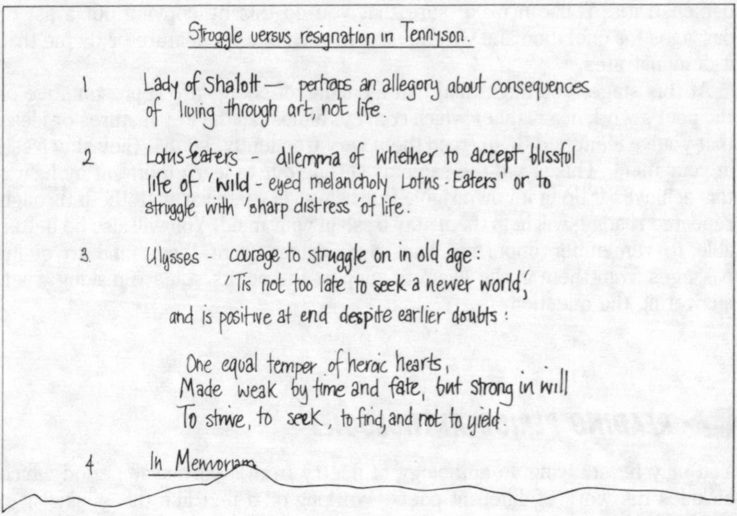
Struggle versus resignation in Tennyson.

1 Lady of Shalott — perhaps an allegory about consequences of living through art, not life.

2 Lotus-Eaters - dilemma of whether to accept blissful life of 'wild-eyed melancholy Lotus-Eaters' or to struggle with 'sharp distress of life.

3. Ulysses - courage to struggle on in old age:

'Tis not too late to seek a newer world',

and is positive at end despite earlier doubts:

One equal temper of heroic hearts,
Made weak by time and fate, but strong in will
To strive, to seek, to find, and not to yield.

4 In Memoriam

Fig. P.6

Checking your themes

When you have made your series of notes on themes, you need to check them carefully to make sure that you have covered all the important features and topics of the collection. Check by:

1 Thinking carefully yourself about the text, reading through it again to see if there are any other topics or features that you've missed.
2 Discussing the text with other people – your teacher, or fellow-students – to make sure that you haven't missed anything of importance.
3 Reading the introduction to your edition, to check if the editor mentions important themes or features that you've missed.
4 Reading critical commentaries for the same reason – though be careful not to be overwhelmed by the interpretation they offer.

Once you have gone through these stages, you should have a fairly thorough acquaintance with the poems and the topics they deal with. You can now take your revision a stage further by selecting a number of poems which you can use as the basis of your revision, and which you can discuss in detail in an exam.

Do this by:

a) selecting those which are the best examples of each topic or feature;
b) looking for poems which appear as examples of several different topics or features.

In this way, you will arrive at a small group of poems, or passages from poems, which you can learn. There's no point in doing this, though, unless you know *why* you are learning them – that is, what features or themes they demonstrate. You can make sure that you do this by copying out a list of passages for quotation and writing next to each one the feature or theme that it demonstrates.

At this stage, you might find that a handful of poems are representative of the poet's work in a manner which conveys almost all the key features or ideas that you've identified. If so, read them very frequently, so that they stay fresh in your mind. This is *not* the same as setting out to learn them off by heart; this achieves little in its own right. But being very familiar with them through repeated reading will help them stay fresh in your mind. You will also be better able to remember important lines and images from them, and to quote passages from them in the exam to support the points you are making when answering the question.

READING PERIOD ANTHOLOGIES

You may be studying an anthology of poetry from a particular period which includes the work of different poets. Working on a text like this is similar in many ways to studying a collection by one poet, but there are certain other points to bear in mind.

1 *Look for points of contrast*
Anthologies often include a wide range of poems which discuss the same themes in very different ways. If you group poems together according to subject, make sure that you note the differences between them in style or attitude.

2 *Be aware of individual poets*
In the exam you may be asked to discuss the treatment of a theme by two or more poets. Make sure that you include, in your groups of poems, work by individual figures, with notes on their characteristic features of style, subject and attitude.

3 *Note familiarities and differences of style*
In some periods, poetry *shares* features of style and attitude. The eighteenth century, for example, was a period of much formality in poetry, with a large number of poems written in rhyming couplets of ten syllables to a line. By contrast, the poetry of the nineteen-thirties is very diverse in form, with very few structures in common between poets.
Include in your notes a sheet showing how the styles of the poems you are studying are similar, and a sheet showing their range and diversity, so that you can answer a question on these aspects should it arise.

4 *Beware of 'background'*
When studying an anthology of work from a particular period, it's easy to get carried away with 'background studies'. Reading about the social history of the thirties, or the conditions in the trenches in the first world war, can become more absorbing than reading the poems themselves.

Be careful about this. If you find the period interesting, by all means read about it; but make sure that this doesn't become a substitute for the close study of the poems themselves. This should always be the main focus of your work, and the background should never change into the 'foreground' of your work.

WRITING ABOUT POETRY

If you have read the material on **essays** and on the critical appreciation of poetry (**poetry**) you should have a good idea of what's required in essays about poetry. The key points to remember are those that were made under those headings:

1. Read the question carefully and know what you are asked to do.
2. Marshal your knowledge of the text and relate it to the questions.
3. Organise your material in concepts – a list of eight or so points which directly engage the question.
4. Support each point with a quotation or close reference to a text.

As well as these points, remember that simply quoting a poem will achieve nothing unless you *use* it – relate it to a critical point which directly answers the question. Remember, too, that quotations which are longer than a few words should be set out as they are in the printed poem – as separate lines, usually with a capital letter at the start of each.

Finally, remember that your knowledge of the poems will achieve little unless you actually answer the question; you must make everything relevant. This means leaving out biographical or 'background' material, and points which, while perfectly valid about the poems, do not engage with the question.

What you *can* do, however, is to make clear your own opinions. If you are asked to discuss the effectiveness of a poet's work or treatment of a theme, give your opinion clearly and directly. Simple statements of liking or disliking are clearly out of place, but a *reasoned evaluation* of the work *is* a valid part of your response, so don't be afraid to make it.

◀ Essays, Poetry ▶

PRAGMATICS

As a branch of linguistics, pragmatics is a fairly recent development though it has been regarded as a branch of **semiotics** for the last fifty years or so. In both fields, pragmatics is concerned with the influence of social context and psychological interaction on the ways in which language users understand the meanings being constructed during a conversation or a meeting. It is very easy to assume that everyday conversations, for example, just happen without any structure or rules to guide them. In fact the reverse is true.

Conversations are extremely subject to social rules which are learned in childhood, developed in later years and maintained throughout life. The study of the various strategies and structures of conversation is the business of *discourse analysis* which describes ways in which conversations are begun and ended, how topics are changed, how questions are asked, how interruptions and hesitations occur, how turntaking is established. Features such as these are as observable in everyday chat as they are in more formal meetings. You could usefully consider what we have to learn in order to take part effectively in a committee, in a job interview, in a seminar or tutorial, in a consultation, in a press or police interview, or in a doctor's surgery. What are the features of such conversations? and how do they differ?

Pragmatics, whilst taking into account what discourse analysis has to offer, additionally considers the social contexts of discourse and some psychological features. The status of speakers in relation to each other is often important (e.g. child/parent, teacher/pupil, employer/employee). Power has to be negotiated, degrees of politeness or frankness established; implicit agreement on the agenda will be necessary if the conversation is to continue. Note that the term agenda can be applied to topics that occur in informal conversation, as well as to the listed topics of formal meetings. The signalled agenda for a conversation may be last weekend's soccer game but one participant in the conversation may wish to change the agenda to the forthcoming cricket season. There may also be a hidden agenda to a conversation, not explicitly discussed, but implicit in the speakers' mind.

There are a number of popular expressions that reflect an underlying awareness of pragmatic features of conversation: e.g.

Within these four walls . . .
Between you and me . . .
Who do you think you are talking to?
You always want the last word.
Let's talk man to man.
I must caution you that anything you say . . .
Off the record . . .
Give it to me straight.
You shouldn't say things like that.
Without a word of a lie, I'm telling you . . .
I am obliged to say that . . .
I am going to pretend I didn't hear that . . .
What right have you to say that?

There seems to be an endless range of social circumstances in which we can investigate pragmatic features of conversation: e.g.

- expressing condolences to a bereaved person
- telling somebody off, gently
- establishing one's right to disagree
- making complaints
- asking for personal information
- proposing marriage
- breaking bad news
- negotiating a business deal.

An interesting area of pragmatics is the study of the short conversational exchanges that cumulatively make up a discourse. Greetings such as 'How are you?' normally expect brief responses not long accounts of minor operations. When people observe that the weather 'is mild today' they do not normally expect detailed comparisons of temperature and humidity readings for the preceding week. Young children have to learn how to handle the pragmatics of a telephone conversation. The question from a caller, 'Is your mother in?' could elicit from a five-year-old the reply 'Yes', after which the child would replace the receiver. It requires a certain amount of social learning to realise that a question like that is really a request to speak to someone and implicitly requires you to do something about it.

Modes of address are another important aspect of conversations. All GCSE French students will be familiar with the distinction between 'tu' and 'vous' to express familiarity and formality. What effect does the impersonal pronoun have on English conversations? e.g.

One does not do that sort of thing.

You could consider how and why the word 'mate' is used in conversations, or why a word like 'pal' is often used in a threatening way, e.g.

Move your car, pal (spoken with menace).

PRE-MODIFICATION (AND POST MODIFICATION)

A *pre-modifying* word or construction qualifies, describes or modifies a noun before the noun is stated:

a large, expensive, green car.
a loud-mouthed, red- faced woman.
a distinguished, elderly man.

A *post-modifying* construction qualifies, describes or modifies the noun afterwards:

The car was **large, expensive** and **green**.
The woman was **loud-mouthed** and **red-faced**.
The man was **distinguished** and **elderly**.

It is not difficult to see the different rhetorical effects of the two strategies (see **rhetoric**). One predisposes a response to whatever noun is about to be used while the other delays the modification.

PREPOSITIONS

Prepositions are grammatical words that usually go before a noun or a pronoun (e.g. about, onto, until, beside, over, under, with).

Sometimes prepositions can consist of more than one word (e.g. up to, instead of, with reference to).

They are also an inseparable part of English phrasal verbs (see **verb**). Sometimes students are unsure whether a word is a preposition or an adverb. Consider for example the words 'under', 'over', 'up' and 'inside'. Used as prepositions you would expect these words in such sentences as:

a) She found a bottle *under* the stone.
b) Trench soldiers must have dreaded going *over* the top.
c) He climbed *up* the tree.
d) She found a key *inside* the box.

They could also occur in the following sentences:

a) He never expected to go *under*.
b) The balance was carried *over*.
c) The balloon went *up*.
d) She spent five years *inside*.

Notice that their use here does not precede a noun. When used in this way they are sometimes called *prepositional adverbs*. Notice too that they tend to be adverbs of place.

PRESCRIPTIVE GRAMMAR

◀ Descriptive grammar, Grammar ▶

PRONOUNS

Pronouns can be used to substitute for nouns or noun phrases. They perform a variety of functions and are named accordingly.

Personal pronouns (I, you, me, they etc).
Possessive pronouns (my, mine, your, their etc).
Demonstrative pronouns (this, that etc).
Interrogative pronouns (who, which, what etc).
Reflective pronouns (myself, themselves, yourself etc).
Relative pronouns (who, whom, that etc).
Indefinite pronouns (anyone, nobody etc).

You will have noticed that the same pronoun can have two functions. Consider the following sentences:

a) *That* one is mine (demonstrative pronoun).
b) This is the car *that* won the race (relative pronoun).

c) *Who* did this? (interrogative pronoun).
d) I am the one *who* started it all (relative pronoun).

In a) the pronoun demonstrates exactly which one is mine.
In b) the pronoun relates the car to winning the race.
In c) the pronoun asks a question.
In d) the pronoun relates 'I' to the person who started it all.

Relative pronouns often cause argument about usage. 'Who' and 'whom', for example, have a flexible use according to whether they are being used in writing and formal speech or in informal speech:

a) This is the woman who he was talking to. (informal)
b) This is the woman whom he was talking to. (formal)
c) This is the woman to whom he was talking. (very formal)

To avoid problems of this kind English employs what is referred to as a *zero relative pronoun* which means that the pronoun is only implied:

d) This is the woman he was talking to.

It is also possible in this example to use the pronoun 'that':

e) This is the woman that he was talking to.

The relative pronoun that could not be used is 'which':

f) This is the woman which he was talking to.

'Which' is reserved for non personal uses:

g) This is the book which he gave to the woman he was talking to.

PROSE

Defined simply, prose is any kind of writing which is not poetry – it is the ordinary, straightforward writing that we all read every day in letters, newspaper reports, novels and instructions for computer games. In itself, there's nothing special about prose – and, perhaps for that reason, many people find it hard to analyse prose, describe its features and say how it makes the effects it's aiming for.

There is, however, no reason why prose should be difficult to analyse. Although it is set out in a different way from poetry – not as separate lines but in continuous paragraphs – prose shares many of the devices and techniques of poetic writing. The problem often lies not in the prose itself, but in our attitude towards it – we're not used to looking analytically at a medium in which we read the football results or ask the milkman for two extra pints. So the first thing to do when confronted with a piece of prose is to make a slight, but significant, shift of attitude – think about it is as a complex, subtle piece of expression, in which every word has a function to perform and nothing happens by accident. If you approach it in this way you will find that you will have no shortage of points to make about it.

CRITICAL APPRECIATION

As well as a poem and a passage from a play, the critical appreciation exam usually includes a piece of prose for you to analyse and comment on. You may have a choice between tackling the prose and tackling the dramatic passage. Even if, in the end, you choose not to write about the prose you need to be aware of the techniques of reading and analysing prose to give you a proper choice in the paper.

In addition, you need to know the basic techniques of reading and analysing prose so that you can study your set texts properly. You will almost certainly be studying one or more novels, and may also have a descriptive or analytical prose work to study. The techniques discussed in this section will give you help in working on these texts – and also, incidentally, help in reading critical works about your set texts should you do this as part of your study programme. For all these reasons, then, knowing how to read and appreciate prose should be an essential part of your critical skills.

This section discusses the nature of prose writing and shows you how to:

- identify the essential nature of the passage – whether it is descriptive, narrative, comic or has another main purpose;
- analyse the features of the passage by which it makes its main effects;
- read a passage with care and precision, looking at its various features and bringing them together to form your own coherent reading of the whole piece of writing.

Features to note (techniques and devices)

Meaning

Because of the nature of prose and the purposes for which it is most often used, we are more accustomed to look for its meaning first and its qualities of expression later, if at all. Indeed, many questions which ask you to look at prose passages in appreciation papers will actually mention the meaning or argument of the text as one of the main topics you should consider.

As a result, gaining a clear understanding of what the passage is *about* is a major priority when reading a prose text. It's not the *only* one; but it is one from which many of the others will follow since, once you *have* a grasp of the passage's purpose, you will be better able to analyse the features it uses to achieve that purpose. Looking for the meaning and significance of the passage, then, will be of much importance when you are reading a prose passage set for appreciation.

Grammar and syntax

In a poem, you may have to tease out the grammatical structure before you can grasp the significance of a line or longer passage. Although there will often be fewer complex structures – like inversions of syntax, for example – just the same is true in a prose passage. Understanding the grammar means finding the subject, main verb and object of each sentence, as we do automatically when reading.

In prose, you need also to consider various other questions about how the writer has constructed a particular passage:

How are the various clauses and phrases related to each other? In other words, which is the *main clause* or phrase in a sentence? Unless you know this, you will find it very difficult to write coherently about the passage since you will not be in a position to grasp the basic points it is making.

Does the writer use *balanced clauses* to show the relationship between the two points under discussion? Often a writer will deliberately put two points next to each other in two clauses of equal weight in a sentence, to show that they are of equal importance in the argument or description. You need to be able to recognise such features, and so show how the writer matches expression to content in the passage.

Does the *position of a sentence* within a paragraph indicate its importance? Usually the first sentence in a paragraph will give the paragraph's main point, and those which come after will elaborate or clarify various aspects of it. Use this as a guide to the way the prose develops its points.

Diction

Just as the choice of words is important in poetry and drama, so it is in prose.

Tone

A poem or dramatic passage will most likely be read aloud or performed by a speaking voice. The prose writer does not have this in mind, except when writing for the stage, and so the tone has to be conveyed just by choice of words and the way they are put together.

Rhythm, pace and sound

Although the rhythm of a piece of poetry is more obvious than that of a piece of prose, this quality may nevertheless be just as important in conveying an essential element of the significance of a piece of prose. Rhythm might, for instance, be used in any of the following ways:

To establish suspense by using long, slow-moving sentences.

To clarify a complex argument by using sentences with a number of clauses and phrases of equal weight.

To suggest a reflective mood by using long, slow words, often in conjunction with sounds which are long and slow too.

To create fast action by the use of short, simple words and brief, efficient sentences.

None of these effects would be created by rhythm alone, of course. Sounds, meanings and associations of words would also have a great deal to contribute in many cases.

A sudden *change* of rhythm or pace can also be very effective in prose. A shift from long, slow words and sentences to short, brisk ones can suggest the switch from contemplation to action; a change from complicated diction and irregular rhythm to simple, clear words and straightforward, conversational rhythms can show the change in a character's mind as a result, say, of taking an important decision or hearing some reassuring news.

As with diction and tone, rhythm needs to be considered in conjunction with other aspects of a piece of writing, so make sure that you are aware of all of these features working in combination while you are reading a piece of prose for appreciation.

Figurative language

Prose generally uses fewer **metaphors, similes** and **images** than poetry. But comparison and **figurative language** is an essential part of everyday conversation. We talk about being 'as dead as a doornail' or 'as deaf as a post', and stay at home 'snug as a bug in a rug' while outside it is 'raining stair-rods'. These are simple, conversational expressions – but they are also one kind of figurative language which you might well find in a piece of prose.

Alternatively, prose may make long, complex comparisons, every facet of which is explored separately, so that one metaphor may take up a whole paragraph. This is especially the case with many novels which use extended comparisons to present an object or relationship in a startling new guise: E M Forster uses figurative language, for example, to describe the strange nature of the Marabar Caves in *A Passage to India*.

Not every piece of prose which you are asked to comment on will do this – but you must be aware that a prose writer can use figurative language which is just as rich and various as that found in poetry, so keep alive to the metaphorical dimension while you are reading.

As with poetry and dramatic writing, it is not these features in isolation which create an effect in prose writing. It is the way in which they combine which gives the writing its special nature.

KINDS OF PROSE

One major way in which prose differs from writing of the other kinds which you will be studying is in its *purpose*. When you are reading a piece of prose it is often useful to try to categorise it. This does not mean simply labelling it, as a Victorian butterfly collector would identify a butterfly and pin it lifeless onto a board for display. Instead it means trying to find the underlying purpose and intention of a piece of writing, so that this, and your awareness of those features described in the last section, will come together to give you a far greater sense of what the piece is concerned with and how it achieves its purpose.

The following list of categories is not exhaustive – and neither should you assume that every piece of prose can be slotted into one of the pigeonholes it represents. Instead, look on these categories as a series of possibilities to run through while reading, so that you will arrive at a closer awareness of the passage by seeing what kind of prose it might or might not resemble, or which features it might share.

Narrative prose

This is one of the most familiar kinds of prose. It simply tells a story, as in a novel or short story. Narrative prose can be written in different ways. There may, for example, be a single figure who tells the story. In the Victorian novel, this is usually an 'omniscient narrator' – the figure of the writer who tells the story but is not involved in the action in any way, and of whose nature and personality we directly learn nothing. Alternatively, the story may be told by someone who *is* involved with the action – a 'first person' narrative, so called because it is controlled by someone who writes as the 'I' of the story.

In addition there are various combinations of these two. The novels of Joseph Conrad, for example, are often narrated by a figure who is identified early in the book, so that we are given the effect of listening to a story-teller. Some novels will change the narrator at various stages in the story, so that we see things from various different viewpoints.

An awareness of the person who is doing the narrating is an important element in appreciating fiction. When writing about a piece of narrative prose, you should try to be aware of the nature of the narrator, as it is revealed by the style of prose. Do this by studying closely the features described in the foregoing section.

Conversational prose

Here the piece will record all or some of a conversation. Instead of just putting the name of each character at the left before he or she speaks, however, a piece of conversational prose will identify each speaker in more complex ways. Sometimes the words of the two speakers will be presented on alternate lines, so that the reader knows when a new person is speaking. Nevertheless, at times it can be quite difficult to work out *who* it is who has said something, making it necessary for you to work back to the last identified speech to be sure about the identity of the speaker.

The text may simply say 'George replied' or 'Alice spoke reflectively' before or after the actual words. More often, however, there will be sentences which will comment on what the characters are thinking while they are speaking. This makes the passage more complex, adding analysis of character and situation, as well as perhaps some further elements of narrative, to the passage. Be aware of this complex mixed purpose while you are reading, and always give special attention to short sentences between elements of conversation, as they may convey a lot of information in a very short space.

Descriptive prose

The main purpose here is to give an account of a geographical location, character or other phenomenon rather than to recount a series of events. It's unlikely that you'll have a piece of prose to comment on which does nothing other than describe, but description will often form a component of more complex writing. Writing about other countries or geographical exploration, for example, may well have a strong descriptive content; so, too, may writing about personal experiences such as learning to fly or feeling strong emotions.

Learning to tell when the descriptive shades off into the analytical or emotional is something which will come with experience. So, too, will the skill of knowing to what *use* apparently simple description is being put. Often, for example, a description of weather conditions will be in part a metaphor for a mood or feeling, or a preparation for an event or series of events to follow shortly in the piece of writing. In this way, descriptive writing is often more complex than it seems. Whenever you read a passage which appears to be largely descriptive, ask yourself whether the description could also have another, larger meaning as well as its surface one.

Atmospheric

This sort of writing is closely related to the descriptive. Very often, novelists wish to create a mood or atmosphere to prepare for or enhance the effect of a particular event; often, too, a travel writer will wish to convey not only the appearance of, say, a remote valley, but also to give an idea of the peculiar nature of being there.

Atmospheric writing may well make use of figurative language to make its effect, but not always; moods and feelings can be conveyed just as well by hard, apparently factual writing as by chains of imaginative images, so be aware that the style of writing such as this is not always ornate and flowery.

Explanatory prose

This is writing which seeks to explain. The subject might be a particular principle or concept, or the operation of a process.

Since writing of this kind is often found in the sciences or social sciences, or in writing which tries to give reasons for historical events and processes, it often occurs in combination with other kinds of writing. A passage might, for example, begin with a narrative of a sequence of events – perhaps with some atmospheric writing to create a sense of immediacy in the reader – and then move on to some explicative writing to attempt to explain the process just described.

As previous sections have stressed, you need to be aware of the changing tone of the passage to show how it may shift from descriptive to atmospheric and then to explicative, all with the aim of discussing fully a particular sequence of events.

Discursive prose

The aim of discursive writing is to present a logical argument. Each stage is presented with clarity and precision, and the overall intention is to clarify the logical sequence by stating firmly:

the individual points;
the relationship they bear to each other;
the larger truths which evolve when the separate points are combined;
the final conclusion of this logical process.

Occasionally you may be asked to explain the stages of a logical development of this sort. To do so demands careful reading in order to separate each strand, and careful planning: take plenty of notes, listing the stages and clarifying the progression. Do not begin your final version until you are sure that you have a clear idea of each stage, the way it is related to the others and the overall logical progress.

Other kinds of writing

You may also come across writing of other sorts – comic, analytic, critical, meditative or instructional, for example. The main aim, remember, is not simply to *identify* a passage by hanging one of these labels round its neck, but to *use* your awareness of its purpose to clarify your knowledge of its aim and techniques.

Above all, remember that a passage may change in nature and aim during its course – just as the situation may change in a piece of dramatic writing.

READING A PROSE PASSAGE (EXAM)

Approaching a prose passage in an exam is very similar to the process of reading a poem or dramatic excerpt which has been discussed under these headings. While reading, be aware of any specific demands made by the question – does it ask, for example, for an account of the argument of the passage, or an outline of the techniques and features which make it suitable as the opening of a novel?

With this firmly – but not exclusively – in mind, read through the passage in detail. Look out for the features discussed in the first part of this chapter – diction, tone, rhythm and so on – and also for the various kinds and purposes of prose listed above. Develop an awareness of the individual 'moment' and its relation to the whole, and the way in which the expression of the writing matches its content. Ask yourself, too, how the passage changes in nature or intent as it progresses.

While you are reading, you need to take notes in the way discussed under Notes in the drama section.

1 Jot down points as they occur to you.
2 Make pattern notes or lists – whichever technique you find best.
3 Underline or highlight key words on the passage.
4 Number your points.

While you are doing this, after you have read the passage several times, finalise your own interpretation, based on the hypothesis you will have been developing and modifying in your earlier readings. If the questions ask for your response, make sure that you are clear about your own feelings and attitudes to the passage. Then write your appreciation, using the techniques and approaches laid out under poetry.

Comparing prose passages

Some examining boards may set a question which asks you to *compare* two passages of prose. To do this fully, you need to read both with equal care, and to use the techniques of critical comparison discussed with reference to poetry.

Throughout the process of reading and writing remember to bring the two passages together, showing similarities and differences between them in a clear and quite explicit fashion. Only if you do this will you fulfil the demands of the question. Don't approach one passage and then the other one separately.

READING A NOVEL

When most of us read a novel for recreation, we try hard to become closely involved in the world it creates. People talk of 'really getting into a good book', and the most popular novels are those which allow people to escape into the alternative reality they offer. When you're reading a novel for study purposes, however, you need to read it in rather a different way.

Never forget that it's written by a novelist, who is inventing the world that is being written about and controlling the characters who inhabit it. This enables him or her to use the framework of the novel in a lot of ways – to discuss ideas, explore human relationships, make historical or philosophical points, or be satirical, for example.

First reading

When you begin to study a novel, you should read it through fairly quickly to get a general idea of what it's about. This can be a little difficult if you're not used to reading long novels – and a Victorian novel can be easily 800 pages in length. But don't be daunted.

Try to timetable your reading – so many chapters each day, for example. Many eighteenth and nineteenth century novels are divided into separate 'books' or parts: try to read each one of these as a single unit in a fairly concentrated time-span, so that you can hold larger bits of the novel in your mind.

By all means get involved with the plot to the extent of wondering what happens next, but don't get *too* engrossed. Always remember the directing consciousness of the writer who planned it – this isn't 'real life' but a work of art that you're reading.

Think about the way the novel is written. This doesn't only mean style and language, although these are important – but also the themes and ideas which you think the novelist might be discussing. Don't, as yet, spend too long on this, but have these areas of thought always there at the back of your mind when reading.

Detailed reading

Now you should go through all the processes mentioned under the heading **study skills**, looking closely at the way that the expression and themes are developed in each stage of the novel.

While you are doing this, take notes in the manner suggested under the heading **drama**, recording points of interest as they come up in your exploration of the text. Just what you might find here is explored in more detail in the section 'What to Look For'.

You may find it easier to take notes by writing on the text itself, perhaps using the approach suggested in Fig. S.5. Be careful, though: you'll have at some stage to draw together the points you make about individual chapters, and it might be easier to start taking separate notes right from the start – a sheaf of papers is much easier to work through than a large, bulky novel when you're looking for one specific point. (**Notes**).

A detailed reading of a novel is bound to take time. Even the shortest novel will probably take three weeks to work through in the necessary depth – perhaps by working through it in classes and then consolidating your work in the evenings and writing essays on important aspects and themes. A full-length Victorian or eighteenth-century novel will take longer; so don't be too impatient when studying a novel. Take it gently, and give yourself plenty of time for the ideas and their treatment to sink in.

Reading to revise

Once you've read the book through, first to grasp what happens, and then to undertake detailed reading and study, it's a good idea to draw together your work by again reading through the whole novel quickly. A good approach is to set aside a whole weekend and to just read the novel. You'll find that this will bring together the work very effectively, and help you to grasp its themes and development more completely than if you spread the third reading over a longer period.

This is something that you should do when you've just finished the detailed reading stage. When you come to revise the work, perhaps after not having read it for a few months, you should try the same approach: shut yourself away and just read through the novel rapidly, using your notes to refresh your memory of the ideas and themes you noted when studying it in detail.

At this stage, too, you might like to make a 'map' of the novel – an outline which tells you very briefly what happens in each chapter and lists any other important features so that you know where they come from and can find them quickly when you need to. More advice is given on this under **study skills**, and **revision**. It's a useful technique, when you're revising, as it helps you to get an overall grasp of the novel.

USING ADAPTATIONS

Many novels have been adapted into different forms. Stage plays, films and radio performances have frequently been made of well known (and some less well known) novels, and properly used these can be of value to you when revising. But see **adaptations** for a warning about the limitations of many adaptations.

Narrative voice

Who is telling the story has a considerable effect on what the story is like.

1 Omniscient Narrator – story told by a figure who is not identified.
2 An identified story- teller.
3 First-person narrative – named after the grammatical term 'first-person', meaning 'I'.

(See **narrative voice**)

When you are reading you should always make sure that you know *who* is telling the story, and what effect this has on the novel as a whole in terms of the view we are given of events, the tone of voice that is used, and the attitudes that are presented.

Narrative stance

As well as who is speaking or writing the narrative, you need to know his or her attitude towards it. (See **narrative stance**)

WRITING ABOUT NOVELS

When you're writing about a novel, you need to plan and structure your essay in exactly the same way as when writing about a play or a collection of poems. There are, however, some other points to remember.

1 Don't tell the story

It's easy to get bogged down in narrative when you're trying to answer a question, simply because you want to explain where a theme is covered or how an attitude is shown and need to refer closely to the text. Remember, though, that the examiner will know the story well and will need only the shortest suggestion of the passage you mean.

Avoid narrative by always making your point *first*, and then citing evidence from the text to support it. Make sure, too, that the idea or concept is the main clause of the sentence, and the evidence is a subordinate clause like this:

> Greene's use of symbolic detail, shown for example in Scobie's rusty handcuffs, is a major technique in the novel.

This will ensure that you get the balance right and do not write long accounts of the story of the novel, for which you'll get no reward in the exam.

2 Don't write about characters as people

As the last section made clear, you won't be asked to write about characters as real people. You may be asked *how* a novelist creates a character, or what the character adds to the discussion of a theme or idea in the novel, in which case you need to treat the characters very much within this context and not spend any time on unnecessary description.

3 Avoid 'background'

As with any other kind of text, you should not spend time in writing accounts of the novelist's circumstances when the novel was produced, or the historical setting in which it is placed, or any other elements of its 'background'. As always, go straight to the text.

4 Use the present tense

When writing about a novel, always write in the *present tense*. Don't for example, say:

> Pip's first meeting with Magwitch on the marshes showed the impact the convict was to have on him.

but instead:

> Pip's first meeting with Magwitch on the marshes *shows* the impact the convict *is* to have on him.

This will make the writing much clearer and also show that you understand the existence of the novel as a work of literature, not just a 'story' or sequence of events from real life.

Reading and studying a novel is not easy. For all of the reasons made clear in this chapter, it demands close attention and careful thought, in order to understand the main themes and ideas being covered as well as the writer's attitude to them. It also demands the ability to select passages which are representative of important ideas, and to write clearly and briefly to establish the key points in the narrative, so freeing you to discuss these ideas in your essay.

As always, the basis of success is close textual reading. Follow the advice given here about careful, detailed reading, and you should find that your knowledge of the prescribed novels will deepen considerably.

Types of question on prose

Questions on prose works will be of three main types.

1 Questions which give you a passage from a text, with an accompanying question.
In most cases, the aim of these is to get you to read a passage closely, to write about it in detail and to *relate* it to the text as a whole. You may, for example, be asked to show what it contributes to the discussion of a particular theme,

how it is typical of the writer's use of humour, or how it demonstrates the tone or approach of the whole work.

Tackle these questions by reading the whole text and by identifying the specific features it demonstrates. Then find examples of these in the rest of the work, plan your answer under concepts or techniques, and write the essay.

Sometimes, you will be asked two questions about a passage and its relation to the work. Generally, the first will be longer and more complex, the second shorter and more straightforward. You can always tell the relative importance of such questions by looking at the number of marks allotted to each section. If the first has, say, fifteen and the second five, you will know the first part should be three times as long as the second – a very rough guide which should help you to plan the time you spend on each. Remember, too, that you will probably be able to answer the second in two or three sentences – so don't spend too long searching out hidden significances in the question: there usually aren't any.

In plain text papers, the questions will generally be of this sort, except that you will be given the page or chapter numbers for the passage involved instead of having it printed on the exam paper.

2 Questions with a quotation.

Like similar questions on poetry or plays, these will make a statement about the work and then give you instructions about how to treat it – either to discuss it in general, or to relate it to a more specific theme or part of the text.

As before, you must *read* the quotation carefully and make sure that you understand it before thinking about the task that you're asked to perform in response to it. Once you have done this, you need to work out exactly what you're asked to do. This will usually be one of the two alternatives given above. Then, think about the work as a whole, make a list of points each with supporting evidence from the text, and write your essay.

3 Questions on a particular aspect or theme of the book.

These are usually fairly straightforward – if you know the text you should have no difficulty in using this knowledge by bringing it to bear on the topic given.

Once again, read the question carefully to define the topic; think about the book and make a list of points which *relate* it to the given subject; support each one with textual reference or quotation; and then write the essay.

◀ Diction, Drama, Essays, Revision, Study skills ▶

PROSODY (AND PROSODIC FEATURES)

Prosody originally referred to **metre** in verse. In linguistics it refers to stress and intonation in speech.

Phoneme theory identifies and describes individual sound units that have meaning. When these units are produced in sequences they also exhibit variation in amplitude (loudness), tempo (pace or speed), rhythm and pitch (rising and falling intonation). *Prosodic features* are sometimes referred to as *supra-segmental* because they cross over individual phonemes in their effects.

PYRRHIC

◀ Metre ▶

QUATRAIN

A four-line unit of verse within a longer stanza. Many sonnets, for example, are formed of three quatrains and a couplet, like this example from the beginning of a sonnet by John Donne:

> Death, be not proud, though some have called thee
> Mighty and dreadful, for thou are not so;
> For those whom thou think'st thou dost overthrow
> Die not, poor death; nor yet canst thou kill me.

QUESTIONS

SHORT ANSWER QUESTIONS

If the paper has a *short-answer question*, in which you are asked several questions on a given passage, it makes sense to do this first. It gets your concentration working, as it makes you think about small, significant details in a passage and their relation to the whole. It also means that you can get something *done* fairly quickly at the start: even if it's only a question which earns you two or three marks, it is still an achievement, and this will build your confidence and get you into your stride for the more arduous questions to follow.

Some papers start with a compulsory section which is a series of *short questions on a passage* from the text you have studied. This is most common in papers on Shakespeare or Chaucer, although it can appear on other papers – check your syllabus and past papers carefully. This type of question should not be confused with the type of essay question which gives you a passage to discuss as typical of the work as a whole, or a poem to discuss as typical of a selection you have studied.

The short questions on a passage come in various types. They may ask for:

Comments on the meaning or effect of *individual words*.
Comments on the meaning or effect of *phrases*.
Analyses of *particular kinds of language* – chains of images or metaphors, for example – which are found in the passage.
An explanation of the *place of this passage in the text as a whole*.
Comments on the *main themes or issues* the passage discusses.
Discussion of the *dramatic effect* of the passage.

You may be asked three or four questions of one or more of these types, or two questions about themes, languages, character or the function of the passage which will require longer answers.

The essential way to prepare for such questions is by knowing the text thoroughly by repeated reading and analysis.

Reading the passage

The first thing to do when you see a question like this is to spend quite a lot of time *reading the passage*. Your first instinct will be to get something on paper as quickly as possible, especially if – as is often the case – this question is the first one on the paper. Resist the temptation. Your answers will be superficial and limited, or even downright wrong, if they are based on a superficial reading of the passage. So, read the passage very carefully.

How long should you spend reading? It's not possible to give a hard and fast rule here, but if you have thirty minutes for this question you could well spend ten of them reading the passage *before* you tackle the questions.

How do I read? This question isn't as daft as it sounds – reading a passage in an exam isn't at all the same as reading a newspaper or a novel for recreation. Try to follow this approach:

a) Read it through quickly just to get familiar with it.
b) Read it again more slowly. While you do this, ask yourself questions to aid concentration and get the analytical process started. Here are some to try:
   Where does it come in the play or tale?
   How does it advance the development of particular themes?
   What does it *add* to the text as a whole – a key change in the plot, a theme treated in a new way, a character revealed, a new strand of imagery?
   What do individual words and images mean? What effect do they have on the passage?
   How does the writer use sound, rhythm, diction, tone and the other techniques to create different effects?
c) Read it again fairly quickly to pull together the ideas you've had when reading in more detail.

Don't be alarmed – this doesn't mean that you have to write a full-length critical analysis of the piece in your head. But it *does* mean that you should be alert to all these things while you're reading. Notice why a particular word is used; whether it's part of a pattern of language and how everything comes together in this passage and how it, in turn, contributes to the progress of the text as a whole.

Just thinking like this will sharpen your critical faculties a good deal and prepare you for the sort of detailed work you'll be asked to do in the questions. It shouldn't take too long, either – in the concentrated atmosphere of an exam, you can get a lot done in ten minutes.

Reading the questions

Once you have read the *passage* carefully, you need to read all of the *questions*. Don't start to answer the first one before you have read them all. You need to read them all for these reasons:

a) to work out what each one wants by way of answer;
b) to make sure that you don't answer two questions in one answer – something that is easily done. For example, if the third or fourth question asks you what the passage contributes to the imagery of the whole play, don't explain this in an earlier question which asks you just to explain the function of **one** image in this passage;
c) to be sure that you know how important each question is, by looking at the number of marks it has next to it. Questions which have only one or two marks will need only a sentence or even a word or two for a satisfactory answer; those which have five, eight or ten marks will need a short paragraph.

Again, don't be alarmed. You can do this in a matter of seconds in an exam and just knowing what kind of things are required will save you wasted effort, repeated material and the possible loss of nerve that this might bring on at the start of your paper.

Let us illustrate the various types of short answer questions by using the passage below and the questions which follow.

Falstaff.

If I be not ashamed of my soldiers, I am a soused gurnet. I have misused the King's press damnably. I have got, in exchange of a hundred and fifty soldiers, three hundred and odd pounds. I press me none but good householders, yeomen's sons; inquire me out contracted bachelors, such as had been asked twice on the baness such a commodity of warm slaves as had a lief hear the devil as a drum, such as fear the report of a caliver worse than a struck fowl or a hurt wild duck. I pressed me none but such toasts-and-butter, with hearts in their bellies no bigger than pins' heads, and they have bought out their services; and now my whole charge consists of ancients, corporals, lieutenants, gentlemen of companies – slaves as ragged as Lazarus in the painted cloth, where the glutton's dogs licked his sores; and such as indeed were never soldiers, but discarded unjust serving-men, younger sons to younger brothers, revolted tapsters, and ostlers trade-fall'n; the cankers of a calm world and a long peace; ten times more dishonourable ragged than an old fazed ancient; and such have I to fill up the rooms of them as have bought out their services that you would think that I had a hundred and fifty tattered prodigals lately come from swine-keeping, from eating draff and husks.

i) Explain 'a soused gurnet' (l.1), and 'Lazarus in the painted cloth' (l.10–11). *(3)*
ii) Comment on the images of animals in lines 6–8 *(3)*
iii) Why does Falstaff want soldiers? *(1½)*
iv) Comment briefly on the statement that, in this passage, Falstaff is no longer a comic character. *(5)*

Questions on words and phrases

These can ask you to do various things. The simplest are those which ask you to 'explain' or 'translate', but these are getting less likely. For such questions you should simply say what the phrases mean. Consider the first part of question (i) on the passage quoted above for example:

Q: Explain a 'soused gurnet' (line 1).
A: A soused gurnet is a pickled fish.

More complicated questions can ask about the *effect* of a particular phrase in its context. These need slightly longer answers, to make quite clear how the phrases work. Take the following example:

Q: What is the effect of 'a soused gurnet' (line 1)?
A: A gurnet was a fish with a big head and a small body which when soused or pickled was a great delicacy. It is ridiculous to think of Falstaff like this, and so it makes the idea that he is ashamed of his soldiers quite absurd.

This is a longer answer, but is still only a single paragraph of a few lines, and it gets across both the meaning of the phrase and its effect in its context.

Questions on imagery

You might be asked about one particular image, or about a chain of images or metaphors which occurs in a passage. In the earlier passage, for example, you were asked in question (ii);

Q: Comment on the images of animals in lines 6–8.

First you need to *find* the animal images here. If you've read the passage carefully in the way suggested above, you should already have noticed them, so it's only a matter of going through and finding them.

But just finding the images isn't enough. You need to say what they *do* – what particular shade of meaning or effect they add to the main point of the passage. Here, what's happening is that Falstaff is talking about his soldiers in terms of animals – a struck fowl and a hurt wild duck. These are animals which suggest fear and flight, rather than courage and fight, so the comparison makes the soldiers sound very weak.

A good answer to this question might go like this:

A: Falstaff says he has chosen only people who fear a 'caliver' or musket as much as would a 'struck fowl' or 'hurt wild duck'. This makes clear that they are weak, cowardly people, who willingly 'bought out their services' – paid to be released from fighting.

This answer does three things:

it *identifies* the images;
it *explains* the way they colour the impression we get of the objects they are used to describe – here, the soldiers;
it *puts them in context* by showing how they contribute to the larger meaning and progression of the passage.

An answer like this would get full marks; one which did only the first two would probably get two-thirds; one which simply identified the images would get only a third of the marks, or perhaps less.

Questions on the passage's place in the whole text

You *won't* usually be asked to give a detailed explanation of where a passage comes in a play, although you might have to say briefly what happens just before it and what comes immediately afterwards. But you might well be asked to explain the importance of the passage in the text as a whole – say how it contributes to themes and ideas, or develops a pattern of language, for example.

To do this, you have to know where it comes in the whole play or tale. But you do not need to say this *unless* it is essential in making clear the importance of the passage.

Always give the way in which the passage is important and *then* give your reason for saying this, if necessary showing where it comes in the play. That way, you'll keep the priorities right – the idea first, then the evidence for it. For example:

A: This passage is important in showing Falstaff as the comic figure he is throughout the play. His language is comic in its references to animals, and his references to the kind of people he presses introduce the familiar element of comic trickery and dishonour.

Keep your answers **short** – don't go into long, complicated explanations or give long narratives of the story. Usually all the questions on a passage together will be worth half the marks of an essay question, so they should be less than half the length of an essay. For most people, that means about a side and a half of A4 paper at the very most, and often half a page per question will be enough if you make your points clearly.

First, make a rough *list of reasons* why you think it is important or what it adds to the play. This can be done in single words – comedy; irony; character extension; suspense – which will be enough to establish the point.

Secondly, find some *evidence* to support each point – a line which is funny, an ironic statement, a way in which a character is extended, an element of suspense. Here you may need to refer to earlier or later stages in the play – but be careful. Make sure that you really use the references and don't just tell the story.
Thirdly, get the points in *order*. This may be no more than just scribbling a number next to each key word you wrote down, but it's worth doing as it makes sure that your points are connected and keep to the point of the question.
Finally, you can *write* your answer, following the points clearly and stating the ideas first before supporting each one with evidence.

Here's an example, again based on the earlier passage:

Q: How is this passage important in the play?
A: The passage is important because it shows the character of Falstaff within the changing circumstances of the move towards war at the end of the play. Falstaff's character is still bluff, comic and self-interested, shown in his forthright delight in using his powers as a recruiter to his own advantage (II. 1–3) and his images of animals (ll. 6–7) and food and drink (ll.1, 7–8). The language is still that of the low life we have encountered in the Boar's Head Tavern where Hal visits Falstaff. Yet the audience knows that things have changed. In the scene immediately before this one, we have heard Vernon describe the army raised by Prince Hal as 'gorgeous as the sun at midsummer', suggesting that he is now too serious to take part in Falstaff's joking. The passage also adds suspense, in coming before the preparations for war in the rebel camp. In all these ways it is an important contribution to the play's dramatic movement.

Questions on themes and issues discussed

You may be asked to say what *themes* and *issues* of the play are discussed in the passage you are given. Here again, you should make a list of them, or a set of pattern notes. Single words will usually be enough for each point; write them down with a reference to the evidence which supports them, get them in order and then write the answer.

Remember that there may be only one or two themes which a passage discusses or extends, so don't spend a lot of time looking for others once you've found a couple of strong, firm ideas. Here's an example based on our passage:

Q: What themes of the play does the passage continue?
A: The main theme is the discussion of the idea of honour. The soldiers Falstaff collected are very different from the courageous army of Prince Hal which Vernon has just described. This shows that Falstaff is more concerned with comfort than with fighting.

Notice that only one theme has been discussed here. That's fine; the passage is only concerned with one. Other passages may require longer answers; again, be guided by the number of marks available.

Questions on dramatic effectiveness

You may be asked how the passage is *dramatically effective* – that is, how it succeeds in the theatre.

To answer this question, you need to think about how the scene would look on stage, and how the audience would respond. Spend a few minutes trying to picture the stage in your mind. Then jot down a few key words (Fig. Q.1), find some evidence to support each one, and get them in order.

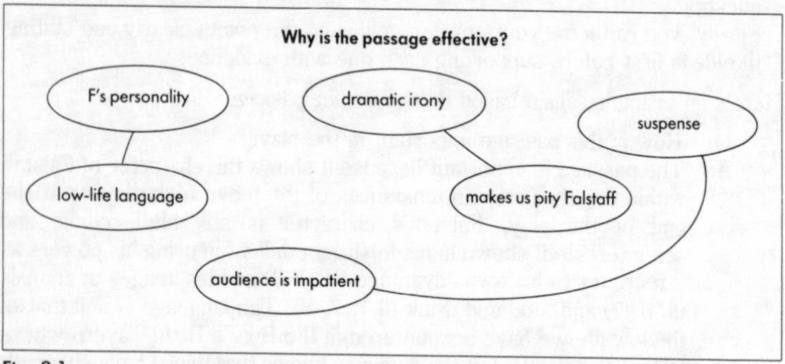

Fig. Q.1

Now write your answer, like this:

Q: How is the passage effective on stage?
A: The passage is mainly effective because of the force of Falstaff's personality which comes across in this monologue. He has completely overturned the proper procedure for recruiting soldiers, and talks of them in the low-life language of the Boar's Head Tavern. Yet there is also dramatic irony in the passage's effect. The audience knows that Falstaff's behaviour is quite out of place in the coming fighting and this makes us feel differently towards him – perhaps with pity or with impatience. A third way in which the passage is effective is in adding suspense to the play. We know that fighting is about to take place, but Falstaff's leisurely speech holds up the action and makes us want to know what will happen next.

Questions on a passage will normally come in a clear order, with the more straightforward first – those on single words or phrases – and the more complicated at the end. Go through them in the correct order, as this will help you to go from single details to a larger view of the passage. Questions about a single word or image should be answered first, as they help you to look at the passage in detail. Later ones will ask you to draw together readings of many such words – so it makes sense to get the sequence right.

Here we have looked at most of the kinds of question which might arise, using the passage from *Henry IV* Part 1 as an example and inventing questions of the main types which will come up. In a real exam, you might have four questions, one of which might be of the more complex type we have outlined, demanding a side or so for a full answer. Alternatively, you might find a passage with just two questions, both of the longer sort, which will require answers of about a side and a half each, and so on.

ESSAY QUESTIONS

The first thing to do when approaching an *essay question* is to *read* it carefully and thoroughly. If you mis-read it the first time you look at it, the likelihood is that you'll continue to mis-read it – so make sure that you get it right.

Different kinds of essays, and the responses they require, can often be identified by the **verb** which gives the instructions. Those which ask you simply to 'list' for example would be fairly straightforward, but it's unlikely that you'll see any as simple as that on an English paper. Instead, you'll probably be asked to analyse, discuss or explain, generally with reference to an idea stated in the question.

Often you'll encounter questions which are quotations or statements about the text. You may be asked 'How far do you agree?' or 'To what extent is this true?', for example. In almost all cases, these demand what is often called a 'Yes, but . . . ' answer. They are true up to a point, but need to be limited and qualified.

Be aware, too, of what the question does *not* say. Look at this question:

> 'The main significance of *The Rainbow* is in its picture of North-country working life.' How far is this true?

You could answer this by giving a long account of how the novel treats working life. But this wouldn't be a full answer. To answer completely, you'd have to think of other significances of the novel – as an exploration of human relationships, for example, or as a study of the relationship between humankind and nature. You'd then need to evaluate the statement, to say whether or not this really was the main significance, and, if it was not, which of the others was the major theme of the novel.

You should also be sure not to confuse what the question says with what you think it says. It is easy, for example, to think that this question

> Discuss Wordsworth's concept of nature in *The Prelude* Books 1 and 2

means simply

> Discuss nature in *The Prelude* Books 1 and 2.

The former is concerned with philosophical attitudes; the latter simply with a catalogue of geographical features.

Remember, then, that reading the question is of the utmost importance; a few seconds spent concentrating hard on working out what the question really means here can be immensely valuable in ensuring the relevance of your answer.

Planning, writing and checking

An exam essay, like any other piece of writing, consists of three stages – planning, writing and checking. Of these the most important is probably the first since, if you don't have the ideas clearly formed and well ordered before you start, you run the risk of omitting key points or including irrelevant ones. Try to divide the time available for each essay so that you have time for all three activities, and try to keep calm and give yourself enough time to plan – it pays dividends in the long run.

Planning an essay

The process of essay planning is described in depth under the heading **essays**: in an exam, you simply go through it a little more quickly, using your memory as the source of information rather than a detailed reading of the text. You may feel tempted to go straight into an essay, as the time is very limited. But resist the temptation for just a few minutes and make a clear, detailed plan which you can follow when you write the essay. This has many advantages:

1 It lets you sort out all the points first without the added task of having to write clearly about them.
2 You can put them down in any order, and then change it to the most suitable one, before you write.
3 You can cross out irrelevant points without wasting time.
4 Once you've got a plan to follow, you can relax and concentrate only on writing the essay.
5 If you make mistakes here, you can change things quickly; if you make a mistake in an essay, you will have lost time and it may be difficult to get back on target and finish the paper.

Your plan should include the main points together with brief details of quotations and other references to make in the essay, as shown in the illustration (see Fig. Q.2). In this way, *before* you start writing, you will be able to work out a clear, reasoned argument, to check the relevance of your points and to list quotations, all in a matter of moments, leaving yourself free to write the essay and to concentrate on expressing yourself clearly.

The importance of relevance

What you *say* in your plan will of course depend on the question, but it's vital that you remember one thing: relevance is all. The aim of the examiner is to get you to show your knowledge of the text by applying it to the issues raised in the questions. If all goes well, you should know the text; understand the question and use your knowledge in order to answer the question.

The whole process, then, is one of **application** of knowledge to the given topic or statement. If you do **not** make your answer relevant, however much you know the text, you will not do well. As a result, you should **avoid** the following:

1 'Introductions' which give the story of a novel;
2 Worse still, lengthy biographies of the writer or accounts of how the text came to be written;
3 Summaries of critical interpretations of the text which are not related to the question;

4 Lists of quotations which are not used to make a point.

Your essay should instead be structured around eight or ten key points, each supported by a quotation or close reference to the text. Do not go through the text in chronological order, telling the story as you make points about it. You can safely assume that the examiner knows the story; instead, organise your answer around ideas – make the point first, and then give the evidence to support it.

Writing the essay

The process of writing is really the process of fleshing out the plan into a finished piece of prose. Try to follow this advice: write in a clear, straightforward style; make frequent reference to the text, either by quoting it or by referring to episodes within it; use the words of the question frequently to show that you are really engaging with the issues it raises.

"The sad elegiac note is seldom absent from Tennyson's poetry."
Discuss.

Often present – not always a note, sometimes entire subject matter.

1. Elegiac 'note'
   i) 'Rizpah' a note: narrative poetry
   ii) 'Passing of Arthur' – lamentation of Arthur's death. 'From the great deep to the great deep he goes': only note: obedience contemplation and action.
   iii) 'Lotus Eaters': lamentation of war's existence in 'confusion worse than death';
   note: Richness, languidity, sweet exoticness. Contemplation worse than death.

2. In some, more than just a 'note'
   i) In Memoriam: entire poem an elegy
   ii) 'Garden of Swanston' – entirely concerned with the 'three men have I loved'.

3. Absence of elegiac note: 'Ulysses' – more concern, dissatisfaction, yearning 'I cannot rest from travel'.

Conclusion:

Sad elegiac note sometimes present – often though more than a note – not present at all in 'Ulysses'.

Fig. Q.2

As you have already established the points you are going to make in the plan, in the essay you can write a very brief outline of your approach in the first paragraph. This will give the examiner an indication of your main ideas, and also show that you have considered the points carefully. In addition, should you be unable to finish the essay you will gain some credit for stating these ideas at the outset. Similarly, the final paragraph should summarise the points you have made or reach a clear conclusion in direct response to the question. Other points about essay-writing are made under the separate heading **essays**, they are all of importance in an exam.

Checking your essay

Always try to read through an essay after you have finished to check for errors. You may, for example, have inadvertently used one character's name instead of another's, or made a statement which you thought was clear but, on second reading, is really rather ambiguous.

There will not be much time for this, however, and you may prefer to go on and write the second essay before going back to check the first. This has several advantages:

It gives you time to move away from the essay before checking it – if you were to read it immediately after finishing it, you would probably read what you *thought* you said, rather than what is actually there;

It provides a short break from writing roughly in the middle of the exam – a very welcome breather before the final onslaught on the remaining questions.

If you follow these principles and, above all, if you know your texts thoroughly, you should be able to answer all of the questions in the time allotted.

With carefully-planned study and revision, you should be able to approach the exam without too much terror. Once you have started to write, try to relax – remember, you have been working for this for several months, so you might as well enjoy it!

◀ Drama, Essays, Poetry, Prose, Revising, Study skills ▶

QUIRK, RANDOLPH

The grammatical scholarship undertaken by this distinguished British linguist (b 1920) is discussed under **grammar**.

In 1960 he began a survey of how educated, adult, native speakers of English in Britain use their language. In particular he was interested in the grammatical structures they used, and from the data collected he compiled his comprehensive grammar of the English language.

He also wrote a book for students and teachers of English called *The Use of English* (1962). It remains an excellent, simple introduction to some helpful linguistic concepts. In it he discusses, for example, the notion that English words may be divided into two kinds: *lexical* and *grammatical*. Lexical words have recognisable content and external reference – they are the bulk of nouns, verbs, adjectives, adverbs that make up an English dictionary. They are sometimes called *content words*. Grammatical words connect lexical words into the sentences or utterances we wish to make. Articles, conjunctions, prepositions are examples of words which have no identifiable content meaning but which have specific grammatical functions. They are sometimes called *function words*.

QUOTATIONS

A quotation is a short passage taken from a longer text. When you are writing about a text you have studied, you should use quotations to support your points. Get into the habit of remembering short phrases which reveal a feature so that you can incorporate them in your writing. Remember that there is no value in just quoting long passages – you have to *use* them to demonstrate an important point about the text. The following is a passage from a critical essay which shows how to set out quotations, and how they can be used to support a point or idea in your writing.

1 In many ways 'Strange meeting' is a poignant and confused completion of 'Hyperion', the fourth and final book Keats himself never wrote. In simplified terms, the major theme of Hyperion is the process of evolutionary change through succesive generations, exemplified in the ousting of the Titanic Gods by the Olympian to produce a finer race of deities, a new loveliness at the expense of the power, beauty and strength of that preceding. The Keatsian themes of beauty and the vale of soul-making are strongly present in 'Strange meeting' – the war is even referred to as 'Titanic' – and it is in the way in which they contribute to the notion of rebirth through sacrifice and death that the poem is most profoundly effective. A Keatsian hope for beauty and its intrinsic sadness is imminent in Owen's idea and expression:

> I went hunting wild
> After the wildest beauty in the world,
> 3 Which lies not calm in eyes, or braided hair,
> But mocks the steady running of the hour,
> And if it grieves, grieves richlier than here.

Yet there is little hope that a better race will emerge from the loss
2 of this beauty. There is some, certainly, in the line 'Now men will go content with what they spoiled'. But the notion of future content seems short-lived, and in any case refers to a renewal of the existing pattern which has been destroyed by war – perhaps the Arcadian England once again – rather than to a better state made possible by its sacrifice. And the inevitability of a future and communal failure is made clear in the lines which follow it:

> Or, discontent, boil bloody and be spilled.
> 3 They will be swift, with swiftness of the tigress
> None will break ranks, though nations trek from progress.

Here the move towards barbarity – the trek from progress – is national, and unbroken by personal advance or feeling.

In this light, the final 'Let us sleep now' connotes nothing more than resignation, and the whole poem is poignant because of its despair in the face not only of universal slaughter and the destruction of the hope of beauty, but also in the total absence of any movement towards anything finer and better, as in the case with the Hyperion poems. For, despite its sadness, 'Hyperion' is ultimately a hopeful poem, and the apparent hopelessness in Owen is all the more shocking in comparison.

Yet despite this, the poem is hopeful.

---

1 Title of poem is given in single inverted commas. Underline titles of novels, plays or other long works.

2 Short quotations – anything from a single word to two lines – can be given in the text, as part of the syntax of the sentence involved.

3 Longer quotations (three lines or more) are indented, and presented in their original layout. The text of the essay is not interrupted by such quotations – that is, they come at the end of a sentence.

By the way, avoid substantial omissions from passages quoted, but where a word or two are omitted, use three dots (. . .) to show this.

R

RADIO

◀ Adaptations ▶

READING

◀ Drama, Poetry, Prose ▶

REALISM

REALISM IN THE NOVEL

This means the attempt to present the events as if they are really happening, with no presence or comment from the narrator – rather like the presentation of events in a traditional thriller or romance novel, where there is never any question of the role of the narrator but instead we are just told what happened next.

Realism can also refer to a particular school of novel-writing, generally considered to have begun with George Eliot in England and Balzac in France.

◀ Naturalism and realism ▶

RECEIVED PRONUNCIATION (RP)

◀ Accent ▶

REFERENTIAL MEANING

Referents are the objects in the world to which words refer. They could be thought of as the content of lexical words (see **grammar**). It is mistaken to imagine however that referential meaning is the only kind of meaning in language. If it were, how could we explain the meaning of words such as:

> if, should, although, despite, but (all grammatical words)?

Naming and labelling are essential functions of a language but referential meanings have a limited role. Language can do much more than refer to the external world, it can create imaginary words in our minds and it even constructs what we think of as reality.

REIFICATION (VERB 'TO REIFY')

This is a term used by sociologists and psychologists almost as a warning to their readers, their clients and themselves. It is an example of the linguistic process known as nominalisation whereby 'things' are made out of verbs and adjectives. It is also an example of abstraction (see **abstract**).

The word reification comes from the Latin word 're' which means 'thing'. Literally it means turning a quality, or an action into a thing. More particularly it refers to treating something which is abstract as a material thing and forgetting that it was only an idea, a concept, in the first place. Psychology and sociology are full of concepts that we can easily come to regard as concrete things with a separate identity rather than as abstractions or concepts:

> 'inferiority complex', 'super ego', 'cognitive dissonance'.

Reification is not unrelated to labelling whereby people are described in terms of labels attached to them:

> alcoholics, addicts, schizophrenics, manic-depressives.

> In recent years social service officers have begun to discontinue the use of such language as 'has a drug problem' or 'has a drink problem' or 'has a personality problem', 'the family situation', 'the work situation', and employ more verbs and concrete nouns: e.g.
>
> He smokes cannabis twice a day.
> She drinks two bottles of gin a week.
> He does not like the people he lives with.
> When at home, where he lives with his wife and four teenage daughters, he becomes very depressed.
> He makes nuts and bolts in a small factory.

REVISING

Most people think about revising as something that they should do only in the period just before the exam. It's true that you should concentrate your revision in the six weeks or so before the exam; but it's also true that careful organisation of your work throughout your studies will make the process much easier and far more effective.

As you progress through your course, you should always be revising the work that you have done so far. In practice, this means going over the work you've done each day. More particularly, it means pulling together the work you've done on each text as you complete it and before you go on to another one. Do this in the following way:

1 Get your notes in order

Your **notes** will be of various kinds:

notes on specific sections of the text. Taken together, these will form a continuous commentary. Make sure they are clear, legible and complete. Get them in order and copy out pages if necessary. File them and keep them safe.

notes on particular themes and topics. These may be notes that you've made in preparation for class discussion, or the outline plans for essays (see **essays, study skills**). You'll probably have eight or ten sheets of these, each covering a separate aspect of a text. Again, be sure that they're clear, legible and well-titled so that you can recognise straightaway what they are about.

notes from critical texts and commentaries which you've read. You may or may not have these; it depends on how you approach your work. If you *do*, then make sure that they are kept safe and ready for easy reference.

2 Index your notes

Make sure that you know where each sheet is and what it covers. You can do this in a small notebook, under the subject they cover, or as a card index. If you use a card index, you can briefly summarise the contents of each sheet of notes.

3 Read your notes through

Preferably in a single sitting, to refresh your memory of the work you've done. If there's anything you don't understand, check it with the text and put it right NOW. If it's not clear when you've just worked on the text, imagine how confusing it will be some months in the future when you need to revise for the exam. This process will often suggest questions which you can discuss with your teacher or lecturer.

4 Read the text through again quickly

This will bring together your work on it, in the same way as reading through a passage will crystallise the work you do in each study session.

Following these procedures will ensure that you make the best use of the work you've done, by keeping the ideas clear in your mind and the notes safe and in order for when you need them again.

After you've finished your work on a text, try not to forget it completely. Every so often, try to fix a time to look at the notes on a text you studied a few months ago, to make sure that you still remember its main features. If you made a card index, look quickly at the cards and try to recall the main points they contain.

These procedures will help to ensure that you never entirely lose contact with a text or forget about its main points, even while you're working on something different. It won't make revision nearer the exam unnecessary – but it will make it easier, because you'll be able to recall earlier material much more readily.

SORTING OUT THE DETAILS

Between eight and six weeks before the exam, you need to start thinking seriously about your preparations. Before you do any final revision, you need to sort out several basic points.

1 Check the syllabus

You will need to know the full details of the course you're following as they are laid out in the syllabus. As the exam comes closer, have another look at it. Make sure you know:

a) which texts are on which papers;
b) if there are any choices between texts;
c) whether you'll have short-answer questions on passages or essay questions on each text (questions).

This will help you in planning and carrying out your revision. If you *do* have any choices between texts, think very seriously before deciding *not* to revise some of them at all. In the exam you may find that the question on the other text is something you haven't covered, and so are unable to answer properly. It's always best to be as fully prepared as you can, and dropping a text is a very considerable risk to take – so think very carefully before you make a decision like this, and only do so under extreme circumstances.

2 Look at past papers

However detailed the syllabus, it's only past question papers which tell you exactly what the questions look like and the kind of topics that come up. Look at:

a) *the layout of the paper*. If there are alternative sections, make sure you know which you are preparing for. In the exam it's easy to get a little flustered and to mis-read the instructions, so keep the chance of a mistake to a minimum by knowing what you're expected to do in advance.
b) *the number of questions and the time allowed*. This will help you to revise by allowing you to write answers in the time you'll have in the exam – generally it works out at between 30 and 45 minutes for each question, but there are exceptions.
c) *the nature of the questions*. Find out whether you're more likely to be given an excerpt from a text as the basis of a question, or a quotation for discussion. Don't waste time trying to 'spot' questions and predict what's going to come up and base your revision on that: there's little chance that you'll be right. Instead, get a general idea of the topics and the wording used.

3 Look at an examiner's report

Most Examining Boards publish reports which say how candidates actually approached the exam in that year. These can be very useful, as they point out frequent errors and can suggest ways in which answers are more likely to gain good grades.

Planning your revision

At this stage, it's a good idea to do a dummy run of the exam. Try a few past questions and see how much you remember. Look especially at the texts you studied first – you covered them some time ago and were just learning the skills of the subject at the time, so you may need to do more work on them. When you've written the essays, look at your notes to see what you could and should have said. You might find it helpful to work with a classmate on this, to comment on each other's strong and not-so-strong points – but be gentle about it!

When you've done this, you'll know which texts need to be covered in more detail. Don't leave the ones you dislike to the last – tackle them first of all, so that you can remedy deficiencies in your knowledge and build your confidence, instead of having to tackle them just before the exam when you're tired and probably fed up with the whole thing. Nothing gives confidence so much as really knowing your material, so work here will be doubly helpful in the exam.

Make a detailed timetable showing what texts you're going to revise and when. It should cover the four or six weeks before the exam, and set out clearly what texts you will cover on particular days and times. Divide it up into periods like those you are used to at school or college, to give you a set rhythm of work. Don't expect too much, though: starting at eight in the morning and ending at ten at night solidly for four weeks may sound possible, but you won't be able to keep it up – and even if you were to, you'd find that you wouldn't take in a great deal after the first few hours of each day.

REVISION

What do you actually *do* when you revise? There are several approaches which help to bring your work together and prepare you for the exam.

1 Read the text

This is the fundamental process of all revision. However good your notes, you will still need to have a detailed, first-hand knowledge of the books themselves – so a significant part of the revision must be devoted to this. At first, read through the text quickly. Most novels can be read quickly in a day if you have read them already, and most plays in an evening.

Try to vary the approach here. Get together in groups and read through a play with each of you taking a different role – and, if you like, stopping at the end of each scene to discuss it. Read poems aloud, thinking about how they work by using language imaginatively to make their point. If you find that going to a performance of a play helps and you can find one locally, go along – but be careful not to accept it as the *only* way of performing it, and ask yourself how *you* would have directed it if given the chance.

But however you do it, remember that a *knowledge of the text* is the basis of all the questions – so anything you can do to increase that knowledge is going to be valuable at this stage.

2 Make 'maps'

These are *outlines* of the events of a novel, play or long poem. This won't be a substitute for reading the book itself, but it will help you to find particular passages quickly and to clarify the growth of themes and ideas. You could draw a diagram to 'map' a novel, showing its main concerns in a visually striking way.

Another kind of 'map' can be made by listing the chapters and their contents or striking features, like this example:

TOM JONES – section 1, Books 1–V1

Book 1	Notes and Quotes
1 Fielding as omniscient, self-conscious narrator; Human nature as theme; stress on practical philosophy	
2 Allworthy's pragmatic goodness; Bridget's sourness	
3 Tom's appearance; Deborah's pretence and suggested rejection contrasted with Allworthy's delight	
4/5 B approves; angry only with T's mother	

Notice that each chapter is summarised in terms of content or themes in a very few words, with the 'Notes' column free for critical points or references to other notes you may have on particular aspects. Going through a text and *preparing* such a map is a valuable exercise in itself. It will also provide a useful *reference* when it's finished, since it gives you a detailed and fairly rapid overview of the text, which is exactly what you need if you are to answer questions accurately and fully.

3 List key aspects

Structure your revision by making a list of eight or ten *key aspects* which you regard as essential for a knowledge of the text. Some of these may have been covered by essays that you've written; others by notes; and some will be quite new.

4 Make single-page plans

For each of these aspects or topics, make a *single-page plan* which shows anything between six and a dozen key points to make about them (**Essays Fig E.4, plans**). Each point should be supported by a quotation – followed by a page, chapter and line number, or act, scene and line number for easy identification. Add these to your notes on topics in the texts, and to your plans for essays. Eventually you should have a collection of single-sheet accounts of key areas of the text. If you like, arrange to share the work on these with a friend, dividing topics among you – but don't rely too much on other people's work. It can be an excellent way to lose a friend.

5 Meet to swap ideas

As well as for reading plays, getting together can be a useful way of getting new ideas and approaches to texts. Such meetings can be especially useful if you ask each person to prepare a little talk on one aspect of the text, or to write a single-page account of a theme. If you can, photocopy these so that everyone has a copy. Just getting together to share ideas can be very helpful and reassuring – but make sure that you pool your expertise rather than share your ignorance!

6 List passages

Making a list of short passages and quotations sounds a rather cold-blooded approach, and it's important to remember that you'll get no credit for just putting down lines from a text unless you use them appropriately to answer the question. Nevertheless, bringing together the passages you have cited in your single-page accounts can be a useful exercise, and it's much easier to learn lines if you have them on a single sheet of paper.

7 Read critical interpretations

If you're happy with your knowledge of the text, you could extend your knowledge by reading critical essays about it; **but** don't do this unless you're sure you'll understand what they say, and won't take everything they say as the *only* reading. You need to be selective when reading critics, and in absorbing what they say into your own reading of the text, as stressed earlier. It may help your revision to read something new at this stage – but it may also confuse you, so be careful.

8 Answer questions in measured time

One of the best forms of revision is *active* revision – actually doing the task for which you're preparing. In this case, simply sitting down and answering a question in measured time is both necessary and reassuring. Set aside the correct amount of time for the question, and work under strict exam conditions, without access to the text – unless it's an 'open book' examination – or to your notes. If you can, get someone else to set you a question which you won't see until you have to answer it, as this will test the depth and breadth of your revision to the full. Use an alarm clock to tell you when the time's up, and stick rigidly to the limit.

Afterwards, get someone to read through your answer. If you have a teacher to do this, that's obviously best, but a classmate can help too, by pointing out ways in which your answer might be clearer, fuller, or better supported with evidence from the text. Once again, getting together can help a lot here, if it's done carefully and with tact.

9 Read the text

Again. And again. It's the only basis for thorough and complete answers in the exam, so make sure that you know the books thoroughly.

10 Take care of yourself

Revising for an exam is a worrying time, and you can do without health problems. So:

a) get regular, balanced meals;
b) take regular breaks. You won't be able to concentrate for hours on end – five minutes off each hour is a good rule;
c) don't stay up all night – if you plan your revision you shouldn't need to, and you won't perform well in the exam if you're worn out;
d) don't go to bed straight after you finish revising. Try to get half an hour off, to go for a walk, read a magazine, listen to some music, or do anything else that helps you relax;
e) get plenty of exercise. It'll help you sleep and take your mind off things;
f) keep things in proportion. The exam's important, certainly – but it's only an exam, after all.

◀ Examinations, Questions, Study skills ▶

RHETORIC

Rhetoric is an ancient branch of linguistic and literary study though it tends now to be a branch of literary criticism rather than linguistics. As a branch of literary criticism it is concerned with the forms and structures of literary texts and with the way literary effects are achieved.

Rhetoric is also a term for the art of effective speaking and writing.

One area of linguistic investigation that links very well with ideas from rhetoric is public and political speaking. Evidence can be taped from TV party political broadcasts, recorded speeches and trade union conferences. The observation and description of rhetorical constructions and effects is a rich area for language study projects.

Stylistic analysis of texts shares some of the concerns of rhetoric e.g. metaphor and diction (or register).

RHYME

People often think that *rhyme* is much more important than it is. Many examiners are frustrated to find long explanations of a poem's rhyme scheme which have nothing to say about what the rhyme adds to a poem's overall effect. There is no point in simply saying 'This poem rhymes abab cfcd efef gg.'

The only time when you need to talk about rhyme is when it contributes to what a poem is saying in some way. This may be:

a) to give formality to a structure;
b) to draw together words which we would not usually think of as being related, by rhyming one with another to make a point of this sort.

If a poem uses rhyme, but only as a structural principle, by all means mention this in your answer, but don't spend longer than a sentence or two on it: if, however, rhyme is really an important part of the poem's effect, then by all means spend longer in explaining just what it adds to the poem.

RHYTHM

Rhythm – the alternation of strong and weak sounds or 'beats' in a line – can be just as important as sound in conveying an impression or meaning. But there's no point in just going through and marking stresses on some syllables, or talking about lines in terms of '*feet*' or '*spondees*', '*dactyls*' and so on – so if you haven't heard of these terms, don't worry at all about them! Here are some examples of *how* rhythm is used in poetry to create effect.

Stitch – stitch – stitch,
    In poverty, hunger, and dirt
Sewing at once, with a double thread,
    A Shroud as well as a Shirt

The plunging limbers over the shattered track
Racketed with their rusty freight

Listen! You hear the grating roar
Of pebbles which the waves draw back, and fling,
At their return, up the high strand,
Begin, and cease, and then again begin,
With tremulous cadence slow

The first of these examples stresses in its rhythm the repetitive and exhausting nature of the work of a seamstress sewing a shirt; the second presents the uncontrolled lunging of a wagon on uneven ground; the third recreates very subtly the rhythmic patterns of waves moving forward and back on a shore.

As is the case with sounds, rhythms are not always used in a poem to suggest or recreate a mood or movement, but they are another technique which you should be aware of. You can then both identify the rhythms and write about their effect and contribution to the poem, if you are working on a poem in which they are important.

RHYTHM IN PROSE

Although the rhythm of a piece of poetry is more obvious than that of a piece of prose, this quality may nevertheless be just as important in conveying an essential element of the significance of a novel or other prose writing. Rhythm might, for instance, be used in any of the following ways:

- To establish suspense by using long, slow-moving sentences.
- To clarify a complex argument by using sentences with a number of clauses and phrases of equal weight.
- To suggest a reflective mood by using long, slow words, often in conjunction with sounds which are long and slow too.
- To create fast action by the use of short, simple words and brief, efficient sentences.

None of these effects would be created by rhythm alone, of course. Sounds, meanings, the pace or speed of movement of the writing, and associations of words would also have a great deal to contribute in many cases.

A sudden *change* of rhythm or pace can also be very effective in prose. A shift from long, slow words and sentences to short, brisk ones can suggest the switch from contemplation to action; a change from complicated diction and irregular rhythm to simple, clear words and straightforward, conversational rhythms can show the change in a character's mind as a result, say, of taking an important decision or hearing some reassuring news.

As with diction and tone, rhythm needs to be considered in conjunction with other aspects of a piece of writing, so make sure that you are aware of all of these features working in combination while you are reading a piece of prose for appreciation.

ROLE

People very often talk about a role that is played by something in everyday life – the City of London plays a role in the national economy, for example, or youth unemployment plays a role in football violence. The only things that play roles in plays are actors; if you start talking about the role played, for example, by Davies in *The Birthday Party*, you complicate things greatly. Instead, talk about the *contribution* a character or theme makes to the play.

ROUNDED CHARACTER

◀ Flat and rounded characters ▶

RULES

Grammatical rules are often conceived popularly as rules of correctness that should not be broken if at all possible, though it is sometimes lamented that no sooner has a rule about language use been learned but an exception comes along. Rules in language have to be seen as rather elastic, however, they remain rules otherwise a language could not function as a system and meaning would break down. They are not however prescriptive rules in the sense of correctness but observed regularities or strong tendencies. Linguists *describe* what happens in language as a rule; they do not prescribe how language ought to happen.

SAPIR–WHORF HYPOTHESIS

Modern psycholinguistics has been influenced by two major linguistic ideas. One is the Chomskyan notion that language acquisition is an innate process whereby language is learned creatively not imitatively, the other is the Sapir–Whorf hypothesis that the way we think is profoundly affected by the language we learn in childhood. Edward Sapir (1884–1939) and his student Benjamin Lee Whorf (1897–1941) put forward the original view that a native language actually determines the way in which we think. A comparison of American English with an American Indian language like Hopi revealed that both languages use mutually exclusive words. They categorise things in different ways and express concepts of time differently. Quite clearly cultural differences are reflected in language differences, sometimes to a pronounced degree. Eskimos have more words for snow because they have a wider variety of perceptions of it and uses for it, than, say, British or Aboriginal cultures. We may find it unusual to classify trees according to whether we make canoes out of them, hold meetings under them, eat food from them or meet lovers under them. Not so in Samoa or New Guinea. Some Aboriginal languages do not have words for numbers above two. Their counting system is 'one, two, many'. If we find this remarkable, think how inadequate South Sea Islanders or Eskimoes would find our system of classifying 'trees' or 'snow'. It would be wrong to suppose that South Sea Island, or American Indian languages were primitive or culturally inferior because they differ from English.

If we compare languages closer together geographically, we still find interesting linguistic-cultural differences. In English the phrase 'to be right' is used, as in:

- I am right.
- She is right.
- They are right.

In French the equivalent is 'avoir raison' (literally, 'to have reason'). There is certainly a different semantic field for 'being' from the semantic field for 'having'. The differences here are considerable. In the first place the verb 'to be' has quite a different semantic field or set of meanings than the verb 'to have'. Gabriel Marcel, a French philosopher, entitled one of his books 'Being and Having' in which he describes two personalities, one concerned with what kind of person he or she was, the other concerned with what, or how much, he or she possessed. Note too that the words 'reason' and 'right' have very different semantic fields or connotations.

In its extreme, the Sapir–Whorf hypothesis is not tenable. If it were, translation from one language to another would be impossible and field anthropologists would not be able to learn native languages as successfully as they do. The whole question of the relationship between cultural patterns and thought processes as reflected in language use remains fascinating and worthwhile. Frequently, the Sapir–Whorf hypothesis is vindicated when we become aware of just how much of our thinking is conditioned by the language we have learned. Yet humans seem to possess an infinite capacity for overcoming language differences and achieving common understanding, difficult though this often is.

SATIRE

Satire is exposing human vice and folly to laughter and ridicule. Satire can be light or amusing, or savage in the bitterness of tone with which it exposes human frailty. Examples of both can be found in *Gulliver's Travels* by Jonathan Swift. Some satirists believe that by exposing folly to laughter they render it ineffective; its danger and weakness is that it can be wholly negative and destructive, and fail to suggest positive alternatives to what is being criticised.

◀ Irony ▶

SAUSSURE, FERDINAND DE

Saussure (1857–1913) is regarded as the father of modern linguistic theory. He was a respected and influential teacher at the School of Advanced Studies in Paris from 1881 to 1891 and became Professor of Indo-European Linguistics and Sanskrit, later Professor of General Linguistics, at the University of Geneva until his death.

As a young boy he wrote a paper for his uncle, attempting to prove that languages have descended from three basic sounds. It was of course not provable but the theory is a measure of Saussure's academic originality while still only a schoolboy. It is fascinating, or daunting whichever way you choose to look at it, to consider what he might have done for an A-level English Language project!

Later, as a student he wrote another paper on the 'Original System of Vowel Sounds in the Indo-European language' (1879), which established his academic reputation and proved very influential. His life's work amounts to a revolution in language study whereby it was transformed from the philology of the 19th century, where Saussure started, to the linguistics of the 20th century, which he largely initiated. Though a busy and brilliant teacher, and perhaps because of this, he wrote only one publication, the 1879 paper. After his death some of his students collected together his lecture notes and their own notes, and published them as 'The Course in General Linguistics', which he had taught them at Geneva. It is this reconstruction by faithful students that has preserved his influence. Perhaps there is no more fitting tribute to someone who rated teaching so highly. The very existence of A-level English Language examinations is in no small part due to the cumulative influence of his ideas.

SAUSSURIAN LINGUISTICS

There are four sets of ideas that may be called Saussurian linguistics, or principles on which the study of language should be based. They have been explored, practised and debated ever since his death.

1 Diachronic linguistics and synchronic linguistics

To some extent this distinction expresses the shift of emphasis from 19th century philology to 20th century linguistics. *Diachronic* means 'through time' and *diachronic studies* are historical in perspective. Everytime we look up the origin of a word we are making a diachronic enquiry. If we go on to compare the original meaning of a word with any later meanings, we are studying language diachronically. Diachronic studies (etymology, philology) are historically valuable attempts to be objective, and recognise that it is in the nature of language to change as the society that uses it changes. This is not the same thing as the ultra-conservative attitude of English speakers who write disapprovingly to newspapers, or the BBC, everytime a change in meaning or pronunciation is discovered.

Synchronic means 'at one particular time' and *synchronic studies* look at the living language as an organic whole existing at any other time. There is no reason at all to refer to history in synchronic studies because the significant thing for contemporary language users is the way that contemporary meanings are made and contemporary experiences encoded.

For a number of years synchronic linguistics became a revolutionary flag used in support of value judgements and ideologies that rejected history and yesterday's culture. It became virtually an opposite camp to the diachronic. In Saussure's view diachrony and synchrony are complementary dimensions, and continue to be so, especially in modern cultural studies that take a lingusitic perspective. It is sometimes necessary though, for students of language to make practical decisions about the time and energy available, and this may lead to a choice of one, without an ideological exclusion of the other. Inevitably there was an explosion of interest in synchronic studies after Saussure and these have led to the modern fields which we now know as sociolinguistics, pragmatics, and psycholinguistics. The history of English and of how Standard English developed are examples of diachronic elements in language study syllabuses.

2 Langue and parole

Saussure uses these French words to distinguish between the totality of a language and the dialectal and ideolectal variations and possibilities within it. 'Langue' is an abstraction from all the available language data, 'parole' is data itself in specific social contexts. The term 'langue' may be equated with what **Chomsky** means by 'competence' and 'parole' may be equated with what Chomsky means by 'performance'.

3 Syntagmatic and paradigmatic

Everything we say and write exists in two dimensions. That dimension which may be regarded as linear – one word after another – is said to be the *syntagmatic* dimension and the relationship between the words, or groups of words, is governed by rules of syntax. Above and below each word is the vertical or *paradigmatic* dimension, that is to say, all the possible alternatives a speaker or writer has not chosen at any given moment. Some of these words may be synonyms or closely related, others may be contrasts or antonyms. It is not difficult to see that at the beginning of a sentence (the syntagmatic dimension) the range of paradigmatic choice is very wide but as the syntax of the sentence unfolds the range of paradigmatic choice will normally become narrower.

A word like *board* for example could have a very long paradigmatic list indeed:

timber
platform
plank
board
group of people
get on a ship
stage
a bus
a plane
stiff card
note paper
etc.

If a speaker begins a sentence with 'The board . . .' the listener needs much more information before she can close down the range of possibilities. Consider, however, the following:

Cards don't interest me much but I like board . . .

Here the syntagmatic dimension has closed considerably the range of paradigmatic choices so that 'games' seems to be the inevitable choice. Each choice is an exclusion of the alternatives which narrows the focus of attention. Sometimes when re-drafting a piece of original writing you may be searching for an alternative word, at other times you may need to change the syntactic structure of what you are saying. The paradigmatic dimension is shadowed by contrasts and antonyms. If I choose 'he' I have distinguished from 'she'. 'White' is distinguished from 'black', 'good' from 'bad', 'higher' from 'lower'. Every paradigmatic choice can be understood in terms of what has not been chosen. Notice that it is common to hear objections to what people have said, take the form of 'what about this or that?' e.g. 'what about the workers?' In a language system related or contrasted words that are not chosen have an odd way of lining up in the wings. Literature gains much of its resonance from this but so too do political speaking, advertising, comic routines, sermons, letters, popular songs. Even news bulletins can be significant for what they do not say. (See also Syntax)

4 The signifier and the signified

Late in his life Saussure came to the view that the study of language should be subsumed under **semiotics** along with a wide range of other sign and symbol systems in the culture. Semiotics is the science of sign systems and includes just about everything by which we communicate to each other: film, TV, clothes, radio, interior decorating, sculpture, painting, car design, wearing badges, flags, rituals, dancing, emblems, logos, gestures, possessions, make up, etc. The *signifier* is the word itself (spoken or written), not its content, but its sound or appearance. The *signified* is the concept in the mind to which the signifier gives expression.

Signification is a key concept of modern semiotics and linguistics.

SCANSION

The analysis of metrical patterns in poetry.

SCHOOL

A term used of a group of authors who are seen to share certain features in their work. The term needs to be treated with caution; members of the same school can be very different, and authors are usually grouped into a school by critics, rather than by the authors themselves.

SEMANTICS

Semantics is the study of meaning, of how it is constructed, communicated, comprehended through language. The word 'semantic' is used as an adjective pertaining to 'meaning'.

Look, for example, at the following sentence put together by the linguist Noam Chomsky:

Colourless green ideas sleep furiously.

From the lexical point of view it is made up of familiar words; from the grammatical point of view it is a perfectly sound construction. But from the semantic point of view, *what* on earth does it mean? *How* can it mean anything? It was a philosopher, Ludwig Wittgenstein who remarked that grammar was not a sure guide to meaning. The overlap in the work of philosophers and the work of linguists has become especially interesting in recent years. Looking back over the history of western philosophy it is perfectly reasonable to describe it as a history of abstract nouns (e.g. truth, justice, freedom, beauty, divinity) to which different people have assigned a variety of meanings. It was the linguistic philosopher Wittgenstein, again, who remarked that the meaning of a word is its function i.e. what people want to do with the word, or what they want it to mean. Since however, a language is the common property of its speakers, the interpretation of abstract nouns, or of maxims such as 'All men are born equal', will always be a matter of debate. But whilst it is possible to define what is meant by 'equality' in any given context, it remains exceedingly difficult, if not wholly impossible, to construct a meaning for the Chomsky sentence despite its grammaticality.

For A-level students the whole point of studying English language or literature is to learn more about the ways in which human beings make meanings. This of course raises vast semantic issues that often require an interdisciplinary approach. Media studies, philosophy, logic, scientific theory, sociology, psychology, anthropology all have contributions to make. In order not to get lost in generalisations from insufficient knowledge, the best thing an A- level student of language can do is to identify some areas of semantics that are manageable and which will add to their knowledge about language and to concentrate on these. The following list consists of topics you should certainly have thought about:

1 How many different ways are there in which we use the word 'mean'? The variety is illustrated by the following:

- do you get my meaning?
- I didn't mean that
- mean what you say and say what you mean
- 'felicitous' means 'happy'
- we have a meaningful relationship
- I don't know what this poem means
- his departure meant the end of the whole project
- life has become meaningless
- she gave meaning to everything she touched
- but what does he really mean?

2 Meaning does not reside in the language itself. The language is a system of signals and symbols with which humans *make meanings*.

The sounds and letters that make up the word 'play', for example, are quite arbitrary. There is nothing about the concept 'play' in the word itself. It could just as easily be the French 'jeu'. Consider then how it is made to mean something in the following uses:

- rain stopped play
- I went to see the play tonight
- the play of light and shade
- it played on my nerves
- we learn through play
- she's wearing a play suit
- playbox, playground, playtime, playact, playschool, playscript
- don't play at it
- 'All the world's a stage and all the men and women merely players'.

3 Dictionaries are sources where we normally look for word meanings. It is an interesting exercise to take a number of different dictionaries and compare the ways in which their information is presented. Do this with reference to selected words. Meanings offered by dictionaries are usually referred to as *denotative meanings*. A dictionary will tell you for example that a stallion is a 'male horse' but in the minds of different people the word 'stallion' will *connote* many other meanings which will vary according to individual experience. *Connotative* meanings are a rich part of our experience of reading literature but they are equally important in everyday life. Connotation and association can generate or reflect a wide range of emotional states. For one person, the word stallion may connote ideas of power, freedom and wild nature; for another it may mean a lot of money invested in a stud farm; for a third completely uninterested in horses, it may mean little or nothing at all.

4 Despite the fact that there are such things as dictionaries of *synonyms*, it can be argued that there are no synonyms in the English language. Every variant of a meaning is needed because it contains a significant difference. The fact that the difference is subtle should alert us to its importance since language and social interaction work all the time through subtlety. You could explore, in Roget's Thesaurus for example, the range of variation and nuance in a selected area of word meanings. A well known comic example of how different meanings are assigned to similar words is the following:

> He is pigheaded, she is stubborn, they are bloody minded, but I am resolute.

What's the difference? Why is 'resolute' more flattering?

What are the differences between a wally, a wimp, a wet, a berk and a prat?

5 You could also explore the idea of *antonymy* (oppositeness). Look at some morphological ways of creating opposites e.g.

colourful	– colourless
own	– disown
thesis	– antithesis

There is a strong element of *negativity* here.

When you consider the use of different words to express *opposition* you will need to ask what is the feature that is being contrasted e.g.

black	– white
authoritarian	– egalitarian
romantic	– classic
masculine	– feminine
warmonger	– pacifist

6 A significant feature of language is its susceptibility to change, something that is given considerable attention in the JMB and London A- level syllabuses. *Semantic change* is perhaps the most noticeable kind. It is interesting to note that words like 'gothic', 'romantic' and 'impressionist', for example, which were originally used to convey disapproval, have now become distinctive names of periods and schools of art, and are usually spelt with an initial capital letter, 'Gothic', 'Romantic', 'Impressionist'.

The word 'disinterested' used to mean 'impartial' but has now come to mean 'uninterested' or 'switched off'.

If it is the case that one aspect of the meaning of a word is the idea it first brings to people's minds then we have only to consider words like 'gay', 'midi' (hi- fi) and 'fibre' to note significant semantic changes in quite recent years. A good source book for making a start on the extent and variety of semantic change is *Dictionary of Changes in Meaning* by Adrian Roam (RKP, 1986).

7 A term used in linguistics is *semantic field* and it has at least two applications. Originally it referred to the idea that the words of vocabulary of a language should not be thought of as an alphabetically organised dictionary, but rather as an ecology in which groups of words belong together because they were interrelated in semantic ways. This is not so much to do with their historical origins (see **etymology**) but rather a matter of the social and cultural contexts in which they are used. Law, religion, agriculture and technology are examples of human activity where the vocabulary used generates strong semantic fields. Because of this some linguists equate semantic field with *register*.

The term can also be used to describe the context generated by the use of related words in a text e.g. a poem or a novel. Read the opening section of V S Naipaul's *A House for Mr Biswas* and note all the words connected with quantity and number (e.g. time or money). The semantic field created directly affects our emotional response to the beginning of the story.

8 It is also important to understand how *implied meanings* are conveyed in a language. *Implication* and *inferral* are important issues in pragmatics too. How do we know that on some occasions, 'It's hot in here isn't it?' means 'Will somebody open a window?', and 'Have you got a pen?' means 'Will you lend me your pen, please?' The simple answer 'Yes' is not the response expected in either case.

This final point about implication reminds us just how complex the making of meaning is in language, yet how subtly effective.

It is extremely important not to underestimate the complexity of meaning. If it were a simple matter why are there so many unaccountable misunderstandings and why does our everyday language contain so many commonplaces, such as:

- Look at it another way . . .
- What I'm trying to say is . . .
- I didn't mean it quite like that . . .
- Don't misunderstand me but . . .
- You are jumping to conclusions
- About, approximately, sort of thing, a bit like . . .
- And so on.

Often, in conversation, meanings have to be negotiated and we often spend a lot of time getting clear what we do *not* mean. Many textbooks begin with a chapter devoted to statements on what the book is not about.

SEMIOTICS

Under the influence of Saussure's ideas linguistics has increasingly become related to semiotics (see **Saussure**). Semiotics is the general theory of signs and symbols. It is a philosophical discipline but is directly relevant to modern *cultural and media studies. Semiology* is the study of signs, signals and symbols.

Communication studies also draw upon semiotic theory and semiological principles.

How value systems and ideologies are encoded and disseminated in film, advertising, mass media, cultural artefacts, and social behaviour offers fascinating insights into the human condition. The study of language is a good introduction to semiotics because its data consists of the most abstract and arbitrary set of symbols known to man, yet the most familiar and the most taken for granted. When we take symbols, signs and images for granted we also take for granted the values and messages they encode.

SENTENCE

A sentence is more than a string of words. It is essentially a structure which serves a function. It will also be influenced by context. Consider the following conversation:

1 A. Magnificent!
2 B. Too emotional.
3 A. Rubbish!
4 B. Taste never ceases to amaze me.

Within the context of a musical performance it is clear that the function of A's first remark is to praise the performance. The unspoken structure supporting the use of the word 'magnificent' will be something like 'I thought that was . . .' or '. . . is the only word to describe it'. The context sets limits on the grammatical structure underlying what A and B are saying to each other. It is in this sense that we can argue for the existence of one-word sentences. Normally, however, we would regard the last remark as the only complete sentence in the conversation. 'Statistically' would be a better word than 'normally' since it begs fewer questions. The vast majority of what we traditionally refer to as 'sentences' will contain two structural features: a *subject* and a *finite verb*. Consider first the *subject*.

Any act of communication needs to make clear what it is that the reader or listener should attend to. It needs to identify and signal this in an agreed way. Statistically the subject is likely to come, if not at the beginning, then very early in the sentence:

a) *The Beatles* belong very much to the sixties.
b) Yesterday evening *I* watched TV most of the time.
c) *Christmas* is supposed to be a season of good cheer.
d) *Man* bites dog.
e) Although quite ill, *she* continued to go to work everyday.

You should note that in (b) and (e) the subject could very easily be placed at the beginning of the sentence without in any way changing the meaning.

The term subject is used here as a grammatical term signifying a key part of the sentence structure. It should not be understood in too broad a sense as, 'What the sentence is about'. Consider the following sentence:

> The rumour that the lions had escaped from the zoo, alarmed the villagers.

It is quite likely that many people would say that the 'subject' of this sentence is 'lions' since 'lions' is a strong stimulus word. The grammatical subject however is 'The rumour . . .'. It is 'the rumour' that the speaker or writer wishes us to attend to and about which he has something to say. The word 'lions' is admittedly an important piece of information but it is an amplification of the grammatical subject not the subject itself.

You can only be sure about the subject by searching for the finite verb that inextricably belongs to it. In the examples given previously the finite verbs are:

a) The Beatles *belong* . . .
b) . . . I *watched* . . .
c) Christmas *is* . . .
d) Man *bites* . . .
e) . . . she *continued* . . .

Notice that the minimal form of the finite verb has been given in (c) and (e). It would also be acceptable in a preliminary analysis to underline the whole verbal phrase if you were in any doubt:

> . . . is supposed to be
> . . . she continued to go to work . . .

The important thing about finite verbs is that they express committed action done by, or received by, the subject. They could be considered the muscle of the sentence. They form the main statement that the speaker or writer wants to make about the subject. Sometimes the term *predicate* is used for this kind of main statement i.e. what it is that is being said about the subject. The element of commitment is not necessarily dramatic or emphatic; it is a commonplace of everyday language use. Imagine somebody who talked or wrote all the time in the following manner:

Flying birds. The singing wind. Laughing children. Murmering bees. Swaying grass. Whispering trees.

Such language builds up a picture which may seem effectively atmospheric or sentimental tripe according to taste. Notice that there are no finite verbs. It is not possible to continue using language in this way without in the end losing the listener's or reader's interest. It works now and then but the continued absence of a complete sentence (subject plus a finite verb) becomes unacceptable because the speaker or writer has made no committed utterance that our minds can engage with or respond to actively.

SENTENCE TYPES

The classification of sentence types is useful for stylistics and discourse analysis or for noting what a language function is at any give point.

1 Sentences may be classified according to four functions:

a) To make a statement e.g. I like Mozart.
b) To ask a question e.g. Do you like Mozart?
c) To give a command or direction e.g. Go and listen to Mozart!
c) To utter an exclamation e.g. Great!

Statements make up most of the sentences we produce and receive. Questions are frequent, commands a little less so, exclamations are less frequent than statements. You could however check these generalisations by observing and recording. You may know somebody who is always asking questions, a child or an inquisitive friend. You may know somebody else who seems rather bossy because he or she frequently utters commands or directives. Swearing, oaths, curses and expressions of pain or pleasure, approval or disapproval, are the most common forms of exclamations.

2 Sentences may also be classified structurally:

a) *Simple sentences* contain one subject and one finite verb e.g. The car *skidded* round the corner.
b) *Complex sentences* contain two or more subjects and two or more finite verbs, but one subject will be subordinate. e.g. Though my father *loves* fish and chips, my mother *won't have* them in the house. (The word 'Though' signals that the first half of the sentence is subordinate to the second half).

c) *Compound sentences* containing two or more subjects and two or more finite verbs where each subject is equal in status. e.g. My brother *is* a singer and my sister *plays* bass guitar.

Sentences are never more or less complex; they are complex or they are not. Their complexity is determined by the fact that they contain at least one subordinate clause. Subordinate clauses are sometimes called dependent clauses. Compound sentences on the other hand contain two or more independent clauses (see under **clause** for explanation).

SEPTET

A seven line stanza.

SESTET

The last six lines of a sonnet.

SETTINGS

◀ Elizabethan stage ▶

SIGNALS AND SYMBOLS

The distinctions (and connections) between signals and symbols is an important one for language study.

Signals, a term which describes how we normally think of animal communication systems, are limited to the perceptual field of the signaller and the receiver of the signal. There is evidence that some creatures e.g. whales can transmit and receive signals over incredible distances but that does not contradict the view that signals are *percepts*, it simply means that some signals can travel a long way and still be picked up. Percepts depend upon a perception mechanism, eyes, ears, radar, or some other form of sensory perception. The high pitch whistle that dogs can hear and humans cannot, is not extra sensory in any mysterious way, it is simply outside the auditory range of humans.

Humans, along with the rest of the animal kingdom, use signals to communicate. In everyday social interactions, signals will occur. 'Ums' and 'erms', coughing to get attention, rude noises like 'raspberries', 'whistles', 'ahs', and 'oohs', are all examples of non-verbal signals that accompany our verbal language. We can express disapproval by 'tch tch' or 'tut tut' signals, disgust by 'ugh', pleasure by 'mmm' and pain by 'aargh!'. When people have been shot or fall off buildings in adventure comics, 'aargh!' is a favourite way of expressing their scream. There are lots of other non-verbal signals in comics e.g. oof!, gurr!, eek! Laughter, too, is an important set of signals with a wide range of meanings. All these signals are vocal but non-verbal. There is also a range of unintended or half intended signals that we can detect in human conversation. Changes in breathing or the pitch of the voice signify emotional states or impending actions as do changes in pace and volume. *Body language* too plays its part in the total signal network in which communication takes place. Non-verbal and non-vocal signals are referred to by linguists as *paralinguistic features* because they accompany the verbal language. Pointing, nudging, winking, making hand gestures, eye contact, touching, head shaking, backing off, coming in close, are all paralinguistic signals.

Signal systems of this kind are not by any means primitive but highly sophisticated human behaviour. They are so comprehensive that critics of experiments to show that chimpanzees can understand and use human language, point out that the chimpanzee may in fact be learning from human body language, rather than from the meanings of the plastic shapes they are taught to manipulate. What D. H. Lawrence called the 'ebb and flow of human sympathy' between humans is a very effective message carrier without a word being spoken.

Symbols are not dependent upon the perceptual field of the users, they are part of a *conceptual field* in the minds of the users. Symbols are percepts in the sense that they can be seen and heard. We have to be able to see road signs and manufacturers' labels telling us whether a garment may be machine washed or not. But essentially symbols rely upon conceptual knowledge of how they are to be used and interpreted. The fact that the letters of the alphabet have to be seen (or touched in Braille) and that the sound symbols (the phonemes) have to be heard is only the beginning of the message. The meaning-making process depends upon conceptual thinking, not just perceptual response. The sounds and visual symbols of language are a code used to construct meanings. The symbols themselves are quite *arbitrary*. Consider the variety of symbols and patterns of symbols which you can see in Figs. S.1–S.4. They all mean, 'Services guaranteed by the City Council, Manchester City Council'. Each pattern of symbols depends upon collective understanding of an agreed system and a conceptual ability to make meanings with that system. It is important right from the outset for students of English language to recognise the symbolic nature of language and that meanings are made *with* language, they are not contained in the symbols themselves. Ferdinand de **Saussure** compared language to a game of chess. It does not matter what the pieces are made of; it is their symbolic value and the rules governing their use that make the game. You could use shirt buttons, bits of stone, paper, anything to serve as the pieces, provided they were differentiated in some way. They do not have to look like queens, knights and bishops or even be called by those names; they just have to be systematically related so that they can be used effectively in the widest possible range of moves.

যে পরিচর্যাবলী

সিটি কাউন্সিল

নিশ্চিত করে

যে আপনি

যেন সেসব

পান ----

Fig. S.1 Bengali

આ સેવાઓ

તમને મળે

તેની

સિટી કાઉન્સિલ

ખાત્રી

રાખે છે....

Fig. S.2 Gujarati

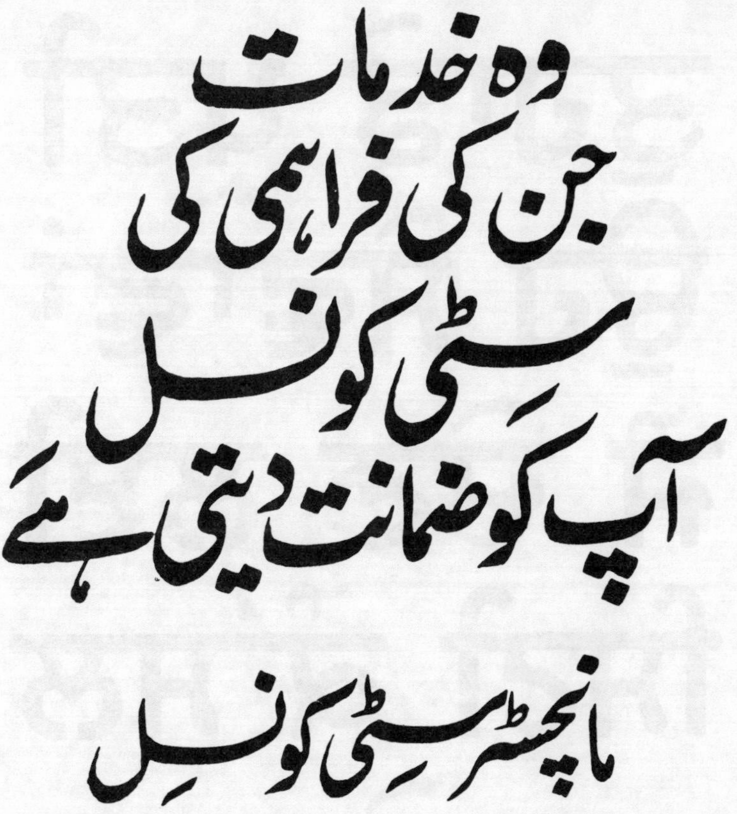
وہ خدمات
جن کی فراہمی کی
سٹی کونسل
آپ کو ضمانت دیتی ہے
مانچسٹر سٹی کونسل

Fig. S.3 Urdu

Saussure also pointed out a peculiarity that illustrates further the symbolic nature of language and the arbitrariness of the symbols used. The 9.15 train from Paris to Geneva does not stop being the 9.15 because it left at 10.20. It still makes sense to say that the 9.15 left at 10.20.

Note that when the word arbitrary is used it does not mean arbitrary from one moment to the next which would be catastrophic. It means that the original set of sound and visual symbols was arrived at arbitrarily. This is a better acount of the origin of language than the ancient notion that words are the origin of language than the ancient notion that words are *onomatopoeic* in origin, that is to say, a word is invented to sound like the thing it signifies. There may be a small area of coincidental truth in this theory (e.g. crack, boom, smack, murmur) but that is all.

ਤੁਹਾਡੇ ਪ੍ਰਤੀ
ਉਹ ਸੇਵਾਵਾਂ
ਜੋ ਦੇਣ ਲਈ
ਸਿਟੀ ਕੌਂਸਲ
ਤੁਹਾਡੇ ਨਾਲ
ਬਚਨ ਬੰਧ ਹੈ

Fig. S.4 Punjabi

The word signal can usefully be used about the function or location of particular words in a text. Grammatical words can *signal* or *mark* shifts in an argument or narrative:

> but, however, meanwhile, thirdly, penultimate, finally, on the other hand, consequently, now.

When reading aloud or delivering a talk, we frequently stress words of this kind, to signal that something significant is about to be said.

SIGNS

A sign is a meaningful unit in a language, though the language need not be verbal. Most often the term is applied to gestures and visual units. Words like 'image', 'icon', 'motif', 'logo' are closely related to the word 'sign' in the context of visual communication. Signs depend upon presentation, a characteristic they share with signals. Dictionaries often explore signs in terms of signals but more detailed entries list distinctions between the two words.

Signs also share an important characteristic of symbols, namely, that they depend for their meaning upon social agreement and conceptual understanding. Sign languages for example are not just inferior aids to help deaf people cope with the fact that they are cut off from the speech community. They are languages in themselves and express *grammatical* as well as *lexical* functions (see **grammar**).

It is a useful exercise to investigate, for example, all the uses you can find of the word sign (and signal) to get a fuller picture of its importance for our thinking about language, media and communication (see also **semiotics**).

Related concepts are signature, 'outward and visible signs of inward and spiritual grace', signing-off and signpost.

Note too that both words, 'sign' and 'signal' can be used as a noun or verb.

SIMILE

Similes are the simplest kind of image, because their comparison is made quite openly. The poet will say, for example:

> My love is like a red, red rose.

This establishes the likeness in a very straightforward manner, and it's hard to miss something like this in a poem. But you still need to point out the effect of the *comparison*. *Why* is she like a rose? Because she is red-faced and has a thorny disposition? Presumably it is something more positive than that; but unless you make clear wherein the similarity lies, the examiner will not be sure that you have grasped the full effect of the language.

SIMPLE WORDS

'Simple' does not mean 'short' anymore than 'complex' means 'long'. A simple word contains no *inflections* or *affixes*. It is self-contained unit. In morphological terms a simple word is a *free morpheme*. It cannot be reduced without destroying its meaning.

SLANG

The term slang has always carried with it disapproval. The use of slang however is an inescapable fact of language and it must therefore serve significant purposes. When slang occurs in everyday contexts it can be very communicative. If someone has raised an unpopular question at a meeting you might say to her afterwards, 'That took a lot of bottle'. By doing so you have expressed admiration and support without being pompous or patronising.

Social disapproval of slang has diminished considerably. The 1960s seem to have been a watershed in linguistic and cultural style. Slang itself shows no sign of diminishing and it is an ideal topic for a language study project. You will need to make an initial decision on whether you are going to study slang that has been incorporated into general use from a specific source, or whether you are going to concentrate on the slang used intensively be a particular social or occupational group, at leisure or at work.

Attitudes to slang is also a fruitful topic of investigation.

SOCIOLINGUISTICS

Sociolinguistics is concerned with the study of relationships between language and society. It is a relatively new branch of language study and has developed considerably in Britain, USA and Australia since the 1960s. Inevitably it is an eclectic, or interdisciplinary, state which is exhilarating for some linguists and worrying for others.

Insofar as language is a prime socialising agent it is of considerable interest to *sociologists*. Language change, and language varieties, can be explained with reference to social processes and social diversity. Attempts to explain social differences (e.g. social class) by reference to language use has not proved so straightforward. The most famous sociolinguistic debate is typified by the contrasted work of Basil Bernstein in Britain and William Labov in the USA. Bernstein has focussed on distinctions of social class in terms of language deficiency (*restricted* versus *elaborated* codes) while Labov has concentrated on the equal effectiveness of different language uses in different social classes and economic groups.

You can read about these points of view in Bernstein's *Class, Codes and Control* (RKP 1965) and Labov's *The Logic of Non-Standard English* in *Language and Social Context* ed by P Giglioli (Penguin). See also Labov's *Language in the Inner City* (on Black English) and *Sociolinguistics* by P Trudgill (Penguin).

Sociolinguistics also overlaps with *anthropology* and *cultural anthropology*. Oldish areas of language study like *stylistics* and newish fields like *pragmatics* are often seen as belonging to sociolinguistics because they are concerned with questions of social interaction, shared understanding, social rules for conversations, accepted conventions for reading and writing. No doubt in the future years boundary lines will be more sharply drawn but by then it is just as likely that new perspectives will have emerged. The present state can only be healthy and has certainly made imaginative as well as scholarly contributions to modern language study.

One exciting area you could begin to explore is the question of language and power. The following studies would give you a good start:

Authority in Language by James and Lesley Milroy (RKP 1987).
Language and Social Networks by Lesley Milroy (RKP 1987).
Language and Power by Norman Fairclough (Longman 1989).

See under **theoretical framework** for more detailed consideration of language and society.

SOLILOQUY

A speech spoken as if revealing his thoughts to himself by a character in a play who is alone on stage. The most famous soliloquy is that of Hamlet which begins 'To be or not to be, that is the question'. Do not confuse this with an **aside**, which is a remark made by a character when there are other characters on stage but which, by convention, is heard only by the audience.

SONNET

A poem of fourteen lines, usually in iambic pentameters (see **Metre**). The form became fashionable in England in the sixteenth century in imitation of love poems by the Italian Petrarch, and originally was formed of two parts, an octave or eight line section and a sestet or six-line section. Shakespeare modified the form by changing it to three quatrains and a couplet, often with a shift of meaning or epigrammatic statement at the end.

The Petrarchan sonnet was concerned solely with love, as were those of the Elizabethans, but later writers, including Milton, Wordsworth, Rossetti and Dylan Thomas, have used the form to write poems on a wider range of themes.

SOUND

Language doesn't only communicate through meaning: it conveys a lot of things through sound. Try reading these lines aloud:

> The moan of doves in immemorial elms
> And murmuring of innumerable bees
>
> Only the stuttering rifles's rapid rattle
> Can patter out their hasty orisons
>
> How a lush-kept, plush-capped sloe
> Will, mouthed to flesh-burst,
> Gush!

The first sounds like the slow, drowsy moaning and humming of bees and doves which it speaks of; the second captures the staccato rattle of gunfire in its harsh 't' sound; the third conveys a sense of great richness in the 'sh' sounds to give an impression of great sensuality.

All of these are achieved by using the sounds of words to reinforce their meanings. Not all poems will use this technique; many make no effort to recreate sound in this way. But you should be alive to the possibility that a poem will work in this way; when it does you should note the fact and explain the effect of the sound when you write about it.

Sound is also important in prose and drama, for the same reason: to recreate or emphasise ideas, feelings or aspects of mood or setting.

◄ Metre, Rhythm, Rhyme ►

SPACE

Organising space is a key skill when studying. You need somewhere to work – ideally, a separate room or part of a room that you can set aside for study. You need:

A desk or a table. Don't think you can work in an easy chair, or out in the country or on the beach – forget it. The only place for serious study is sitting with books and notes in front of you;
Shelves for books. Keep your texts in order, so that you can consult them whenever you need them – which will be very frequently;
Files for notes. It's worth spending a little money on card folders, loose-leaf files and file paper, so that you have plenty of resources for making notes.

Try to use paper that's of good quality and will last the two or more years you'll be studying.

SPEECH

See **phonetics** and **phonology** but also consider what a range of meanings is contained in apparently synonymous words for speech e.g.

talk, conversation, oracy, orality, utterance, locution, the spoken word, the speaking voice, vocalisation.

What are the differences of meaning between these? Consider also the range of social contexts and functions signified so precisely in the following everyday expressions:

chat, chinwag, natter, parley, conference, interview, consultation, talk it over, have words, chat up, gossip, tête à tête, sound you out, don't talk at me, pow wow, full and frank exchange.

How many more could you add to the list?

SPEECH ACTS

The notion of speech acts originated in philosophical investigations of language typified by a famous book, *How To Do Things With Words* (OUP 1960) by J. L. Austin. What sounds like a manual of communication skills is in fact a closely argued, witty account of how language does not just describe action, it can be action in itself. Through the work of Austin and later John R. Searle, what began as a philosophical enquiry has become a significant contribution to **pragmatics** and **semantics**.

The central type of speech act is called an *illocutionary act* and it occurs when language is used to make promises, to warn, to threaten, to thank, to welcome, to bear witness, to baptise, to enrol, to command, to insist, to deny, to request. There are many more but typical examples of illocutionary acts are:

- I. . . take thee. . . to be my husband.
- The Bank of England promises to pay the bearer. . .
- I name this ship.
- I declare this stone well and truly laid.
- I must warn you that anything you say. . .
- I shall be obliged to ask you to leave if you persist.
- I baptise this child in the name of the Father. . .
- I solemnly swear that the evidence I shall give. . .
- We guarantee all our work.

All these examples are acts in themselves; the act of saying is not just informative it has illocutionary force. It is the kind of language which, when written, usually requires a signature and when spoken has a particularly resonant effect. The sayings 'my word is my bond' and 'I mean what I say' are claims that a promise will not be broken, a threat will not be empty, a guarantee will be honoured, a declaration is irrevocable, a warning is not idle. Being a person of one's word is an important aspect of speech acts but the theory also encompasses the everyday aspect of asking questions, demanding attention and making a request – all of which require action from other people.

Note too how important it is, in many social situations, that somebody should propose a vote of thanks, give an official welcome, offer formal congratulations. The business of giving and receiving an apology is an equally important, reciprocal social act.

Finally there is a range of expressions that may be called indirect speech acts. These occur when we say things like 'It's warm in here isn't it?' as a polite way of getting somebody to open a window.

SPONDEE

◀ Metre ▶

STANZA

A group of lines in a poem which are moderately self-contained in either subject or structure – a grouping which is generally referred to as 'verse'.

STREAM OF CONSCIOUSNESS

The attempt in novel writing to recreate the actual flow, pattern and sense of thoughts as they pass through a person's head in real life, or to describe experience as it is actually felt by a person as it is taking place. James Joyce and Virginia Woolf are two well-known exponents of this style.

STRUCTURALISM

The term has been included in this guide not because it is a modern fad but because the study of language is one of the surest ways to come to an understanding of what structuralism is all about. Despite passionate intellectual debates of recent years there is no need to regard structuralism as a credo or exclusive school of thought to which you must declare allegience. Think of it as an extra awareness and a useful set of principles to take into account when studying language use. Sometimes structuralist notions will lead to significant insights, at other times, they will not be very useful.

The base of the word is 'structure' which we tend to think of as a noun. We talk about the structure of literary works, the structure of society, the structure of living organisms. Much linguistic study is concerned with structures (e.g. sentences, discourse, words) and how they serve functions. If on the other hand we think of the word as a verb, something humans do, then it is easy to see how language is a supreme instrument or medium for structuring the world inside our heads. Language literally puts the world inside our heads and structures it in all kinds of ways. It can mix up concrete construction like chairs, elephants, pianos and buildings with abstract constructs (ideas) like family, society, culture, politics, social class, economics, education, industry, God, and fuse them together into value systems which we learn from a very early age.

Language does not just label things it constructs them too. A very influential book by Berger and Luckman called *The Social Construction of Reality* reminds us that reality is not just outside our minds it is also inside our minds so that what we think of as reality is inseparable from the way we talk about it. The fact that we talk about it is what makes it so real. We can talk with passion and conviction about places we have never been to, people we have never met, things we have never seen. The whole of literature provides us with fictions that are just as real and important as the so-called realities of daily life. In *Language and Learning* (Penguin), James Britton describes how we use language to structure and make sense of experiences. Not only do we receive impressions and information from the world via language we also project our minds outward via language. Perception is a two way process.

For everyday purposes language comes to mind quite unbidden and we do not always seem to work out consciously what we are about to say. This may be because language production works in the mind at lightning speed. It need not be depressing to think that we may never say anything original, that somebody else will have said it before. The significance of this, from a structuralist point of view, is that the repertoire of structures encoded in the language also came to the mind unbidden. When we read novels and watch films for example, especially films from an earlier decade, we can see familiar structures and patterns of thought coming through: insiders and outsiders; goodies and baddies; father figures; retribution; quests; love triangles; betrayal. When you write stories for the original writing component of A-level examinations you should try to analyse your story not just in terms of how you have structured it formally (e.g. opening development – climax – conclusion) but in terms of the structures, that have as it were, suggested themselves to you as you wrote. Plotting is not just a matter of planning the formal structure of the story but of working out the internal structures of relationships and events equally satisfactorily. The language you use to create characters for example, or to present dialogue, or to convey thoughts, will be clues to your moral outlook, to the ways in which you think power operates in the world, and to the social patterns you have internalised from childhood.

Deconstruction is a process of trying to examine critically the structures deeply embedded in our language, our social lives, and our culture, and to expose them. Gender roles, for example, are cultural constructs encoded into language. The general use of the term 'mankind' and 'man' to cover both sexes, together with a generalised use of the pronoun 'he' are familiar enough examples. Consider though how such phrases as 'a feminine boy' 'a masculine woman' 'an effeminate man' 'a macho female' can only be possible because gender roles are sociolinguistic constructs and not simply differences of biology.

Remember that structures embedded in language will be embedded in language use. Deconstruction need not be cultural sabotage or intellectual suicide; it can be beneficially purgative.

STUDY SKILLS

ORGANISATION

All the investigations into how the process of study works conclude that you take in more and understand better if you work according to a *regular study timetable*. This is true not only of revising just before your exam, but of the whole process of taking in new ideas and information. Even at the very start of your course you should try to get yourself organised.

So just what is it that you need to organise?

Organise your space

See entry under space.

Organise your time

If you're studying at school or college, much of this will be done for you, with your day being split up into classes on the subjects you're following. But there will be time that *isn't* organised. So get into the habit, right from the start, of deciding what to do with this time, and sticking to a firm timetable. You need time off, certainly – but you can fit this in at times when the work has been done!

If you have free time at school or college, decide how to use it. Divide it between the subjects you're studying. Set aside times for working in a library or study area, and always have an idea of what you're going to *do* during this time – this will be covered in more detail later on.

Organise your time in the evenings and at weekends. Give yourself one evening a week off, and some free time at weekends. The rest of the time needs to be devoted to study.

Organise your notes

See entry under notes.

USING TEXTS

When you're studying literature, everything depends on the *text*. If you have an edition that's old, in small print, difficult to read and generally unattractive, the process of studying will be unpleasant and you'll get little pleasure or help from it.

Always make a point of getting the best text you can. Often your school or college will provide a text for you. If it's a 'school' edition, find out whether there's another version which is better. Many schools use old-fashioned editions of Shakespeare, for example. If you get hold of a first-rate modern edition – such as the *New Arden Shakespeare*, published by Methuen – you'll have a great advantage, because a modern edition will give you a great deal of essential information and help you in your studies.

A good text should have these features:

a) the words of the play, novel or poems edited from the original manuscripts or other reliable sources, presented with the original punctuation or edited to make clear for the modern reader the writer's original intentions. It must be accurate and rest on the latest academic research;
b) full notes to explain difficult words or ideas in the text, and which let you make up your own mind about alternative interpretations;
c) an introduction which will cover the themes and ideas of the text, summarise critical views and in general give you the information you need in order to study, understand, appreciate and interpret the text.

Close critical reading

This is really the essence of literary study at all levels. What you need to do when reading critically is to work through the text, using all the features of your critical edition to make sure that you grasp fully what the writer is saying. When you are involved in close textual study of this sort, you should follow this procedure:

1 Choose a part of the text you are studying – a scene in a play, a chapter of a novel, or a poem. Read it carefully and, at the same time, ask yourself questions about it. The kind of things to look for are dealt with in detail under the heading **reading** for **poetry**, **drama** and for **prose**.
2 Look up difficult words in a glossary or dictionary.
3 Consult the notes of your edition.
4 Think about the important features of expression the passage uses, and consider whether or not these are representative of the whole work.
5 Think about the ways in which the passage contributes to the themes or ideas of the text as a whole.
6 Make brief notes to record these themes and features, either on paper on in the book itself (see Fig. S.5).

7 Think about brief passages (no more that a line or two) which you might like to learn, and so be able to use in the exam to demonstrate key aspects of the text.

8 Read again the passage of the text you've been working on; this will help in bringing together the work you have done on it and in remembering it as a complete unit.

9 Think about how the individual section contributes to the work as a whole; this will help you to make the transition between reading a short passage in detail and knowing the whole of the text in the depth you'll need for the exam.

BOOK THREE

nature, instead of forming originals from the confused heap of matter in their own brains; is not such a book as that which records the achievements of the renowned Don Quixotte more worthy the name of a history than even Mariana's;[129] for whereas the latter is confined to a particular period of time, and to a particular nation; the former is the history of the world in general, at least that part which is polished by laws, arts and sciences; and of that from the time it was first polished to this day; nay and forwards, as long as it shall so remain.

I shall now proceed to apply these observations to the work before us; for indeed I have set them down principally to obviate some constructions, which the good-nature of mankind, who are always forward to see their friends virtues recorded, may put to particular parts. I question not but several of my readers will know the lawyer in the stage-coach, the moment they hear his voice. It is likewise odds, but the wit and the prude meet with some of their acquaintance, as well as all the rest of my characters. To prevent therefore any such malicious applications, I declare here once for all, I describe not men, but manners; not an individual, but a species. Perhaps it will be answered, Are not the characters then taken from life? To which I answer in the affirmative; nay, I believe I might aver, that I have writ little more than I have seen. The lawyer is not only alive, but hath been so these 4000 years, and I hope G..... will indulge his life as many yet to come. He hath not indeed confined himself to one profession, one religion, or one country; but when the first mean selfish creature appeared on the human stage, who made self the centre of the whole creation; would give himself no pain, incur no danger, advance no money to assist, or preserve his fellow-creatures; then was our lawyer born; and whilst such a person as I have described, exists on earth, so long shall he remain upon it. It is therefore doing him little honour, to imagine he endeavours to mimick some little obscure fellow, because he happens to resemble him in one particular feature, or perhaps in his profession; whereas his appearance in the world is calculated for much more general and noble purposes; not to expose one pitiful wretch, to the small and contemptible circle of his acquaintance; but to hold the glass to thousands in their closets, that they may contemplate their deformity, and endeavour to reduce it, and thus by suffering private mortification may avoid public shame. This places the boundary between, and distinguishes the satirist from

cf Lawyer in Book 1 ch 12.

'Prude' in (18) is woman who only pretends to be v. modest but is really corrupt.

v. imp. general statement of author's aim

shows moral purpose of novel: to correct people, not ridicule them

Fig. S.5 A page from 'Joseph Andrews' by Henry Fielding

You will need to undertake close critical reading throughout your period of study, for a range of reasons – to prepare for an essay and to revise, as well as to get to know the text thoroughly. If you are working through a novel or play, it will also help to begin your session of critical reading by quickly going through the passage you read the *day before*, just to revise the points you noted about it and to put the passage you're reading today in context.

Reading in this way may be strange and unfamiliar at first – most of us are used to reading things quickly, and not to looking at words in such depth. But with a little practice you'll soon find that the process comes almost naturally. Doing it *regularly* will help you to read critically with both accuracy and speed.

Reading critical texts

Be careful when reading critical texts:

a) reading a critical text can be confusing, especially if you choose something that goes too deeply into an aspect of the text you're studying;
b) make sure that you don't accept the writer's interpretation at face value; he or she may take one particular view of the many that are usually possible, so don't end up with a limited or one-sided stance to the text;
c) don't assume that critics impress examiners – they don't. Clear, well-thought-out and relevant points of your own will be worth far more in an exam than impressive-sounding references to critics, or restatements of half-digested critical views which have nothing to do with the question;
d) *above all* don't assume that you can read a critical text or set of notes *instead of* the text if you want to do well. Remember that a knowledge of the texts themselves, your ability to understand the question and to apply your knowledge of the texts to the question set, are all that's needed in the exam. Careful knowledge and intelligent application are far more important than some pseudo-sophisticated and name-dropping.

To sum up: if it stimulates your own thoughts and you can read critically, by all means read what others have to say. But if you're unsure about major points, go back to the text or get help from your teacher. And *never* put reading a critical essay or guide before reading and thinking about the text itself.

USING CLASS TIME

If you're following a course, you'll spend quite a lot of your time going to *classes*. In them, you'll be reading through your set texts, discussing their authors' ideas and your responses to them, looking at the techniques the writers use, and generally getting to know these texts. In addition, you'll be writing essays based on the texts. So you might think that you're already doing all that you need in order to cover the ground thoroughly.

A BEFORE THE SESSION

1 Make sure you have enough paper, 2 pens, and perhaps carbon paper (in case a friend's away)
2 Know the context of the class – discussion or formal lecture.

B DURING THE SESSION

1 Don't write all the time: listen for the complete point before writing.
2 Listen carefully, questioning what you hear.
3 Try to distinguish between new points and enlargements of old ones.
4 Be selective with examples – go for main points first.
5 Use digressions/questions/anecdotes to get points down.

C THE SPEAKER

1 Get to know how the speaker works. Does he/she:
- list main points at start of class;
- allow points to emerge during class;
- pause regularly to sum up or draw points together;
- give final summaries;
- give references for the points made.

2 Vary your note-making technique according to the speaker's approach.

D LAYOUT

1 Note time, date, speaker and subject.
2 Leave plenty of space when writing. This allows for later additions.
3 Use any abbreviations & codes you can.
4 Use main headings, sub-headings & numbered points as far as possible.
5 Alternatively, use 'pattern' or 'spidergram' notes.
6 Note questions, uncertainties and points for checking as you go.
7 Put names and unfamiliar terms in capitals.
8 If speaker permits, ask about unfamiliar terms.

E AFTER THE SESSION

1 Re-write using clear layout at first opportunity.
2 Check names, dates, spellings and other uncertainties with reference books and re-write.
3 Ask speaker if unsure of anything.
4 Add points and comments of your own, making sure they're separated from speaker's points.
5 Compare notes with friends if subject is difficult.

Fig. S.6

Certainly all this will give you a basic knowledge of your texts, but the process shouldn't stop there. As well as going along to classes, you should set aside a time *every day* to go through the work you've covered in your class earlier that day.

In this time, you should:

a) copy out the notes that you've taken, making sure that you have all the points in the best order, and that all your points are clear – both in terms of their meaning and in the way that you write them down. Write legibly – remember that you may have to revise from these notes over a year away;
b) read the passages of the text you've covered during the day, using the critical reading procedure outlined in the last section;
c) if time permits, read *ahead* to cover that part of the text you'll study in your next class.

This whole process shouldn't take longer than forty-five minutes. And if you do it every day, you'll end up with a full set of notes which record your work on each text you're studying. You can then use these notes as the basis for essays as well as for revision when the exam is near. Fig. S.6 sets out in rather more detail how you can make the best use of your class time.

As well as this, of course, you'll need to gather material for the essays which will form an important ingredient in your course. Don't forget, too, that you will have your essays returned by your teacher or lecturer with comments about what went well, and which areas need more attention. When you get an essay back, don't just look at the grade and hide it in your file. Instead:

read the comments, and think carefully about them;
make notes on points which your teacher suggests you've neglected;
find quotations or other evidence to support the points you've made, if the comments suggest that these are needed.

In this way you'll capitalise on the work you did for the essay and be able to incorporate it into your other work – such as the notes on the text you made in class, and those that you took yourself as part of the critical reading process.

Another part of your study regime will involve the process of bringing together the work you have done on a text – the kind of continuous revision which stops you from ever really losing touch with the work you have done in the past. This will be covered in more detail in the next section of this chapter – but remember that there are really three key elements to a study session. Not each session will necessarily contain all three, but you need to be aware that all are just as important.

1 Close critical reading.
2 Work preparing an essay, or extending an essay already written, in the light of your teacher's comments.
3 Revising and bringing together your work so that you have a clearer view of the whole text.

◀ Notes, Poetry, Prose, Questions, Reading, Revising ▶

STYLISTICS

All examination papers that set unseen passages for analysis are demanding of candidates some knowledge of stylistics. In linguistics, stylistics is a general term referring to studies which account for the differences between varieties of English use. It can be applied equally to talk or to written texts. Some examination papers present candidates with transcripts of spoken English, data which lie somewhere between talk and conventional written texts.

Under the general term of stylistics is subsumed the term *literary stylistics*, which refers to studies of literary texts and includes features of *style* discernible in individual poets, novelists and playwrights. *Style* is also a general term applicable in non-linguistic contexts. In literary criticism it can include aesthetic features of structure and imagery as well as personal idiosyncrasies in an authors tone of voice and choice of vocabulary.

Many students ask what is the difference between doing a *stylistic analysis* for English language at A-level and a *literary critical analysis* for English literature. The question is a fair one but in view of the frequency with which literature examiners lament the scant attention many literature candidates pay to the ways in which language is being used, it is a pity more time could not be spent looking at the interconnections rather than trying to pigeon hole the differences.

Since, however, languages examiners are equally critical about a lack of attention to linguistic features by language candidates it will obviously be helpful to draw some guidelines. Language examiners have also been critical of the inadequate theoretical framework that candidates bring to their analysis, and perhaps that is the best place to begin.

a) Your framework needs to encompass a *macro* point of view that will put the text in a social context. It must also encompass a *micro* point of view whereby you focus on individual features in the text. Your examination answer will move between these two points of view in a variety of ways according to the order in which you make your points.

b) Your sociolinguistic framework should ask such questions as *Why was the text written? For whom? When and where might it be read? What form does it employ? To what genre does it belong?* All these are factors which depend upon readers' assumptions, assumptions which are often made very quickly and which will determine how we read the whole text. Sometimes it is better to reserve statements about these matters until the end of your answer even though you are bearing them in mind as you read. It can be fatal to begin with statements like:

'This is obviously a recipe, an instructional piece of writing for housewives.'
'This is obviously a letter. It contains a lot of information and is written to inform the residents of Hope Street.'

Both of these remarks draw on knowledge that puts the texts in social contexts by describing form, purpose and audience. There are many more things that could now be said about the specific forms, purposes and audiences but a start has been made. The problem however of committing yourself so early is that you start looking for micro features to 'prove' what you have stated as being so obvious in the first place. This hardly constitutes an open minded investigation of a text.

Look now at the two texts to which these initial responses have been made. (Fig. S.7 and Fig. S.8)

There are a number of linguistic features in Fig. S.7 that are characteristic of a recipe ranging from the enticing name 'Tropical Trifle' to the detailed

Tropical Trifle (Serves 4)

1 Jamaican ginger cake
225g/8oz canned pineapple in its own juice
568ml/1 pint fresh milk
2 level tablespoons custard powder
25g/1oz sugar
2 size 3 eggs, separated
100g/4oz caster sugar
Selection of fresh fruit (optional)

1 Cut the cake into slices and arrange in a heatproof dish. Soak the cake with the pineapple juice. Chop the fruit and place over the cake.
2 Blend the custard powder with 25g/1oz sugar, the egg yolks and a little of the milk. Bring the remaining milk to the boil.
3 Stir hot milk into the blended mixture, return to the saucepan, heat until custard boils. Simmer for two minutes. Pour over fruit and cake.
4 Whisk the egg whites until stiff, gradually whisk in the caster sugar. Spread or pipe over the custard, brown under a hot grill. Serve immediately.
5 Alternatively, pipe meringue round the edge of the dish, brown quickly, allow to cool. Fill the centre with a selection of fresh fruit.

For a selection of recipes using fresh milk, send a 9″×7″ SAE to Dept RL/Z, The National Dairy Council, 5–7 John Princes St., London W1M 0AP.

Good food's gotta lotta bottle when your cooking's gotta lotta milk.

Fig. S.7

Peter Smith BA MPhil MRTPI

Warfield
Borough
Council

Chief Planning Officer

Box No 40
Blake House
King Edward Road
Warfield
Lancashire LS9 4YD
Tel Warfield 21955

Please reply to	MR D W Long	Date 13 March 1986
Extension	128	Application No 44429P
Our reference	P.DWL/GC/44429P	Your reference

Dear Sir/Madam

Description
TWO NON FOOD RETAIL STORES ONE PART RETAIL FOOD STORE WITH ANCILLARY ACCOMMODATION WITH BELOW STORE CAR PARK SURFACE SERVICE AREA AND ELECTRIC SUBSTATION

Location
LAND BOUNDED BY CROWN ROAD/MATTHEW STREET/QUEEN STREET/ NELSON STREET WARFIELD

I refer to the above planning application which has recently been submitted and which will comprise the redevelopment of the land opposite your house.

The proposed development, which includes modifications to the line of Matthew Street is available for inspection during normal workings hours at the Warfield Service Centre in the Town Hall or in this Department.

Should you wish to comment on the proposals I would be obliged if you would do so in writing prior to 4 April 1986 so that they may be taken into account by the Planning Committee when they consider the submitted plans.

Yours faithfully

for Chief Planning Officer

THE OCCUPIER
MATTHEW STREET
WARFIELD
LANCASHIRE

Fig. S.8

sequence of practical instructions using command (or imperative) from verbs (cut, soak, chop, blend, bring, simmer, pour, whisk, spread, pipe, allow, fill). At the end, however, in the boldest type there is a statement about milk and since the recipe depends very much upon milk, we realise that the purpose of the text is to advertise (and sell) milk. *Thus it is not 'obviously' an instructional text but a persuasive one too,* all the more effective for giving the reader something useful, namely the recipe. There is in a sense a text within a text and the familiar form of the recipe obscures the fact that the text framing everything is in fact an advertisement for milk. You might even go on to argue that once the reader's mind is set along following instructions the final response might well be to go out and buy a bottle – as implicitly instructed! The slogan is in the form of a statement (a micro detail) and it uses phonetic spelling and a rhyme – 'gotta' and 'lotta' (two more micro details). These observations lead to more general (macro) comments about the functions of slogans as persuasive structures and about how they lodge in the memory and take on a life of their own in the popular culture. They reinforce a positive disposition toward milk.

In Fig. S.8 there are a number of micro details that can be observed: the authority of the heading; the exact description and location; the phrase 'I refer to. . . .'; the invitation to inspect plans; the use of the verb form 'Should you wish. . . .'; the setting of an exact reply date. The register features here are those of local government bureaucracy. There is a good deal of information but notice who the letter is from and to whom it is addressed. Its purpose is not only to inform, there is an underlying and more important purpose contained, once again, in the final words. The letter is in fact a *legal instrument* fulfilling a legal requirement. Residents of the affected street have to be informed and have to be given the opportunity to object 'in writing'. This is almost a warning, notice that the time given is not very long, 'prior to 4 April 1986'. Oddly enough the letter is as much an instruction as the recipe is the advertisement. It is an instruction in that the recipient is being told what to do if he wishes to comment. Notice the neutrality of a word like 'comment' and the formal politeness of, 'I would be obliged' (two more micro details).

An *adequate theoretical framework is one that enables a student to move from wider issues of social context and functions to specific linguistic details in the text, making connections between them in either direction*.

c) When you take an initial overview of the text do not immediately jump to a conclusion about it but note how it is laid out and structured. Is there a heading? Is there a signing off or other type of ending? How many paragraphs? Is there any variation of typescript?

d) Provided you write in continuous prose (rather than notes that may not be comprehensible) it is a good strategy to take the examiner through your own reading journey noting on the way micro and macro features that you find interesting.

e) Save your most important point until the end when you have had some time to reflect upon your conclusions. Do not forget that it is perfectly acceptable to revise any point of view you have expressed on your journey through the text.

f) Try also to think how other people might read the text. This can act as a check on your own viewpoint and help you to be more objective.

g) Always keep this checklist in the back of your mind:
lexis
grammar
discourse structure.

You don't have to comment on these every time or for the sake of it, but it is likely that you will find the evidence for your macro impressions somewhere in the linguistic detail of lexis, grammar and discourse structure. They will enable you to answer the one important question not detailed in ii) above, namely, how is the language used?

h) When working on a literary text there will be some important differences between it and other sorts of texts. Questions about who wrote it? for whom? why? to be read where and when? are not so easily answered. In the two examples discussed earlier there is an element of transaction between a writer and readers, toward specific ends. It is therefore important to be sure about immediate social context and purpose. Literary texts to some extent create their own imaginative contexts in which the reader is a spectator (or a listener to a narrative) rather than a participant in a transaction of information, instruction or persuasion.

Consider the following poem:

love is more thicker than forget
more thinner than recall
more seldom than a wave is wet
more frequent than to fail
it is most mad and moonly
and less it shall unbe
than all the sea which only
is deeper than the sea

love is less always than to win
less never than alive
less bigger than the least begin
less littler than forgive

it is most sane and sunly
and more it cannot die
than all the sky which only
is higher than the sky

e e cummings

Now imagine taking the examiner on your reading journey through the poem:

At first the poem seems like a joke. There is no punctuation and no capital letters. There is no title either but the name of the poet is given, e e cummings. I have no knowledge whatsoever of this poet but intend to take the poem seriously and explore it further. [**or** I have met the poet before and know that he often writes in this way].

The first line of anything is important since it prepares you for the rest. The trouble with this first line is that it is so puzzling. 'More thicker' is unusual to say the least and the word 'forget' does not make sense either. 'Forgetting' would make it a noun which is what should be there, but then the idea of love being thicker than forgetting is very difficult to follow.

Any reader seeing that first line for the first time is bound to be surprised. A quick scanning of the poem however shows that it is quite a formal little poem very carefully put together in four verses. The attention paid to structure and the apparent nonsense of the content are a strange contrast. The more you look at the poem the more pattern you can see in it. The pattern 'more. . . . than' occurs in every line of verse one and the words 'more', 'most' and 'less' occur in other verses.

It is also noticeable how, throughout the poem, opposites are contrasted e.g. thicker/thinner, seldom/frequent, mad/sane, moonly/sunly, bigger/littler, alive/die, deeper/higher, always/never, sea/sky, forget/recall.

Such deliberate contrasts suggest that the poet knows exactly what he is doing. The invented words (sunly, moonly, unbe) are not difficult to understand but I find some lines very difficult:

'more seldom than a wave is wet'
'all the sea which only is deeper than the sea'
'love is less always than to win'
'less bigger than the least begin'.

Possibly the last verse is the most straightforward and since last verses often sum up the meaning of a poem it might provide a starting point for a better understanding. 'It' refers to love, as it does in the second verse, and seems to be saying that love cannot die. It will last forever like the sky, and is a much higher thing than the sky.

The poem is about love. 'Love' being the grammatical subject of each verse. The whole poem is a bit like a list of statements, each beginning 'Love is. . .'.

I can now see how clever the poem is but am still not sure what it means. At first it was difficult to take seriously but the more you read it the more serious it sounds. Possibly the poet finds it difficult to say just how strong love can be. It is as if he has run out of comparisons. He is deliberately misusing English perhaps to make the reader think. It is easy to read in the sense that words are simple, the lines are short and the rhyming scheme is very regular.

At this point the candidate would already have achieved a great deal and an examiner could not but be impressed. It is not likely that a poem so awkward at first sight would be set in an examination. The comments given here are a composite of observations made by students about the poem in seminars. There follows a list of further comments which though related specifically to Cumming's poem, provide a theoretical framework for approaching other literary texts:

1 What literary genre does this belong to?

It is a love lyric which means it will be read in the light of other love lyrics we know, traditional or modern. There is a long tradition in love poetry and love songs in which love is compared to other things in nature – the sky, the sea, the stars, a red rose. Many love poems are very extravagant in their profession of love, perhaps Cummings is being a little satirical. Nevertheless it ends on a happy note with a conventional image. The more you read the poem the less important the oddities become.

2 In what ways does the language differ from everyday use of language?

Cumming's poem deviates from Standard English quite considerably whilst at the same following a strict pattern which would never occur in everyday English use. By using language in unusual ways a poet can achieve effects which make the reader view his subject or theme differently. Readers bring a great deal to poems before they have even read them. This particular one does not have a title but expectations are immediately roused by the first word 'love'. To prevent the reader from reading the poem in the way in which love poems might habitually be read, Cummings breaks a number of conventions (e.g. 'more thicker') and in doing so makes the reader think again about the whole tradition of hyperbolic (i.e. exaggerated) love lyrics.

3 What lexical and grammatical features are evident?

In 2 we considered features which characterise literary language i.e. make it different from everyday English. Here we consider those basic features of English to be found in all forms of English.

The antonyms have already been mentioned and the invention of new words could more appropriately be discussed under 2. Note, though, that the only verb used until the last verse is the verb 'to be' ('love is', 'it is'). In the last verse there is one modal verb 'it cannot die'. This has the effect of making the poem a declaration. There is no motion, it makes up stop and think.

Be careful here not to make it sound as though the poet *intended* every effect in the language. Poets use language in ways that combine instinct, accident and hard work. If you say something like, 'The poet uses such and such a word because he wants to make the reader feel sad', you are treating the poem as a message between poet and reader and speculating too much on the intention behind the message. The best evidence, or data, that you have is the lexis and the grammar and their effect upon you, the reader. Forget writers supposed intentions and concentrate on your responses which will be partly those of a 'typical' reader and partly those of your own personality. Finally do not think of lexis as unusual or special words. Remember that significant things occur in a text when very ordinary words are used: yet, but, finally, once upon a time, however, either. . . or, if, so that, etc.

4 What tone of voice do you detect?

This question is never an easy one to answer because tone works in subtle yet very effective ways. We can respond to tone without realising it. Language originates in speech and however formal a piece of writing may be someone is addressing somebody, somewhere. We often say of official reports that they have been written by a committee because we detect a collective, impersonal voice. They are sometimes jokingly referred to as Dalek documents. On the other hand, letters, memos and notices, written by one person can convey a tone of voice quite unintended by the writer who may be surprised to discover that whilst nobody objects to the content, the tone has offended.

With plays and TV scripts tone is not always a useful concept because the writer speaks through many voices but in a novel, tone may be detected straightaway in the opening paragraph. In the poem discussed here there is a temptation to say that the tone of voice is matter of fact because the lines are short and consist of listed statements. It is possible for a list to peter out but it can also have a cumulative effect which seems to happen here. Notice how comparative forms are emphasised in the first three verses while in the final verse a superlative is introduced – '*most* sane and sunly'. By the end of the poem there is a seriousness in the tone that overrides the quirky deviations. Brevity need not be matter of fact. Here tone has been detected in the positiveness of the statements, and in their cumulative effect. You could also argue that Cumming's tone is serious because the cumulative effect of so many qualifications and comparisons suggest that love is a very difficult thing to write about. The poet is saying, in effect, that love is much greater than anything else in the world.

5 What structural features may be observed?

Many structural features have already been identified because this particular poem is so precisely structured internally (via the language of comparison) and externally (via its layout on the page in regular, rhyming verses). There are other internal metaphorical structures in the contrast of 'deeper than the sea' with 'higher than the sky' which give a sense of space, while other contrasts (frequent, seldom, never, eternity – 'it cannot die') create a time dimension.

Repetitions are worth noting here because there are so many. You could count the repetitions and compare them in terms of lexical and grammatical words (see **grammar**). Which type of word is most repeated?

A helpful way of identifying structural features in a literary or non-literary text is to treat the text as a model or a blueprint and ask, if I wanted to construct a similar one, what would I have to do? Is there a skeletal outline I could sketch out before I think of my own words? What are the rules for writing like this?

Finally, if the text is prose fiction and includes conversation, pay particular attention to tone because you will detect different voices coming through along with the author's or narrator's own voice.

6 A central question in stylistics is what makes literary texts different from other texts.

This question may partly be answered by what you have to say about genre in 1 and about deviant language use in 2. In one sense literary texts are supremely useless. Some parents have even objected to their children reading 'storybooks' and would rather they read encyclopaedias or 'something useful'. Many children's libraries still display books under the headings 'stories' and 'useful information'. It is very easy to have a view of everyday language use which is dominated by transaction: getting things done, not wasting words, useful talk, report writing, business letter writing, record keeping, telephone calls. We know that chat, gossip, natter, yarns, chinwags, heart to hearts are important but we can feel guilty about them if they appear to waste time or if we over-indulge. Yet it is in this very area of human behaviour that literature has its origins. It is true that religion and possibly law figure strongly in the earliest forms of literature but if we look over the vast tradition of the world's secular literature we can see the same recurring preoccupations about human life familiar in everyday gossip, yarn spinning and even jokes. (Read the first three chapters of James Britton's *Language and Learning* (Penguin 1975) for a fuller discussion).

It has already been noted that it is difficult to answer questions about purpose and audience when analysing literary texts. It is equally difficult not to talk about content. One of the essential features of literature is the inseparability of form and content, together with the fact that literature is read outside the normal constraints and contexts of everyday language. We do not transact with a novel or participate in a poem to get things done. In reading literature we share the experiences it has to offer. Literature depends upon us to activate it, to share in its reconstruction by reading it or if it is a play, by watching it. We become accomplices with the author which is why the model of an author on one side of a book transmitting a message to a reader on the other side is such an inaccurate way of looking at reading.

Ultimately all stylistics is about reading but in literary stylistics there are raised questions of cultural value. For if literature can, in one sense, be regarded as supremely useless, it is nevertheless culturally very valuable and all societies in every age have had an insatiable appetite for it. Literature (including TV fiction, popular stories, films) celebrates, criticises and records cultural and social life and encodes it in linguistic forms and in other media. In a sense language is at work in non-literary contexts, whereas it is at play in literature. The play however can be a very serious business as we know from the works of Shakespeare or the novels of Charles Dickens.

This combination of play (entertainment mode) and seriousness (perhaps the only real purpose for literature) was also evident in the Cummings poem. One way of trying to arrive at a list of differences between literary and non-literary texts would be to compare the Cummings poem with the milk advertisement and the Borough Council letter. You could add the letters from the *Beano* comic (Fig. S.9). If you begin by comparing their *content* you will raise far too many issues for a linguistic investigation to cope with. Start with *function* and *form*.

a) What function does each serve? Why was it written?
b) For whom was each written? How do you know?
c) What are the formal (or structural) features of each?

Dear Dennis,	Dear Jerome,
Dear Dennis, ***Do you have a cure for my cats? When the milkman comes, they use him as a scratching post! They are driving him up the wall, and he has threatened to stop delivering the milk!*** ***Yours thirstily,*** ***Jerome Payne,*** ***Aintree,*** ***Liverpool.***	*Dear Jerome,* *What your milkman needs is some cat repellant. I have just the thing, it comes in a black, spiky ball, with lots of sharp teeth and answers to the name of Gnasher!* *Yours helpfully,* *Dennis.*

Fig. S.9

A good exercise with which to sharpen your stylistic analysis is to compare a shopping list with a poem. At first it may sound slightly daft but think about all the factors that produce the language of a shopping list and compare them with the factors that produce poems. One way of tackling this would be to take a shopping list (a genuine one) and see what minimal alterations you would have to make to turn it into a poem. Similarly you could take a poem and either turn it into a shopping list, or make a shopping list of things you would need to make a poem similar to the one you are investigating.

7 The Quantitative aspect

With the advent of computers a new impetus has been given to the quantiative aspects of stylistics. A quantitative survey of a text would count such things as numbers of verbs, abstract nouns or pronouns, for example, and would be interested in sentence length and the frequency of specified grammatical constructions. The trouble with quantitative approaches is the lack of time available in an A-level course. They take up a lot of time and can seem fairly meaningless activities. When you have said that there are 56 verbs in a text out of 200 words you are bound to say that they add up to a lot of action. But will that really be true? and so what? *Stylostatistics*, as this kind of activity is sometimes called, or *computational stylistics* as David Lodge has called it with tongue in cheek (see *Small World* (Penguin 1986)), is time consuming and needs, like phonetics, a lot of data before anything interesting begins to emerge. It is nevertheless a good idea to have a reminder at the back of your mind that flashes a message from time to time saying, 'Have I missed any obvious statistical features that might be worth commenting on?' Certainly it is a worthwhile question to ask of the Cummings poem and it is very relevant to the beginning of V.S. Naipaul's *A House for Mr Biswas*. Keep an eye open in your general reading for statistical features. See how often something turns up. Note for example that in the instructional part of the milk advertisement there are no less than 12 command form verbs followed by a thirteenth, 'send', in the instruction following the recipe.

SUBPLOT

◀ Plot ▶

SYLLABLE

A syllable is a group of letters in a word which can be pronounced together as a single vocal sound. They are most likely to be centred round a vowel but there are no systematic principles guiding their use. They are often used to break a word down into smaller pronounceable units, though, unlike *morphemes*, they have no meaning in themselves. For generations they have been used in the belief that they help learners to read, spell or say words correctly. It is a perfectly understandable, undeniably rule-of-thumb way of trying to provide practical help. Some people do teach themselves spellings by paying attention to syllables, which is also a helpful way of learning to pronounce and remember long foreign words.

The problem with syllables is that they are rather arbitrary vocal sounds which when applied to the written word (especially in English) show little correspondence between spelling and pronunciation. It is one thing to make up your own syllabic aids and mnemonics, quite another to prescribe them wholesale for other people. Books for beginning readers are probably the most familiar examples of words written in syllables. They are written that way in the belief that young children learn to read by decoding a text letter by letter, syllable by syllable, word by word, until they arrive at the meaning. But children learn to read in a variety of ways and they certainly look for much bigger units than syllables. Modern reading books for young children do not use syllables but encourage readers to focus on whole words and sentences.

In secondary schools, some English teachers teach spelling syllabically:

e.g. ob+li+ga+tion.

Others however encourage a morphological approach drawing attention to units that have meaning

e.g. oblig(e)+ation.

Breaking words into syllables cannot be called analysis because there is little underlying principle or reference to meaning. For this reason syllables should never be confused with morphemes.

◀ Morphology ▶

SYLLABUS

This is an outline of the exact topics on which you will be tested in an exam. For English Literature it will usually be a list of set texts; for English Language, it may take the form of a definition of the areas you need to know and the skills which you'll be asked to demonstrate.

You need to know exactly what's required of you in the exam, and the best way to find this out is by obtaining a copy of the syllabus produced by your Examining Board. At the same time, you should be able to buy copies of past examination papers, which will give you an idea of what the questions will be like and give you practice in answering them.

To obtain a syllabus, you should write to the Publications Department of the Examining Board with which you're entered – your teacher will be able to tell you which one this is.

Addresses of the Exam Boards

Associated Examining Board (AEB)
Stag Hill House
Guildford
Surrey GU2 5XJ

University of Cambridge Local Examinations Syndicate (UCLES)
Syndicate Buildings
1 Hills Road
Cambridge CB1 1YB

Joint Matriculation Board (JMB)
Devas St
Manchester M15 6EU

University of London Schools Examination Board (ULSEB)
Stewart House
32 Russell Square
London WC1B 5DN

Northern Ireland Schools Examination Council (NISEC)
Beechill House
42 Beechill Road
Belfast BT8 4RS

Oxford and Cambridge Schools Examination Board (OCSEB)
10 Trumpington Street
Cambridge CB2 1QB

Oxford Delegacy of Local Examinations (ODLE)
Ewert Place
Summertown
Oxford OX2 7BX

Scottish Examination Board (SEB)
Ironmills Road
Dalkeith
Midlothian EH22 1BR

Welsh Joint Education Committee (WJEC)
245 Western Avenue
Cardiff CF5 2YX

SYMBOL

This is rather like a metaphor for which we can't easily find an exact meaning. For example, when W. B. Yeats writes

> Surely thine hour has come, thy great wind blows,
> Far off, most secret, and inviolate Rose,

we cannot identify exactly what it is that he is discussing. In a similar way, the symbols used by William Blake in his poems generally defy complete explanation, although they are very precise in their context. The symbols of 'the invisible worm' and the rose in the poem 'The Sick Rose', for instance, stand for corruption and purity, experience and innocence, evil and good – large, general qualities which cannot be precisely 'translated', but which are clear enough to *feel* on reading the poem.

If you are confronted by a poem which seems to use language in this way, you should be aware of the *range* of possible meanings, and also of the fact that the symbol cannot be expressed fully in any other way. A sentence like this would be an acceptable response:

> Although the exact significance of 'Rose' cannot be made clear, it seems that Yeats here is referring to a time of great beauty and spiritual perfection which he hopes is about to dawn.

◀ Figurative language ▶

SYNONYM

Synonyms are words in the same language which have the same, or nearly the same, meaning.

SYNTAX

Some linguists confine the concept **grammar** to words and to the rules that govern their structures and functions. They use the term *syntax* to refer to the structures and function of words acting together. This guide follows a different organisation and subsumes syntax under grammar

GRAMMAR

MORPHOLOGY — words | SYNTAX — words combined

Syntax describes the ways in which words may be combined into larger units and states the rules for combining words and combining larger units. Noun phrases, adverbial clauses, relative clauses, compound sentences are all examples of *syntactic structures* governed by grammatical rules.

Any sentence may be viewed at in two dimensions: the *syntagmatic* (hence 'syntax') and the *paradigmatic*. The syntagmatic dimension is the horizontal or linear axis of a sentence. Though sentences look like one word after another they are not merely strings of words but sequences of words arranged in structures.

The following is a string of words that have no meaning because they have no structure:

> helmet Caruso do thereafter running banana to.

The following is a sentence because it consists of related syntactic structures:

> Just when all seemed lost / Harrison Ford suddenly remembered / the magic button, / pressed it / and disappeared / through an opening / in the roof.

Whatever shapes our thoughts may take, language is produced in a linear timescale and in writing its linearity is especially marked. Even when two people talk at once or one backtracks over what has been said, time marches on and both listeners and speakers, readers and writers have to process language in a time sequence. Units in the syntagmatic dimension must not be too long, for example, else we forget how they began and begin to lose continuity. Nor can they be too repetitive else they become boring or monotonous. Nor must they be unconnected else we cannot make cohesive sense of them. In writing we expect syntax to be well formed and cohesive because writers normally have time to attend to such matters in a more formal way and readers expect to be given a readable text. In speech the syntagmatic line may be discontinuous or irregular and will sometimes peter out. Usually however there is a grammatical complicity between speaker and listener that ensures an overall syntactic continuity even when sentences begun by the speaker are sometimes completed by the listener. The sentence above, about Harrison Ford, is a well formed sentence typical of writing. The subject of the sentence, Harrison Ford, has been deferred by the introduction of another piece of information ('Just when all seemed lost'). The finite verb comes soon after the subject ('remembered') and is followed by two more finite verbs both performed by the subject ('pressed' and 'disappeared'). Inserted at appropriate points are adverbial information ('when all seemed lost' and 'suddenly'), noun phrases ('the magic button' and 'an opening in the roof'), prepositional information ('through' and 'in'). A direct object is included ('the magic button') which is then referred to by the pronoun 'it'.

If a speaker had been telling the story, the sentence might have come out like this:

> Suddenly – er – Harrison Ford (long pause) just when – er – all seemed lost – he – er – remembered the magic button – and pressed it – and disappeared through the roof – there was an opening in it.

The same syntactic relationships are being generated but there has not been time, as in writing, to tidy up the structure.

The *paradigmatic dimension* is a vertical one and refers to choice of vocabulary at each stage of the syntagmatic dimension. At the very beginning of a sentence there is an extremely wide range of paradigmatic choice. You could start a sentence with any word, even 'and' or 'but'. Initial choice will be made in the light of syntactic planning but with each successive paradigmatic choice the range of choice narrows at each stage along the syntagmatic dimension which is why a listener or reader finds it easier to guess how a sentence will end than how it is likely to begin.

The two dimensions may be represented diagramatically; as in Fig. S.10.

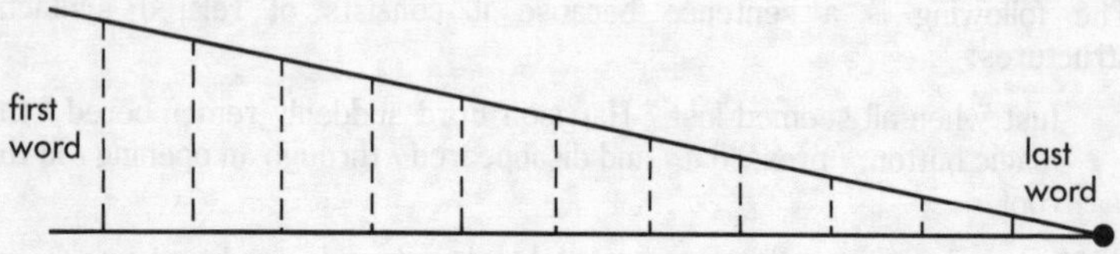

Fig. S.10

T

TETRAMETER

◀ Metre ▶

TEXT

The word text is derived from the Latin *texere*, meaning *to weave*. Most commonly it refers to writing and in particular, writing of a fairly permanent kind. It is a word familiar to English literature students whose examination syllabuses will contain 'set texts' or 'set books', usually a selection of novels, poems and plays. Knowledge of the text is essential for success in examinations and a traditional mode of examining is to give candidates excerpts from a prescribed text for identification, comment and intrepretation. Some boards also set 'unseen texts' to which candidates are expected to make critical responses.

Literary texts

These have acquired considerable authority and prestige, and scrupulous respect for their integrity and authenticity is expected of students. Many works of literature are published in the form of scholarly texts complete with textual variants (e.g. between earlier and later editions) which permit close critical scrutiny. Doubtful texts (e.g. a pirate copy of a Shakespeare play) are referred to as corrupt texts and where there are a number of different versions, alternative readings are given as footnotes and appendices.

The word 'text' also has a wider *educational use*: most subjects are taught and learned with the aid of a *textbook* designed to cover all the knowledge and skills prescribed in a particular syllabus e.g. Geography, Psychology,

European History, Physics, Computer Studies. It is possible for texts of this kind to acquire classic or definitive status but there is also the danger that knowledge of a subject can become fossilised, outdated or severely restricted if there is too great a reliance on a single textbook. All textbooks need frequent revision, especially in the physical and social sciences, and even annotated editions of *David Copperfield* or *Lord of the Flies* can become old fashioned in a surprisingly short time. In recent years there has been a noticeable shift away from comprehensive textbooks especially where syllabuses require a lot of coursework. Collections of documents, source material and varieties of textual presentation are increasingly more evident in place of conventional textbooks.

Religious and ecclesiastical use

In this context the word 'text' has very definite sacred connotations e.g. Holy Writ, the Word of God, the Scriptures. The word 'Bible'means a collection of books, or texts and is usually written, 'The Holy Bible'. The ten commandments, for example, were texts of such importance to the Jewish faith that they were inscribed on stone and preserved in the Ark of the Covenant. The Bible owes its very existence to the labour and vision of Jewish and Christian forefathers who saw the need to preserve oral tradition in the form of more permanent texts, especially at a time when Jews were being forcibly dispersed throughout the middle east, or later, when Christians were being prosecuted. Another important feature of Hebrew tradition is the Talmud, or 'authoritative writings'. *Talmud* is the Hebrew word for 'instruction'.

The sacred text of the Muslims is the Koran, containing revelations made to Mohammad by Allah. The Arabic word 'qur'an' means 'to recite, or to read aloud from the text'.

The Upanishads and the Bhagavadgita are sacred Hindu texts.

Religious texts generate and sustain faith yet some of the bitterest controversies have occurred over the status and interpretation of texts. Who has the right to read them? Can they be translated? Whose interpretation is the right one? Familiar Christian disputes hve concerned such things as the scientific validity of the Genesis account of creation, the ethical content of the ten commandments, the meaning of the parables, the historical truth of the Gospels, and the interpretation of predictions contained in the Book of Revelation.

It is interesting to note the legal, instructional and persuasive character of religious texts. The important thing is not so much what is written as why it was written. It is important too to recognise that religious texts have survived from great antiquity and have often been woven together from a variety of ancient sources, for different purposes other than those originally intended. The Bible, for example, consists of an Old and a New Testament and a key to the nature and function of religious texts is contained in the word 'testament' which means a binding and legal covenant or agreement. In the case of the Bible the covenant is between man and God, and it must be witnessed in much the same way as a last will and testament. This legal aspect of text is continued in present day law and commerce where the texts of important agreements and undertakings have to be signed, countersigned and preserved for future reference. The same is true of more commonplace texts such as certificates, licenses, registration documents and membership cards.

Modern uses of the term

Everyday uses of the word 'text' usually refer to such things as the small print of hire purchase agreements or to a set of instructions. It can also refer to the words in greetings cards or to inscriptions.

Sermons sometimes begin with a text taken from the Bible ('My text for today is taken from the Book of . . . .') and this notion is carried on in the modern day fashion for displaying texts in the home or the office:

e.g. East, West, home's best.
You don't have to be daft to work here, but it helps.
Silence is golden.
The difficult we can do, the impossible takes a little longer.

The advent of the computer has also brought the word into frequent use in offices given over to word processing and information technology. 'Super-text', for example, refers to an editing program, while Hyportext is a sophisticated text construction programme.

In a literate culture texts are powerful artefacts. We have vast libraries and archives to preserve valuable texts e.g. Magna Carta, and also to record every citizen's birth. It is even possible to construct an individual's life history from the texts that survive after death.

So far attention has been paid to literary texts i.e. texts written down. In modern linguistics the term text is also used to refer to spoken discourse. Once a conversation, for example, has begun, the speakers weave a text just as effectively as a writer writes a text. So far as the participants are concerned at the time, spoken texts depend upon the short term memory for their links with what has previously been said just as they depend upon co-operativeness for their continuation. When a conversation has been tape recorded and transcribed the text can be read very easily but conversations are no less texts for not having been recorded or transcribed.

Another modern use of the term text occurs in media studies. Media texts are advertisements, TV programmes, news bulletins, magazine layouts, photographs. They may or may not contain verbal language but they are treated as texts because of the non-verbal language in their construction and its capacity to signify meanings in a systematic way. You could compare for example two media texts such as the Australian soap operas, *Neighbours* and *Home and Away*. In particular you could investigate how teenagers are presented in relation to the value systems and authority represented by adults. A working hypothesis could be that teenagers in *Home and Away* are not presented in terms of adult approval and disapproval but more in terms of their own values, whereas teenagers in *Neighbours* are more likely to be framed within contexts of adult approval or disapproval. The textual evidence would be found in who talks to whom? about what? and how? and also in the images and actions associated with, or performed by, the characters.

In common with written and spoken texts, media texts are accessible to discourse analysis.

Texts and contexts

The most familiar use of the term 'context', for students of English, refers to the overall circumstances of plot, character, situation or theme in which any excerpt from a text needs to be understood. Relating a speech, or a single stanza or part of a chapter within the context of the whole play, poem or novel is part of the literature student's stock in trade. Just as it is objectionable, in everyday life, to be quoted out of context, so are interpretations of textual excerpts objectionable if they ignore matters of context.

Like sacred texts, literary texts have the power to create their own cultural contexts and are highly charged with social, moral and aesthetic values. The reading of a novel, for example, involves so much more than just knowing how to read. There is the question of **genre**, knowing what kind of a novel it is and *how* the reader may be expected to read it. There is the willing suspension of disbelief on the one hand, while on the other, there is a constant matching of new fictions with familiar old facts of life. A good deal of knowledge and experience of the world comes into play with cumulative habits of reading.

Questions of social context and purpose such as:

> Who was it written for?
> Why was it written?
> Under what circumstances is it to be read?

– if not oddly irrelevant, are certainly not immediate ones. The first two may be answered with reference to the common reader wishing to share literary experiences or to the casual reader seeking to while away the time. The third is even more difficult to formulate in any specific way.

The existence of the two words 'text' and 'context' implies a separation between the two but close study of non-literary texts reveals a very close inter-dependence of text and context. When considering function and audience it is often very difficult to separate text from context so influential is context on both text and reader.

Look for example at the Warfield letter and the milk advertisement (Figs. S.7 and S.8) discussed under **stylistics** and list all the contextual factors, in each case, that determine how and why anyone should read the texts in the first place. How dependent are features of the texts on factors outside the texts?

THEATRICAL

Rather like 'dramatic', this is used popularly to mean something very flamboyant or unusual. If you use it of a play, it will be unclear whether you mean this, or 'pertaining to the theatre', its strict meaning. This will make things unclear for the reader and confuse or obscure a point in your essay. Avoid such ambiguity and possible loss of marks by using 'theatric', or by talking about how the play works in the theatre.

THEORETICAL FRAMEWORK

One of the problems of studying a language syllabus is the sheer range of topics that language raises when we start to look at it seriously. After the first term or two it is likely that students will begin to feel a little overwhelmed by the variety of knowledge about language they can see opening up.

One way to check how your studies are progressing and how your own framework is beginning to develop, is to use a matrix such as the one below for the JMB syllabus:

	Language & Society	Language Acquisition	Language Varieties	Language Change
Phonology				
Lexis				
Grammar				
Discourse/ Pragmatics				
Semantics				

The four areas of study are indicated across the top of the matrix. These are the areas in which you will read theoretical and practical studies about the nature and functions of language and where you would choose to focus your language study project. There are also opportunities here for shorter informative, persuasive or instructional pieces of original writing. JMB candidates would also choose one of these areas to discuss in Section A of Paper One.

The vertical column on the left of the matrix contains the various disciplines and knowledge that studies of language draw upon in order to form a hypothesis, devise a procedure, and analyse data. They could all be applied in some way to each of the four areas but some are more often and more appropriately used in selected areas.

First, consider why the four areas have been chosen: Language & Society; Language Acquisition; Language Varieties; Language Change.

All four areas have a separate identity in that many studies have been done in each one which form a corpus of knowledge and research method for each area. It should be clear though that all four areas are interconnected.

Knowledge in any one area has implications for knowledge in the others. Taking the broadest view of language studies, it is possible to subsume Language Acquisition, Language Varieties and Language Change under the heading Language and Society but that view simply provides an overarching perspective, it does not contradict the model given above.

Below are some questions that illustrate kinds of study appropriate to each area.

Language and society

How does language influence and reflect social values?
How may languages be said to construct social reality?
Language is a prime agent of socialisation – how does it work?
Language defines social groups; how?
How is language a key element in the negotiation of power?
What are the connections between language and prejudice?
What forms does the persuasive power of language take?

Language acquisition

How does language acquisition distinguish us from animals?
What are the stages of language development in young children?
How do we learn to read and write?
Why is speech so significant in the acquisition process?

Language varieties

What is the range of language variation?
What are the differences and connections between the two major varieties – speech and writing?
How do we account for diversity? e.g. of occupational dialects, literary forms.
What attitudes exist toward language diversity?

Language change

Why is change an inevitable state of language?
What then is permanent?
How does language change over long periods of time? (a socio-cultural history).
How does language change over short periods of time? (an autobiographical approach).
How does language change from place to place?
What kinds of language change take place?
What factors precipitate change?
What attitudes exist toward language change?

One way of illustrating how interconnected the four areas are is to consider the social influences on the life of an infant and how they will affect the ways in which that infant will acquire and develop language. Consider the varieties of language uses, dialects, attitudes, forms that will impinge on the growing child, and consider, the changes that will take place in the child's language development (e.g. education) alongside changes that will be taking place in the wider society. A biographical perspective such as this links the four areas but also shows how appropriately we can focus on any one of them.

The disciplines, knowledge and terminologies of the vertical column are described elsewhere in this guide. They are all appropriate in some way to each area of study but there follows a list of suggestions where there is a particular relevance.

Language and society

the grammar of 'them' and 'us'
attitude toward correctness in grammar
taboo words and euphemisms (lexis and semantics)
gender coding (grammar, lexis, semantics)
language and power (pragmatics)
speech acts (pragmatics)
the status of speech and writing (discourse).

Language acquisition

acquiring speech sounds (phonology)
developing syntax (grammar)
learning how to hold a conversation (pragmatics)
young children's writing (grammar; discourse)
learning to read (discourse; semantics; acquisition).

Language varieties

difference between speech and writing (grammar; discourse)
accent and dialect (phonology; lexis; grammar)
different genre; literary and non-literary (discourse)
occupational register (lexis; discourse; pragmatics).

Language change

the creation of new words (lexis; semantics)
changes of meaning (semantics)
sound changes (phonology)
emergence of new English dialects e.g. Asian/Afro Caribbean English (phonology; lexis; grammar).

See also under **stylistics** for micro- and macro-perspectives.

TONE

Poetry

Here, the word really means the kind of *voice* in which the poem is written. Is it, for example, tender, gentle, angry, vigourous, comic, self-mocking, or none of these? The best way to approach tone is to read the poem carefully and try to *hear* it. Then try to think of a way to describe it. There will be no single 'right answer' for this, so it's up to you to choose an adjective which fits the tone well. Be aware, too, that the tone of a poem might change quite a lot during its course, just as there may be two or more 'speakers'. Thomas Hardy's 'The Ruined Maid', for example, is a dialogue between two women; Edward Thomas' 'As the team's head brass', a conversation between an observer and a farmer.

Drama

Tone in drama is if anything more important than it is in poetry, since at the heart of most plays is the exchange of *ideas and feelings* between the characters. In everyday life, we communicate as much by the tone of our voices as by our words – so tone is of great importance in the theatre.

The tone of a speech can be indicated in various ways. The simplest is a stage direction, making clear how a character is speaking, like this:

DUNOIS [*furiously disappointed*]: Is that all? You infernal young idiot; I have a mind to pitch you into the river.

THE PAGE [*not afraid, knowing his man*]: It looked frightfully jolly, that flash of blue. . . .

But more often, you'll have to work out the tone for yourself. Think about the setting, situation and what you have so far worked out about the characters and their relationships. Be aware, too, that a character might be using sarcasm or irony – meaning the opposite of what he or she is saying. A careful reading of *all* the aspects of a scene, then, is necessary to arrive at an understanding of the tone of voice a character is using – and an awareness of the tone will help you to understand the overall importance and significance of the scene.

Prose

The tone of a piece of prose will be rather different from that of a poem or dramatic passage, since both these will most likely be read aloud or performed by a speaking voice. The prose writer does *not* have this in mind, except when writing for the stage, and so the tone has to be conveyed just by the choice of words and the way they are put together.

The tone of a piece of writing may be tender, ironic, distant, formal; it may be playful, comic, offensive or provocative. Most often, it will be a combination of many of these – reflective and gently self-mocking, perhaps, or formal yet considerate. Be aware, too, that a passage may pass through several different tones of voice, especially if it is telling a story, or describing a series of characters or a situation unfolding between them. The death of Little Nell in Dickens' *Old Curiosity Shop*, for example, is gentle and tender in its tone – within the sentimental conventions of Victorian writing. Passages in William Golding's *The Spire* have a tone of ecstasy which matches the mood of Dean Jocelin's vision.

Don't assume, then, that the tone of a prose passage can be described in one word, which you can hang like a label around its neck. Good prose, like good poetry or dramatic writing, will change and develop, and convey a subtle mixture of different tones, which need care and thought if they are to be analysed fully and described clearly.

TRAGEDY

This is perhaps the most misused word of all in drama. In common speech, a tragedy is an unfortunate or distressing event – the sinking of a ship, say, or the early death of a brilliant man or woman. In the theatre, it means something very different. There are many theories about what the word means: in Elizabethan theatre, for example, it can be said to refer to the gradual fall of a hero as a result of his or her own actions or a nature which, though great, is also impaired or limited. If you use the word, make sure that you know what specific meaning you are giving it: if you read it in an exam question, make sure that you know how it is being used there. Never use it in its everyday sense when writing about a play; this could make all the difference between a pass and a fail grade on that question.

TRANSFORMATIONAL-GENERATIVE GRAMMAR

Transformational-generative, or TG, grammar derives from the seminal work of Noam **Chomsky**. Its origin lies in Chomsky's notions of a *deep structure* where utterances and sentences are created, and a *surface structure* which is the form in which they are finally produced.

To take the second half of the name first, the generative part of the grammar lies in the deep structure. What is important about this notion is that it does not treat language use as a mechanical system at the top of the mind as it were, but as a creative, generative speech planning process at a more fundamental level of thinking.

The word *transformational* refers to the capacity in language for making transformations: e.g.

subject into object
passive into active
past into present
negative into positive
statement into question
and vice versa.

These are fundamental grammatical processes and constructions. TG grammars account for the rules that generate them.

The relation between *surface structure* and *deep structure*, between which the transformations pass is described by Chomsky in the following examples:

John is eager to please.
John is easy to please.

The surface structures of these are identical and they can be analysed (or parsed) in the same way. The meanings however are almost opposites and when analysed according to how their different meanings may be generated it is only then that their fundamental difference of meaning can be described. It is in the deep structure that the conditions will be specified for how the sentence should be understood.

TG grammar is also interested in identifying universal features of language (*language universals*) that may underlie all the world's languages.

TRIMETER

◀ Metre ▶

TROCHEE

A trochee is a **foot** consisting of a stressed syllable followed by an unstressed syllable.

V

VERSE

◀ Metre ▶

VERB

The traditional schoolchild's definition of a verb, i.e. a doing word is still useful since it draws attention to the necessity for action. Until you have had some practice at identifying word classes, and made a lot of mistakes, it is very easy, on the basis of this definition, to be misled by the usual meaning of the verb in question. Consider the following sentences:

They seem nice enough people.
He suffered a serious setback.
She experienced a lot of opposition.
They received their just deserts.

The italicised words all contain verbs but they are not obviously 'doing words'. They do nevertheless signify action in the grammatical sense in that they are the main thing the speaker or writer wants to say about the subject of each sentence.

Problems are also caused by the verbs 'to be ' and 'to have' which contrast markedly with the idea of 'doing' or 'action' in the obvious sense. If however we consider the central importance of these verbs in our language, how much commitment they express, then there can be no doubt about the grammatical action they give to a clause or sentence. Whenever we use words like 'is', 'are', 'have', 'had', 'will be', 'were', we are using verbs. Verbs then, refer to states as well as actions.

Because of their central importance verbs have to convey a wide range of meanings.

a) If we view grammar as a mapping out of time, space and relationships through language then one of the main purposes of variation in verb forms is to convey *past time*, *present time* and *future time*.

b) Verbs also express the *active* and *passive*. Actions are received as well as performed.

He *kicked* the ball. (active)
The ball *was kicked* by him. (passive)

c) Verbs may also be classifed into *finite* or *non-finite* forms. Finite verbs are the ones that express commitment directly.

She ran away.
She opened the book.
She will go home.
She had a bad cold.
She has given a recital at Wigmore Hall.

Non-finite verbs are *participles* e.g. having, going, being and *infinitives* e.g. to have, to go, to be.
In a sentence such as the following:

- Going to the garage, Sarah dropped her car keys.

The speaker or writer has not explicitly predicated an action to Sarah but has implied that she was going to the garage. The explicit, committed or finite verb is 'Sarah dropped', the implied action by Sarah is the participle 'going' which could in fact be replaced by a non verb form such as 'On her way. . . '

d) Verbs are classified as *regular* and *irregular*. Usually young children learn the regular verbs easily and first because they are governed by a rule. Once the rule is learned or activated, the verb forms can be produced when necessary. A child will learn, for example, that the regular past tense is formed by adding the morpheme -ed to the end:

he opens – he opened
he walks – he walked
he plays – he played.

When young children say such things as:

I eated it all.
We buyed some sweets.
He runned away.
She singed to me.

they are not making gramamtical errors in the adult sense but applying a rule they have used quite successfully on many other occasions. Unfortunately there are about three hundred irregular verbs in English, four of which are illustrated above, which do not take the '-ed' form in the past tense. They take other forms e.g.

I *ate* it all.
We *bought* some sweets.
He *ran* away.
She *sang* to me.

e) The three commonest English verbs are 'to be', 'to have' and 'to do'. Not only are they used on their own but they also serve as *auxiliaries* to other verbs to express specific nuances of meaning within the general meaning of the verb:

I am going (continuous present form distinguished from simple present form, *I go*).
I had given it to him (different from *I gave*).
It does open your eyes (different from *It opens*).

There are also *modal auxiliaries* which enable users to express shades of meaning such as the possibility (*can* go), permission (*may* go), habit (*would* go), ability (*could* go), obligation (*must* go; *ought to* go), uncertainty (*should* go).

f) Just as nouns are likely to occur in noun phrases (NP) (see **noun**) so verbs frequently occur in verb phrases (VP):

. . . . would have gone. . . .
. . . . will be about to go. . . .
. . . . would have had. . . .

When analysing these it is best to keep the phrase together rather than split it up. The important thing is to be able to recognise that it is a verb phrase with a function of its own in the sentence.

g) Verb phrases should not be confused with the term *phrasal verbs* which has quite a different meaning. Examples are: give in, get up, go off, get on with, send up, play down, make over, make up, lay down, show off. Whole dictionaries are devoted to English phrasal verbs, of which there are many, because they present difficulties to people learning English as a second language. (See the *Longman Dictionary of Phrasal Verbs*.) The chief reason for this difficulty is their idiomatic nature. Their meaning is not simply a combination of the meaning of the verb and the **preposition**. How would you explain, for example, 'give in', 'make off', or 'send up'?

h) Complete sentences are distinguished by the possession of a finite verb but sometimes the verb is conspicuous by its absence as in such sentences as:

i) How about a cup of tea?
ii) Why not?
iii) More coffee?
iv) Sorry mate.
v) Marvellous performance!

Notice that these sentences are *very* characteristic of everyday conversation. Notice too that they fulfil specific sentence functions i), ii) and iii) are questions, iv) is a statement (of apology), v) is an exclamation.

i) The term *concord* is often used about verbs. It refers to agreement between a verb and its subject. Singular subjects are expected to take *singular form verbs* (e.g. The man walks **not** The man walk). Plural subjects are expected to take *plural form verbs* (e.g. The women sing **not** The women sings). 'The man walks' and 'The women sing' represent Standard

English forms but the non-standard forms may be found consistently used in regional dialects.

The issue of concord (or agreement) is complicated by the existence of consistently used dialectal forms (e.g. He make me laugh).

There are also a few problems of agreement which occur in both writing and speech:

If 'and' is used to connect two individual items in the subject of the sentence then a plural verb is used:

My brother and sister *are* both at school.

Yet we say 'Bread and butter is delicious' because bread and butter in this context are thought of as one thing.

If two singular objects are joined by 'or', the verb takes the singular form:

TV or Trivial Pursuit takes up most of their evenings.

Where the subject of a sentence is a word like 'any', 'either', 'neither' and 'none' there is no clear consensus.

We can say for example:

I didn't think either of them were any good.

or

I didn't think either of them was any good.

Group nouns such as 'family', 'government', 'committee', 'majority', 'audience', and 'team' often cause argument among English speakers. Should it be:

- the committee have decided (or 'has decided')?
- the family are all very happy (or 'the family is very happy')?
- the government believe (or 'believes')?
- the audience was unimpressed (or 'were unimpressed')?
- the team plays well (or 'play well')?

j) Finally a caution about the word *verbal* which is sometimes used as an adjective referring to 'words' in general as well as 'verbs' in particular. You may, for example, on the JMB English Language Paper One, the London Board's Varieties of English Paper, or the AEB Literature/Language Paper, want to remark of an unseen passage that there are some interesting verbal features, meaning that you are drawing attention to the writer's use of verbs. Beware using the word if it could be thought that you mean verbal in the sense of any kind of words. Make sure you know the difference.

VOWEL

◄ Phonology ►

W

WIT

A term which has gone through several meanings. It can mean intelligence or wisdom, or the application of those features to experience. It can mean 'quick-witted', implying excellent imagination, originality, and the capacity to think quickly. It can mean excellence of judgement and a reasoned, balanced outlook. Pope's lines

True wit is Nature to advantage dres't
What oft was thought, but ne'er so well exprest'

refer to an eighteenth-century idea of wit: the poetry of Donne, with its complex chains of preposterous logic, have an intellectual energy and verbal dexterity which exemplifies an earlier view.

WITTGENSTEIN, LUDWIG

Austrian born philosopher, Ludwig Wittgenstein (1889–1951), lived in England from 1911 and proved very influential in this country on the development of what came to be known as linguistic philosophy. Very early in his work he came to the view that language was extraordinarily complex mental behaviour and that a simple referential theory of meaning (words standing for 'things') was quite inadequate. He also saw the relationship between meaning and grammar as far more subtle than a mechanistic theory of parts could explain.

His thinking relates to that of **Saussure** in that he saw language as part of a much larger communication network rather as Saussure subsumed the science of language under the science of semiotics. His thought also resembles Saussure's in that both thought of language as a kind of game. Saussure used the analogy of chess, Wittgenstein saw language as a compendium of games, all different but all governed by rules of one kind or another. 'Language games' came to be a recurrent phrase in the discussions of linguistic philosophers. It should not be thought of as a trivial or trivialising concept but rather as an attempt to relate the abstractions of language to the practical effects of everyday communications. He was especially interested in the vocabulary we use to describe mental states e.g. happiness, pain, thinking, feeling, sadness, certainty. He argued that if the language we use is to be understood, it cannot get its meaning from essentially private states of mind but from social agreement about how such words as 'happy' may be used.

WORD

◀ Morphology ▶

WRITING

◀ Drama, Essays, Poetry, Prose, Study skills ▶